## How to build a winning sales proposal in five steps

1. **Learn all you can about the buyer. Find a key "improvement opportunity" within the buyer's operations.** Check out Chapters 4 and 5.

2. **Propose a workable, financially attractive way to unlock the buyer's improvement opportunity.** See Chapters 6 and 7.

3. **Propose a sensible way to implement the solution you propose in step 2.** See Chapter 8.

4. **Raise the buyer's comfort level in selecting you as the seller. Sketch in your record of success.** Refer to Chapter 9.

5. **Cover all the necessary stuff — assumptions, fees, invoicing schedule, and so on.** Use Chapter 10 to double-check.

The diagram below gives you the big picture.

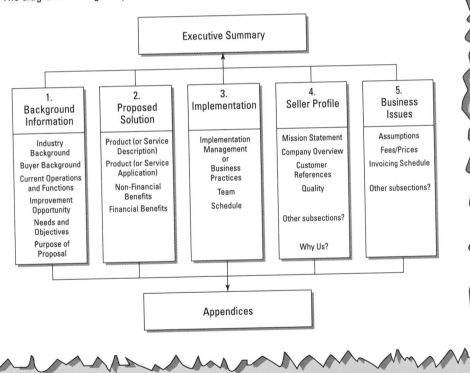

# Sales Proposals Kit For Dummies®

**Cheat Sheet**

## Checklist of what goes into a proposal transmittal letter

- Tells why you are submitting the proposal (because you've been invited to!).
- Highlights the buyer's improvement opportunity and explains that implementing your proposed solution will reduce or avoid costs, increase revenues, or improve operations.
- Explains why your company is a good choice.
- Includes an offer to provide additional information or assistance if requested by the buyer.
- Thanks your contact for his or her time and efforts in helping you gather the information needed to write the proposal.

See Chapter 11.

## When to use a letter as your entire sales proposal

Consider using a letter as your proposal when:

- You're selling an uncomplicated product with a low dollar value.
- The customer has received and accepted one of your standard proposals and what you're selling now is an add-on benefit.
- The product or service is not an add-on but a smaller sale between larger sales to the same customer.
- The buyer's organization has only one or two decision makers and they want a simple proposal to document an understanding that they're already reached with you.

See Chapter 13.

## How to write a winning title on your proposal

To create a great title for your proposal, answer these two questions and combine the answers:

- What's the buyer's improvement opportunity?
- What's the primary benefit of installing your product?

*Example:* The improvement opportunity is the need to raise employee accuracy, and the benefit of your unique electric widget is that it does just that. So the title is "Increasing Employee Accuracy by Installing Electric Widgets."

See Chapter 11.

## Four steps to a solid executive summary

- Write it last.
- Provide a concise synopsis of your entire proposal.
- Give readers a heads up to the important issues presented in the main body of the proposal.
- Keep it short.

See Chapter 11.

Hungry Minds™

*For Dummies: Bestselling Book Series for Beginners*

# Sales Proposals Kit

## FOR

# DUMMIES®

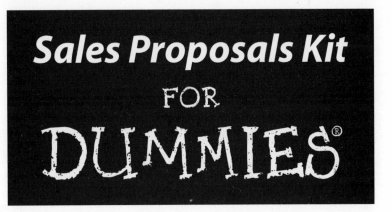

# Sales Proposals Kit FOR DUMMIES®

## by Bob Kantin

**Hungry Minds**™

Best-Selling Books • Digital Downloads • e-Books • Answer Networks • e-Newsletters • Branded Web Sites • e-Learning

New York, NY ◆ Cleveland, OH ◆ Indianapolis, IN

**Sales Proposals Kit For Dummies®**

Published by:
Hungry Minds, Inc.
909 Third Avenue
New York, NY 10022
www.hungryminds.com
www.dummies.com

Library of Congress Control Number: 2001089321

ISBN: 0-7645-5375-5

Printed in the United States of America

10 9 8 7 6 5 4 3 2 1

1B/RT/QX/QR/IN

Distributed in the United States by Hungry Minds, Inc.

Distributed by CDG Books Canada Inc. for Canada; by Transworld Publishers Limited in the United Kingdom; by IDG Norge Books for Norway; by IDG Sweden Books for Sweden; by IDG Books Australia Publishing Corporation Pty. Ltd. for Australia and New Zealand; by TransQuest Publishers Pte Ltd. for Singapore, Malaysia, Thailand, Indonesia, and Hong Kong; by Gotop Information Inc. for Taiwan; by ICG Muse, Inc. for Japan; by Intersoft for South Africa; by Eyrolles for France; by International Thomson Publishing for Germany, Austria and Switzerland; by Distribuidora Cuspide for Argentina; by LR International for Brazil; by Galileo Libros for Chile; by Ediciones ZETA S.C.R. Ltda. for Peru; by WS Computer Publishing Corporation, Inc., for the Philippines; by Contemporanea de Ediciones for Venezuela; by Express Computer Distributors for the Caribbean and West Indies; by Micronesia Media Distributor, Inc. for Micronesia; by Chips Computadoras S.A. de C.V. for Mexico; by Editorial Norma de Panama S.A. for Panama; by American Bookshops for Finland.

For general information on Hungry Minds' products and services please contact our Customer Care department; within the U.S. at 800-762-2974, outside the U.S. at 317-572-3993 or fax 317-572-4002.

For sales inquiries and resellers information, including discounts, premium and bulk quantity sales and foreign language translations please contact our Customer Care department at 800-434-3422, fax 317-572-4002 or write to Hungry Minds, Inc., Attn: Customer Care department, 10475 Crosspoint Boulevard, Indianapolis, IN 46256.

For information on licensing foreign or domestic rights, please contact our Sub-Rights Customer Care department at 212-884-5000.

For information on using Hungry Minds' products and services in the classroom or for ordering examination copies, please contact our Educational Sales department at 800-434-2086 or fax 317-572-4005.

Please contact our Public Relations department at 212-884-5163 for press review copies or 212-884-5000 for author interviews and other publicity information or fax 212-884-5400.

For authorization to photocopy items for corporate, personal, or educational use, please contact Copyright Clearance Center, 222 Rosewood Drive, Danvers, MA 01923, or fax 978-750-4470.

Hungry Minds™ is a trademark of Hungry Minds, Inc.

# About the Author

**Bob Kantin** is a founder and principal of SalesProposals.com (www. salesproposals.com), a firm focused on increasing clients' sales by improving their sales proposal development processes. Bob consults in the areas of proposal design and sales process integration, marketing, and new product development. In 1991, he coauthored his first book on sales proposals, *Quality Selling through Quality Proposals*. Bob's second book, *Strategic Proposals, Closing the Big Deal* was published in 1999. His company also has developed a software product, *Sales Proposal Architect*, which automates the sales proposal design process. This Windows-based software product is based on Bob's proven five-section proposal model presented in this book.

Before starting his consulting practice, Bob was Director of the Professional Services Group-Southwest Region for Goal Systems International, Inc. At Goal, Bob was responsible for client and corporate administration and new business development. In 1987, Bob founded Electronic Learning Systems, a computer-based training consulting and development organization, which was purchased by Goal Systems in 1989. Before founding Electronic Learning Systems, Bob was Vice President and Manager of MTech's Computer-Based Training (CBT) business unit. He was responsible for identifying and successfully developing CBT as a new product line for this large financial services provider. Prior to his involvement with CBT, Bob was a Vice President in product development and management for MTech's commercial banking application systems.

Before joining MTech, Bob held positions with two large commercial banks. At The Arizona Bank, he was a Project Manager for major projects and then Vice President and Manager of the Electronic Banking Systems. At M&I Marshall and Ilsley Bank (Milwaukee, Wisconsin), Bob held various positions in sales and marketing, product development, and customer service in M&I's Data Services Division. Bob has a BBA in finance from the University of Wisconsin-Oshkosh.

# Dedication

This book is dedicated to my wife, Marylee — my best friend and fellow snow skiing addict. Thank you for your love, encouragement, and unwavering support.

# Acknowledgments

Many thanks to Kathy Welton and Holly McGuire at Hungry Minds for deciding I was the right person to write this book. Also, many thanks to Norm Crampton, Project Editor, and Ben Nussbaum, Copy Editor, who edited my work. Believe me, this book is much better because of their extraordinary talents. Finally, thanks to Jim Donovan of Jim Donovan Literary for his support, encouragement, and expertise.

Special thanks to Bill Concevitch, now Senior Vice President of Strategic Development at Mentergy, Inc. I met Bill several years ago when I was consulting with ExecuTrain Corporation. Bill had an opportunity to meet Kathy Welton and he mentioned my approach to sales proposal design and development. Bill identified the need for *Sales Proposals Kit for Dummies.* Bill's meeting with Kathy and his endorsement of my approach started the process.

## Publisher's Acknowledgments

We're proud of this book; please send us your comments through our Online Registration Form located at www.hungryminds.com

Some of the people who helped bring this book to market include the following:

*Acquisitions, Editorial, and Media Development*

**Project Editor:** Norm Crampton

**Acquisitions Editor:** Holly McGuire

**Copy Editor:** Ben Nussbaum

**Technical Editor:** William L. Cron, PhD

**Senior Permissions Editor:** Carmen Krikorian

**Media Development Specialist:** Megan Decraene

**Editorial Manager:** Pam Mourouzis

**Media Development Manager:** Laura Carpenter

**Editorial Assistant:** Carol Strickland

**Cover Photos:** Robin Davies/FPG International

*Production*

**Project Coordinator:** Nancee Reeves

**Layout and Graphics:** Joyce Haughey, LeAndra Johnson, Barry Offringa, Betty Schulte, Julie Trippetti, Brian Torwelle, Jeremey Unger, Erin Zeltner

**Proofreaders:** Susan Moritz, TECHBOOKS Production Services

**Indexer:** TECHBOOKS Production Services

*General and Administrative*

**Hungry Minds, Inc.:** John Kilcullen, CEO; Bill Barry, President and COO; John Ball, Executive VP, Operations & Administration; John Harris, CFO

*Hungry Minds Consumer Reference Group*

**Business:** Kathleen Nebenhaus, Vice President and Publisher; Kevin Thornton, Acquisitions Manager

**Cooking/Gardening:** Jennifer Feldman, Associate Vice President and Publisher; Anne Ficklen, Executive Editor

**Education/Reference:** Diane Graves Steele, Vice President and Publisher

**Lifestyles:** Kathleen Nebenhaus, Vice President and Publisher; Tracy Boggier, Managing Editor

**Pets:** Dominique De Vito, Associate Vice President and Publisher; Tracy Boggier, Managing Editor

**Travel:** Michael Spring, Vice President and Publisher; Brice Gosnell, Publishing Director; Suzanne Jannetta, Editorial Director

**Hungry Minds Consumer Editorial Services:** Kathleen Nebenhaus, Vice President and Publisher; Kristin A. Cocks, Editorial Director; Cindy Kitchel, Editorial Director

**Hungry Minds Consumer Production:** Debbie Stailey, Production Director

◆

The publisher would like to give special thanks to Patrick J. McGovern,
without whom this book would not have been possible.

◆

# Contents at a Glance

# Cartoons at a Glance

## By Rich Tennant

page 271

page 51

page 5

page 225

page 255

page 189

page 151

**Cartoon Information:**
**Fax:** 978-546-7747
**E-Mail:** richtennant@the5thwave.com
**World Wide Web:** www.the5thwave.com

# Table of Contents

# Introduction

••••••••••••••••••••••••••••••••••••••••••••••••••••

*D*o you need to write a sales proposal and never took *Sales Proposals 101* in school?

Can your proposals win an Oscar for "Best Document from a Cut and Paste Production Process"?

Do your sales and proposal writing processes seem to take place in separate departments within your company — and the department that writes proposals isn't the sales department?

Do your proposals look and read like the instructions for completing a tax return?

If you answer yes to just one of these questions, this book can help you write top-notch sales proposals that can close more deals. To the buyer's decision-makers, the sales proposal represents a document on which they must base a critical and often high-cost decision. Often, the more critical the decision is for the buyer's business, the less likely that price is the number one determining factor. A sales proposal that shows a thorough understanding of the buyer's business, presents a viable business solution, and demonstrates the seller's ability to deliver on the contract has a much higher chance for success than the sales proposal that features the lowest price.

A sales proposal must reflect the seller's best efforts at writing, producing, and packaging, because it can represent the first tangible product that a buyer may receive from a seller. In other words, a proposal must communicate a winning value proposition to the buyer and do it in such a manner that the buyer is convinced — although sometimes subtly — that the seller is experienced and able to deliver the product.

## *About This Book*

*Sales Proposals Kit For Dummies* is loaded with information that can help the first-time proposal writer or the seasoned sales professional write winning proposals. This book presents a proven sales proposal structure and content guidelines that have worked for all types and sizes of businesses.

A sales proposal is not an independent business document. It should reflect the results of a sales professional's consultative sales process — it's the prime product from one phase of the sales process. This book shows why and how to integrate a proposal development process with a consultative sales process. The sales proposal structure and writing process presented in this book reinforce the need to follow a consultative sales process.

# How to Use This Book

If you want to improve your selling and proposal-writing skills, then read the book from beginning to end. You can become a much better proposal writer and may pick up a few tips that can help you become a more effective sales professional.

If you promised to have a proposal on the buyer's desk by tomorrow morning, you're in luck. *Sales Proposals Kit For Dummies* is designed to help you get your thoughts and ideas organized and on paper very quickly. The book is divided into segments that break down the proposal into manageable pieces. The enclosed CD also contains templates that can help you make your sales proposal look like a top-notch business document but that don't require a huge investment of your time.

# How This Book Is Organized

*Sales Proposals Kit For Dummies* has six major parts, each of which is divided into chapters covering specific topics. Most chapters are self-contained units of sales and proposal design insight. You don't have to read the chapters in sequence. You can refer to them as needed. However, you may want to read all the chapters in Part II in the order that they're given. Reading these chapters in order helps you understand the recommended sequence for presenting information and ideas to the buyer. The recommended sales proposal structure diagram on the Cheat Sheet (that yellow piece of paper at the front of the book) reappears frequently in Part II to help you design your proposal.

## Part I: Integrating the Sales Process

Part I introduces you to the role a sales proposal plays in the sales process. You find out why the sales proposal should be an integral part of a consultative sales process.

# Part II: Making the Parts of a Great Sales Proposal

This part presents the nuts and bolts for designing and writing winning sales proposals. You get a proven five-section sales proposal structure and content guidelines that positively influence buyers and close more business deals.

# Part III: Details, Details . . . and Presentation!

Besides the recommended five main sections, a winning sales proposal has a transmittal letter, title page, table of contents, executive summary, and appendices. This part explains how to create these elements. Some situations lend themselves to letter proposals. One chapter in Part III explains the when, why, and how of a letter proposal.

# Part IV: Getting It Right the First Time

This part discusses how to use the sales proposal to create a sales partnership with a buyer and write a winning proposal. You may find that your company's sales professionals can use sales proposal models that follow an *80/20 rule* — eighty percent of a proposal's wording is standard for all customers and twenty percent is buyer specific. This part also explains how to design proposal models and sales tools.

# Part V: Selling on the Inside: The Internal Sales Proposal

Got an idea that can reduce or avoid costs or make more money for your own company? Sure you do — everyone who's really paying attention to inside developments seems to have one of these brainstorms from time to time. Part V presents a process and structure for writing a *recommendation report* — an internal sales proposal that senior management will love and that can make you rich and famous.

## Part VI: The Parts of Tens

The Part of Tens is a *For Dummies* classic. Here you find tips to make sure your proposals close more deals, things buyers expect to see in a winning proposal, and tips for presenting your proposal to the buyer.

## Part VII: Appendixes

The two appendixes in Part VII are working tools you can use to find more helpful information about crafting sales proposals. Appendix A lists numerous other reference books and Web resources. Appendix B shows you how to use all the great stuff on the CD that's tucked inside the back cover.

# Icons Used in This Book

This icon appears beside information that sales professionals can use to really make themselves or their proposals stand out from the competition.

This icon identifies handy hints that can make you a more effective salesperson. The information next to this icon gives you shortcuts, ideas, and suggestions for designing and producing winning sales proposals.

This icon flags little pieces of information you'll want to remember, especially when you're working a big deal and you desperately need another fat commission check.

This icon appears next to information, examples, and formats that are also available on the CD included at the back of the book. For example, a twenty-plus page proposal is on the CD. The CD also includes proposal templates that are completely formatted and ready for you to enter your custom content.

This icon flags those things you definitely don't want to do. It helps you steer clear of all the mistakes that can jeopardize the effectiveness of your proposal.

# Part I
# Integrating the Sales Process

The 5th Wave          By Rich Tennant

"I don't take 'no' for an answer. Nor do I take 'whatever', 'as if', or 'duh'."

## In this part . . .

**W**inning sales proposals focus on the buyer, not the
seller. In these chapters, learn why and how you
should integrate writing your proposal with your selling
activities. Also, learn how a well-written sales proposal
helps the buyer's decision makers make an informed
buying decision.

# Chapter 1

# Making the Sale with a Good Proposal

*I*'ll always remember that panicky feeling when the success of my first venture as a business owner was totally dependent on writing a winning proposal.

It was after I'd started a consulting business in the mid-1980s. I'd written sales proposals before then, but they were always based on pieces of other sales proposals. I had never taken a sales proposal writing class. None of my former bosses had seemed concerned about what I put in my proposals, as long as they contained the right price and the customer accepted them. But then, with my own firm, I heard my first potential customer say, "Sounds great, but we need a proposal to get this project approved."

All of a sudden, my new business was in a crisis and I was in a panic.

I mindlessly threw some stuff together. I never even asked the buyer what information it needed to see in the proposal. The first proposal out of my new firm did a great job packaging my fees, but it only sort of told my first customer what I was going to do. I was lucky and the buyer accepted it. But my proposal hadn't made any difference. My first client simply needed someone with my expertise and I was in town and my price was right.

Since then, I've spent a lot of time researching what buyers expect to see in winning proposals. I wrote this book so that you can avoid ever having to feel panicky when writing one. The book shows you how to:

✔ Connect your sales process to your proposal development process.

✔ Act more like a business consultant and less like a salesperson.

✔ Write better proposals that help your customers make better buying decisions.

✔ Maybe — just maybe — close more business deals.

# Selling Like a Consultant

A winning proposal is all about the buyer. In other words, a winning proposal focuses on the buyer's business, how to improve it, and its needs and objectives. To write one, you need to work closely with the buyer during your sales process. Working closely with the buyer means you behave more like a consultant and less like a salesperson, vendor, or peddler. In the process, the buyer may start treating you like a trusted business advisor. That's an enviable position.

If you combine the words *consult* and *sell* you get a new two-part term, *consultative selling.* It sounds fancy, but it's really quite simple: To sell a product or service, a salesperson talks things over with a buyer. They decide how they'll exchange money for property, goods, or services.

Okay, consultative selling is a tad more complicated than that, but not much more. Consultative selling dictates how a sales professional works closely with a buyer to determine such things as:

✔ What the buyer is doing now and whether some opportunity exists to improve the business

✔ How the proposed product can work for the buyer

✔ How the buyer can benefit by buying the product, including how much it can reduce costs or avoid costs or increase revenues

Consultative selling isn't a new idea; it's been around for years. And it goes by various names: *strategic selling, key account selling, collaborative selling, solution selling,* and *conceptual selling,* to name the most popular variations. The words are different but the meaning is the same: You spend enough time with the buyer to really understand his unique business situation. Then you recommend ways to improve the business and the buyer makes an informed decision about purchasing goods or services.

*Note:* In this book, I only use the terms *consultative selling* and *consultative sales process*.

You need to use a consultative sales process to write the kinds of proposals I describe in this book. If you're at all worried about following the consultative sales process, just follow this book's guidelines. Actually, the customer information that you put in your proposals can force you to be consultative when you work with a buyer. In other words, you'll sell consultatively when you gather and process the buyer information needed to write the kind of sales proposals described in this book.

# Wearing Your Consultant Hat while You Make a Proposal

If you want to write better proposals and get more business, you need to integrate two processes: consultative selling and proposal development. *Proposal development* is the process you use to design, write, and produce sales proposals. If you follow a consultative sales process, you end up knowing a lot about your customers. With better and broader customer information, you write better proposals. And as you write better proposals, you naturally become a better gatherer of information from your potential customers. It's circular — the consultative sales process leads to better proposals and better proposals reinforce your consultative sales process.

Is it easy to integrate consultative selling and proposal development? You bet!

Consultative selling requires analyzing that part of the buyer's business that relates to your proposed product. (In this book, I'll just use *product* when I mean either a product or a service.) It also means giving the buyer all the information that it needs to make an informed buying decision *before* you give it the actual sales proposal. In some ways, your sales proposal merely documents the results of your consultative selling activities.

You can work backwards from your proposal to determine what type of consultative sales activities are needed. Suppose you know up front that your proposal will contain, for example, a sophisticated cost-benefit analysis model. Then you know that your sales process needs to include gathering cost analysis data from your customer. In this case, the proposal's content actually defines some very specific consultative selling activities — working backwards from the proposal, you realize that you need to gather and analyze your buyer's current costs.

## A proposal showdown at the corporate corral

A proposal is basically a *customer communication* document — meaning that its purpose is to communicate with the customer. I've seen proposals from some large, well-known companies that were very ineffective customer communications documents. They communicated something about the companies, but not what the companies wanted the proposals to communicate. The proposals made it seem as if the companies had no proposal standards or quality controls. They lacked professional form and substance and did little to help customers make informed buying decisions.

I've always thought someone from the marketing or advertising department (you know, those creative people who specialize in customer communications) could help the sales people do a better job on their proposals. Here's something I've always wanted to do: First, get the vice presidents of sales and marketing in the same room. Then, put one of the company's proposals next to one of its fancy brochures. (You've seen those fancy brochures; they probably cost $5.00 each.)

Then I'd ask only one question: "Both of these documents represent your company. Tell me what kind of impressions your customers will get from each?" After a lengthy discussion, I'd hope that the marketing department would want to help the sales department with some of the content and packaging of sales proposals.

Integrating your consultative sales and proposal development processes can result in this type of reverse engineering. In other words, identifying what you're going to put in your sales proposal early in the sales process influences your selling activities. Your proposal's content actually helps you decide what information you need to get from a buyer and what you need to do with it; you design — or reverse engineer — some of your sales activities using your proposal as the basis for your design.

When you integrate your consultative sales and proposal development processes, you find process connections. By *process connections,* I mean those areas where your selling and writing activities overlap. These process connections are in two main areas:

- ✔ **Buyer information:** Information you need to know about the buyer to understand its business and any opportunities for improvement.

- ✔ **Application of your product:** How your proposed product will work in the buyer's business and what the resulting benefits are.

In Figure 1-1, you can see how this idea of process connections works. The information requirements of your consultative sales process overlap with the information requirements of your proposal development process. The overlap area defines the process connections.

**Figure 1-1:**
*Process connections are where your consultative sales process and proposal development process overlap.*

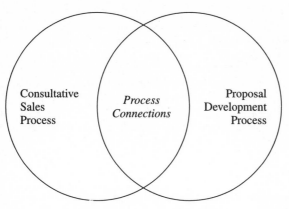

The information that you need to gather as part of the consultative sales process and that you also use in your sales proposals — in other words, the process connections — includes

- ✓ **General buyer information.**

- ✓ **Business improvement opportunity information:** Ways to reduce or avoid costs or increase revenues.

- ✓ **Product or service application:** How the proposed product or service works in the buyer's business.

- ✓ **Buyer benefits:** The financial and non-financial benefit that the buyer receives from the product or service.

- ✓ **Implementation:** How and when the product will be implemented and what the buyer's involvement is.

# Thinking and Speaking like a Consultant

I've introduced *consultative selling* to you. Another term I use throughout this book is *improvement opportunity*.

A key ingredient of consultative selling is helping a customer identify how to fix or improve some part of its business. When you identify the part of the buyer's business that you can improve with your product, you really identify an opportunity that the buyer has.

Look at the situation from a positive viewpoint. I don't use statements such as "The buyer has a problem to resolve" or "The buyer needs to make a change." Instead, I use the term *improvement opportunity* to identify that part of the buyer's business that can be fixed or improved in some way. In many situations, the improvement opportunity reduces the buyer's costs or improves its revenue.

So start thinking like a consultant. Think about how a prospective customer can use your product or service to save or make money. If you work with a buyer to identify and define its improvement opportunity, the buyer may start to treat you like a consultant rather than a vendor. And, by identifying the buyer's improvement opportunity, you obtain a critical piece of information that you need to write a winning proposal.

# Answering Your Buyer's Needs

Your proposal serves two important purposes, whether it's just a price quote or a 30-page, written offer to sell an expensive and complex product. The proposal is

- **A customer communications document:** Your written plan or offer to the buyer to exchange your product or service for money.
- **A decision-making tool:** A document for the buyer's review and analysis from which to make an informed buying decision.

## Customer communications documents

If you get most of your business through proposals, your proposals may be one of your most important forms of customer communications — more important than your brochures, magazine and newspaper ads, press releases, and your Web site. Although it's true that brochures and other customer communications can attract sales leads, they can't close sales. You know that it usually takes a sales proposal that helps the buyer make an informed buying decision.

## Buyer's decision-making tool

You know it's tough for some people to make a decision, especially one that involves a lot of money or is really important for their company. They need to have something to read and study. They want to scribble notes on it or write some questions in its margins.

Here's something to think about: If a proposal is a buyer's decision-making tool, then the better it's written, the better the buyer will feel about making the decision to buy the product.

Put yourself in the decision-maker's place. You have to decide whether or not to buy a complicated product for your company. What would you want and need to know? What would it take to make you feel good about your buying decision? Here are some questions you might ask if you were in that position:

- ✔ How can it reduce costs or avoid costs or increase revenues?
- ✔ Does this product meet our company's needs and objectives?
- ✔ How will the product work in our unique business operation? In other words, what's its application?
- ✔ How will our company benefit, financially and non-financially, from implementing the product?
- ✔ What process does the seller use, and how long will it take, to implement the product for our company?
- ✔ What makes the organization selling the product a good choice for our company?

# Sales Proposals Defined

A *sales proposal* is the seller's written plan or offer presented to a buyer to exchange property, goods, or services for money.

The buyer either accepts or rejects the proposal. Naturally, you hope the buyer accepts!

## Different shapes and sizes

Many companies (and people) use sales proposals in their normal course of business. If you're buying a swimming pool, you expect to get a proposal from the swimming pool builder — maybe not much more than a simple price quote. But the swimming pool proposal should also include information that you can use to compare builders and select the right one. The pool builder's proposal may give you information on such things as the type of concrete that will be used, tile options, and equipment. It may also explain how the pool builder will clean up your yard after construction. And you can bet that the proposal will explain how the builder expects to get paid.

Some companies write sales proposals to sell very costly and complex products or services. A computer systems consulting firm that develops e-commerce applications has to write proposals to get a signed contract, for example. Its proposals often represent one component of a sales process that may have lasted several months and included many sales calls by the sales professional and others from the consulting firm. Its sales process also may have included very detailed analyses of some parts of the customer's business. For costly or complex sales, the seller's proposed product often is an important, high-dollar purchase for the buyer. Because of the cost and complexity of the purchase, one person probably can't make the buying decision. Rather, an executive or buying committee makes the final buying decision.

## Most proposals are proactive

At some point during the sales process, after the sales professional has worked long and hard on the deal, the buyer asks for a proposal. Although the buyer initiates the request, the seller has been actively working with the buyer to get to the point where the buyer wants and needs a proposal to make a decision. It's a *proactive* proposal because the seller has been actively working with the buyer to get it to a point in the sales process where it asks for a proposal.

However, there also are *reactive* proposals out there. A reactive proposal is one where the buyer, usually an organization, formally asks the seller (or a group of sellers) for a proposal. The selling organization or the sales professional may not have had any previous contact with the buyer, but he reacts to their proposal request by writing a proposal.

# Got an RFP? I Wish You Well!

Some companies make purchases after getting competitive bids from two or more sellers. They're looking for the best deal, and who can blame them? They write an RFP, or *request for proposal,* and send it or make it available to sellers. This book is not about how to respond to RFPs. Let me explain why. When a seller writes a proposal in response to the buyer's RFP, the seller is reacting to the RFP and writes, you guessed it, a *reactive* proposal.

So, when a company gets an RFP and responds to it, it's writing a proposal in a reactive mode. The company is not writing reactive proposals because its sales people are just sitting around waiting for customers to call. They're writing reactive sales proposals because some customers are *required* to send RFPs!

RFPs from buyers come in assorted flavors, and so do the reactive proposals that they trigger from sellers. An RFP may just request a proposal for a product or service, in which case the seller can use one of its standard proposal models and take a more proactive sales approach in the response. If you have to respond to an RFP, most sales professionals think this is the preferred situation. This type of RFP is much easier to write than some RFPs that are very strict on what to include and how it must look.

Some responses to RFPs can be downright horrible to write because the buyer's RFP dictates everything about how a seller can write the proposal. These RFPs dictate proposal structure, content, format, and more. Further, this type of RFP often limits whom the sales professional can contact in the buyer's organization. In this situation, the seller must closely follow the RFP's directions or risk being eliminated from the process. Responding to these restrictive, and usually very detailed, RFPs is no fun for the seller or the sales professional. If you ever meet someone who just loves to respond to RFPs, don't get too friendly with him — sooner or later, he's going to lose it.

From the buyer's viewpoint, comparing information from several proposals is easier if all the information is in the same place. But unfortunately, dictating exactly what sellers can include in their proposals and how to write them gets in the way of the sellers' ability to present creative solutions and set their companies apart.

Many federal, state, and local governments make large purchases through only the RFP process. One of the most endearing stories about RFPs goes back to some $600 U.S. Air Force airplane toilet seats that were part of a very creative defense contractor's reactive proposal to a Department of Defense RFP.

# Losing with an Administrative Document

Some companies and their sales professionals write poor sales proposals because they think proposals are just administrative documents. They think a proposal is simply a document written at some point in the sales process. This attitude probably explains why their proposals are usually boring and bland. It also probably explains why their proposals contain little information to help a buyer make an informed buying decision. These sales professionals only use a proposal to package the price and some other basic information.

A proposal that the seller treats as an administrative document makes obvious the fact that the seller hasn't integrated its sales and proposal development processes. The crummy proposals may result from sales professionals who have weak, or maybe no, consultative selling skills; the proposals are poor because the sales professionals *can't* be very consultative.

Maybe you've met an ineffective sales person. He's usually the one who's in over his head trying to sell a complicated product or service. He never seems to get the full picture. He may not know if the prospect actually needs the product or service, but he's always trying hard to sell. Usually he doesn't understand the buyer's improvement opportunity. As an ineffective sales person, he doesn't know most of the critical information that he should about the prospect, especially how the proposed product will work for the buyer. In other words, he misses most of the process connection information.

That this type of sales person views proposals as nothing more than administrative documents isn't surprising. He's probably one of those guys who can crank out a proposal in five minutes. His proposals may even be long and detailed, but they contain very little buyer-specific information. He can probably write proposals by simply making a few global changes to a document on a computer and entering some cursory buyer information. No wonder the resulting proposals read like poorly written brochures!

## Selling to Top Management

Always remember that, in most sales situations, the senior managers from the buyer's organization read your sales proposals. These senior managers are usually the people who make the final buying decisions. In many cases, you have limited or no contact with the decision makers. Your primary contact with the buyer, usually a department or project manager, keeps you from talking directly with any of the company's top management. Many times, you don't get to present your proposal. Instead, your contact sends all the competitive proposals to the decision makers for their review and schedules a meeting to make a decision. Even if you've developed good rapport and built a solid relationship with your contact, that doesn't make any difference to the people making the decision. Your proposal is all that they're looking at. The proposal represents your deal and your company. Now how important is it to have the best proposal on the table?

To an informed decision maker, the winning proposal isn't always the one with the lowest price. The winning proposal may be the one that did the best job of educating the buyer. The winning proposal may be the one that presented the most compelling, buyer-specific reasons to make a change. Or maybe the winning proposal is the one that did a great job differentiating the winning company from the competition.

## My Pitch for Connecting Two Essential Processes

If you integrate a consultative sales process with an effective sales proposal development process, your life becomes easier and you win more business. When you put these processes together correctly, they produce outstanding results. Combining them makes you a more effective sales professional because your customers think that you really know what you're talking about and look to you for some answers to tough questions. If you treat your sales proposals as the end result of the integrated processes, your proposals do a much better job selling and representing your company and its products.

All this integration stuff should lead to more sales for you and your company. And this means you'll probably be over quota. Heck, you'll probably make Presidents Club and get that all-expenses-paid trip to Tahiti. But let me explain the concept a little bit more by showing how *not* integrating the processes works:

- ✔ **Consultative selling not integrated into proposal development.** In most sales situations, if you consistently follow consultative selling practices but neglect to integrate the process with your proposal development process, you can still win a reasonable amount of business. But you're probably missing some sales. Your proposals are probably pretty average; maybe you just write boilerplate proposals. Buyers may think that your proposals are disconnected from your sales process. They most likely think that you're a good business consultant during the sales process, but that you drop the ball when it comes to following through in your sales proposals.

- ✔ **Proposal development not integrated into consultative selling.** If you spend a lot of energy on writing sales proposals and are really good at it, but don't follow good consultative selling practices, you also miss closing some business. You may be skipping some critical sales process steps and moving too quickly. You probably don't spend enough time learning about a buyer's business and understanding its improvement opportunity. You may jump the gun by writing a proposal way too early — the buyer isn't ready to receive a proposal and you aren't ready to write one.

  Maybe you use a sales proposal as a sales process crutch — you spend more time writing a sales proposal than behaving like a consultative sales professional. Your proposals include some good reasons for the buyer to make a change, but they're generic reasons — they don't really fit the buyer's exact situation. They lack the depth that comes from really understanding a buyer's business and knowing exactly how your product can reduce the buyer's costs or increase its revenues. Your buyers probably like some of the stuff in your proposals, but the proposals just don't seem to really apply to their situation. You need to become more consultative.

# Chapter 2

# Getting to Know Your Buyer

· · · · · · · · · · · · · · · · · · · · · · · · · · · · · · · · · · · · · · · · · · · · · · ·

*In This Chapter*

▶ Finding your complex sales and key accounts

▶ Using the five categories of buyer information

▶ Identifying and defining the buyer's key performance indicators

▶ Defining a buyer's selection criteria

▶ Using proposal models and application worksheets

· · · · · · · · · · · · · · · · · · · · · · · · · · · · · · · · · · · · · · · · · · · · · · ·

*U*nderstanding your buyer's business is the starting point for writing winning sales proposals. By using good consultative selling skills, you gather all the information about the buyer that you need to demonstrate to the buyer that it would benefit from purchasing your product.

In fact, if you write a top-notch sales proposal, the information requirements of the proposal will probably force you to gather some buyer information you hadn't considered. In other words, the buyer information requirements needed to write a good proposal probably will make you a better salesperson.

## Recognizing Your Complex Sales and Key Accounts

Before you get to know the buyer, you need to decide just how detailed your knowledge has to be.

One of the key issues affecting how well you need to know your customers is whether you sell a complex product. If you're selling Internet routers, you need to know your customer's business inside and out. If you're selling water coolers, you may not need to know that much about your prospective clients.

## Spotting transactions a mile away

In transaction sales, the salesperson often follows a *technique-based* sales process rather than a consultative process. A technique-based sales process has predefined steps, questions, and techniques. The salesperson uses proven techniques to convince the customer to buy. These sales techniques often require the salesperson to overcome the buyer's objections through forceful selling.

Have you ever been the buyer in a technique-based sales situation? How did it make you feel? Did the salesperson seem like she was trying to hook you into buying? Notice I didn't say anything about used-car salespeople. . . .

Another issue that affects how in-depth your understanding of the buyer's business should be is whether that buyer is a key account. The more important the account, as a general rule, the more time you should spend getting to know the business.

Recognizing complex sales and key accounts ties to the concepts I present in Chapter 1. Integrating the consultative sales and proposal development processes makes complex sales and sales to key accounts a lot easier.

## *A complex sale: It's not a transaction*

A *complex sale* involves the sale of a complicated product that often has a high dollar value. If you're involved in complex sales, more than likely you have to work closely with the buyer so that you can understand something about its business and its improvement opportunity. When you understand the buyer, you can better communicate how your complex product will reduce costs or increase revenues. In other words, you help it make a more informed buying decision by dovetailing your proposal with its needs. Hey, that sounds like consultative selling to me!

A complex sale is the opposite of a *transaction sale*. Most transaction sales don't require much involvement with the buyer. Transaction sales involve the transfer of a *commodity*, meaning something on the low end of the food chain. Selling steel pipe to a manufacturing company is probably an example of a transaction sale, because the buyer is likely more interested in the price and availability of the pipe than in the features and benefits of the different brands of pipe.

Table 2-1 shows some major differences between transaction sales and complex sales.

| Table 2-1 | Transaction versus Complex Sales | |
|---|---|---|
| *Process Variable* | *Transaction Sale* | *Complex Sale* |
| Number of calls | One or two | Many |
| Decision makers | The decision makers are known to the salesperson. There may only be one decision maker. | Many people are involved in the decision. Perhaps a committee makes the final decision. The sales professional may not know all the decision makers. |
| Risk to buyer | The decision maker does not face much personal risk. The decision maker's business also faces fairly low risk. | The risk to the decision maker may be high. The decision to buy or not buy could have serious ramifications for the business. |
| Buyer-seller relationship | Not that important. The salesperson is probably viewed as just another vendor. | Very important. The selling company may be viewed as a business partner and the sales professional as a consultant. |
| Application of product in the buyer's business | Simple. Perhaps the product is just a commodity or raw material in a manufacturing process or the service is something basic, like washing windows. | Complex. Could significantly affect the buyer's business or the product is critical to the buyer's business. |

The types of proposals discussed in this book are designed for the sales professional who's making a complex sale or selling to key accounts. If you only make simple sales, a one or two page price quote may be all that you need to get the business. However, this book can give you some commonsense guidelines for selling and maybe an idea or two that can make your current proposal stand out from the crowd.

## A key account opens doors

A *key account* can be a customer in a complex sale or a transaction sale. Key accounts are also called *prime accounts* or *major accounts.* The definition of a key account is usually different from one seller to the next. If you're an independent business consultant, then you may consider every one of your customers to be key because each is an important revenue source. Other companies may identify their key accounts differently. Here are some of the criteria:

- ✔ **80/20 rule.** Typically, 80 percent of a company's revenue is generated by 20 percent of its customers. Customers in that top 20 percent are considered key.

- ✔ **Impact on buyer's business.** If the product being sold has a major impact or influence on the buyer's business, the buyer is a key account. For example, a manufacturing company is a key account to an enterprise resource planning software vendor because the software is integral to the manufacturer's operations. Or a large, regional financial institution could be a key account to an ATM vendor.

- ✔ **Unique customer relationship.** The buyer is a key account if, by implementing the product, the buyer enters into a long-term relationship with the seller. For example, a manufacturing company that outsources its senior-level management recruiting is a key account to the recruiting firm that provides the service on an exclusive basis. Or a marketing consultant that has an annual retainer with a computer software company would consider the software company a key account.

This book focuses on showing you how to write sales proposals for key accounts and in complex sales situations. If you only make simple sales to relatively unimportant customers, read on — some of the tips presented in this book may give you ideas for moving one or two of your current customers into the key account category.

# Using Five Buyer Information Categories

Some things you just have to know. You can't possibly write a winning proposal unless you know

- ✔ Basic factual information about the buyer
- ✔ The buyer's strategies and tactics
- ✔ The potential application of your product — how it fits in with the buyer's business
- ✔ How the buyer stands to benefit
- ✔ Who makes the decisions at the buying company and how they're made

I give you more information on each of these in the sections that follow.

# Capturing basic buyer information

Before you can sell your product, you have to know who you're selling it to. Basic buyer information is the who, what, and where information that you need before you can start in-depth conversations.

You can gather some basic buyer information before you make your first sales call from annual reports, professional and trade journals, magazine articles, internal marketing reports, trade-show lead cards, the Internet, and so on.

You're looking for the:

- Buyer name and address.
- Business, industry, or profession. Get the type, size, trends, and competition.
- Annual revenues, net profits, number of locations, and number of employees.
- Primary and secondary contact names, titles, mail and e-mail addresses, and phone and fax numbers.

# Connecting to the buyer's strategies and tactics

The buyer has goals. The buyer has probably laid out fairly specific strategies and tactics to reach those goals. You need to find out what those strategies and tactics are so that you can figure out the best way to meet the buyer's needs with your product.

- **Strategies** usually mean plans for making something happen. Most companies have many strategies. They result from strategic planning activities.
- **Tactics** usually mean methods or approaches that the buyer uses to implement the strategies. Think of it this way: Strategies lead to tactics.

You need to know which buyer strategies and tactics are relevant to the product you plan to propose. Don't expect to get this type of information on your first sales call with a new prospect. You first need to build rapport and relationship with the buyer. Behave like a consultant — listen to the buyer and then ask some good questions. You'll be surprised how much information a buyer gives you if the buyer thinks that you may help it with an opportunity.

Here's an example of how to identify strategies and tactics: Say that a large city has a strategy to integrate the Internet into all the city government's functions in order to help people interact with the city government as easily as possible. This strategy becomes very relevant to a software company that sells an electronic bill presentment and payment system in which bills are presented and paid over the Internet. However, this strategy has little relevance to a local automobile dealer who wants to sell pickup trucks to the city's park and recreation department — although the city may have other strategies that are important to the local auto dealer.

Be persistent in trying to identify buyer strategies that are relevant to the product you plan to propose. Don't worry about discovering irrelevant buyer strategies during your sales process. Even information that's irrelevant to your product lets you better understand a buyer's overall organization and business practices.

In addition to understanding strategies and tactics, you should know the role played by needs and objectives. An easy way to keep all this consultative sales stuff straight is to connect the buyer's needs with its tactics and objectives with its strategies. In other words, a buyer's tactics result in short-term needs while its strategies define long-term objectives. This may seem simplistic, but it's always worked for me.

A large healthcare provider plans to grow its business by acquiring other companies — this represents its national acquisition *strategy*. One supporting *tactic* is to develop and analyze company profiles of possible acquisition candidates. To implement this tactic, it *needs* to design and build a system to evaluate and rank the acquisition candidates. The healthcare organization also wants to have this system operational in three months — an *objective*.

In this example, understanding the buyer's relevant strategies and tactics would give a sales professional a critical advantage if she were selling systems development services. She could clearly identify the buyer needs and objectives that can be satisfied by her company's services: designing and developing a system to evaluate and rank acquisition candidates in three months.

## Defining how your product fits the picture

At some point in the process, you need to picture your product in the client's business. Doing so isn't as easy as you may think. First, you need to be an expert on the product that you're selling. Start with the facts — what you really should already know if you're selling the product. The facts can take a long time to gather if you're offering a particularly complex product. Then move on and:

> ✔ Visit your existing customers and find out how they use your products or services — work to understand their unique applications.
>
> ✔ Talk to product or service experts in your company (usually the people who install your products or deliver your services to customers).

After you have this information, think about how the product will operate in the buyer's business. What are the unique elements of the business that affect the installation and use of your product? The variables here are immense — just as there are all sorts of businesses, there are all sorts of ways in which your product can meet the needs of your clients.

A sales professional for an electronic bill presentment and payment software vendor (which I will call EBPP), whose product creates systems whereby bills are presented and paid over the Internet, would probably need to get answers to the following buyer-specific questions before making a proposal:

> ✔ How many customers receive paper-based bills or invoices today?
>
> ✔ What is the expected growth in customers over the next five years?
>
> ✔ How many or what percentage of customers have Internet access?
>
> ✔ How often does the buyer send bills?
>
> ✔ How much does sending a paper bill cost (paper, printing, envelopes, and postage)?
>
> ✔ How much does it cost to receive and process a paper-based payment?
>
> ✔ What type of accounts receivable or billing system is used to calculate and generate the paper-based bills

After gathering these buyer variables, the sales professional can define a unique application of the EBPP software for the buyer. The seller can write a very buyer-focused proposal that could include

> ✔ How the EBPP software could interface to the buyer's accounts receivable or billing system
>
> ✔ How many customers with Internet access might decide to receive and pay their bills over the Internet
>
> ✔ How much sending a bill over the Internet would cost
>
> ✔ How much it would cost the buyer to process a payment sent by a customer over the Internet
>
> ✔ What EBPP hardware the buyer would need to run the vendor's EBPP software

As a general rule, the more complex your product or service is, the more time and effort you have to put into gathering and analyzing buyer application information.

# Using key performance indicators to calculate the buyer's benefits

Buyers want to know how they can benefit financially from your product. To calculate the financial benefits, you first need to measure the current costs and revenues associated with the business's *improvement opportunity*. An improvement opportunity is that part of the buyer's business that you can improve with your product.

You need to know how much *not* having your product costs the buyer today in higher expenses or reduced revenues. This amount is the basis for calculating the financial benefits that the buyer can get from your product.

*Key performance indicators* are the numbers the buyer uses to measure how well its business is doing. Perhaps the ultimate key performance indicator for a publicly traded company is *earnings per share* (EPS) — how much net income the company earned for each share of outstanding stock. But most companies have many key numbers that affect EPS. For example, a company's *employee turnover rate* can represent a key performance indicator. A high turnover rate means the company is spending a lot of money recruiting, hiring, and training new employees. The company needs to reduce its employee turnover rate and lower it costs — sounds like an improvement opportunity to me. If the company doesn't have to recruit, hire, and train as many new employees, its EPS can go up.

Knowing the buyer's key performance indicators is important. This financial information, the buyer's increased costs or lower revenues, gives you the best basis you can have for calculating the financial benefits of the proposed product.

Identifying a buyer's key performance indicators can be difficult. You may find that the buyer doesn't really know how to measure the financial impact of its improvement opportunity. In some cases, it may not want to identify its key performance indicators (doing so could be controversial or embarrassing). You may run into a situation where the buyer knows what its key performance indicators are, but it doesn't want to share that information with you. When this happens, you may not be able to calculate the financial benefits of your proposed product or service. (Chapter 7 discusses financial benefits in detail and includes information on how to handle any bumps in the road caused by an inability to obtain needed information.)

To understand how to gather the information needed to measure the financial impact of the buyer's improvement opportunity you need to follow a few steps. This might seem like a lot of work at first, but the more you do it the easier it should become.

 1. **Make sure you understand how the application of your proposed product can make or save money for a buyer.**

2. **Develop a financial benefits calculation that measures how your product can reduce the buyer's costs or increase its revenues.**

   This financial benefits calculation requires some buyer-specific financial variables. These are the key performance indicators that you need to get from your buyer. Use them to calculate the financial impact of the improvement opportunity and the financial benefits of your proposed product or service.

3. **Make a list of the key performance indicators that you need for your financial benefits calculation.**

   During one of your meetings with the buyer, explain how you can calculate financial benefits using these key financial indicators. Ask the buyer if it currently uses the key performance indicators to measure costs or revenues. If it does, ask it to share its calculations. If it doesn't, put on your consultative selling cap and work with the buyer to measure the financial impact of the improvement opportunity.

Does this make sense? If not, I'll phrase it differently: First, you decide how to calculate the financial benefits of your product or service. While you develop the financial benefits calculation, you discover what financial variables you need from the buyer — the key performance indicators. Then you ask the buyer if it uses these key performance indicators to measure its performance. If it does, you just get the current values. If it doesn't, you need to work with the buyer to calculate them. After you go through the steps a few times in real life, they become pretty easy.

Here's a detailed example of how a sales professional used key performance indicators to make a sale.

A sales professional for a paging company sold alphanumeric paging services that offered the ability to send text messages to people equipped with standard alphanumeric pagers. One of her hot prospects was a trucking company that couldn't contact its drivers when they were on the road. As a result, the company missed many opportunities to pick up freight after a truck had left one of the company's terminals or another location.

To help the trucking company understand how alphanumeric paging services could benefit its operation, the sales professional developed a financial benefits calculation. She knew that her calculation needed to include key performance indicators unique to this trucking company.

The sales professional and her contact at the trucking company calculated the improvement opportunity for the trucking company by following this logic:

- They agreed that a partially loaded truck didn't generate the maximum possible revenue for the company.

- They needed to know what the average revenue per mile was for each truck and what the average monthly revenue miles were for each truck so that they could calculate average revenue per truck per month.

✔ They needed to know how much empty space was available in a typical truck while the truck was on the road. The average capacity utilization (expressed as a percentage of a full load) for each truck would allow them to calculate the maximum revenue per truck per month.

They used these three key performance indicators to calculate the trucking company's missed revenue (the improvement opportunity).

| | |
|---|---|
| Average revenue per mile: | $2.00 |
| Average monthly miles per truck: | 10,000 miles |
| Average load percentage: | 80 percent |

Using the three key performance indicators, the average revenue per truck month was

Average revenue per mile × average monthly miles per truck

$2.00 per mile × 10,000 miles per month = $20,000

The maximum revenue per truck per month was

The average revenue per truck per month ÷ average load percentage

$20,000 ÷ 80 percent = $25,000

As such, the average missed income per truck was $5,000.

The trucking company felt that it could easily increase its average load from 80 percent of capacity to 85 percent if it could contact its drivers at any time and send them meaningful text messages and directions using the paging company's alphanumeric paging service. A five percent increase would increase the revenue per truck to $21,250.

The sales professional's proposal included the following information:

✔ The cost to equip a driver with an alphanumeric pager and provide paging service: $78.00 per month, $936.00 per year.

✔ The estimated increased revenues resulting from the use of alphanumeric pagers because the average load capacity increased from 80 percent to 85 percent: $1,250 per month, $15,000 per year.

Do you think the sales professional made a sale?

Identifying a buyer's key performance indicators is a critical activity in your consultative sales process.

# *Pulling the decision in your direction by understanding how the decision gets made*

You can't change your buyer's decision-making process. But you can make some changes to your sales process and tailor the content of your sales proposal to help pull the decision in your direction. You need to understand:

✔ How the company makes buying decisions.

✔ Who the final decision makers are and how each may influence the decision.

✔ How the buyer will evaluate and select a vendor — what are its *selection criteria*.

✔ What the most important selection criteria are.

## *The process and the people*

If you want to sell consultatively, you need to know how the company makes buying decisions. Does one person review all proposals and make a recommendation to a buying committee? Or does each member of a buying committee study each proposal before the committee makes a collective decision? Or is there some other arrangement?

If an executive committee or appointed buying committee, rather than one person, makes the buying decision, you may not get an opportunity to meet every committee member. You certainly can't build rapport or develop a relationship with each person. However, your primary contact will know how his company's buying process works and something about each committee member. You need to ask your contact some good questions and your contact needs to give you some ideas about how each member will decide or how he or she may influence the decision.

Here's another example of why you need to have information about the buyer's decision-making process. If one of the buying committee members has a strong operations background, ask your contact if that committee member might be influenced by a detailed implementation schedule. Again, the answer probably will be yes. So you'll want to put information into the proposal about how your company installs the product.

Your goal should be to know as much as you can about the buyer's decision-making process and who makes the buying decisions. Whether it's one person or a committee, you'll want to shape your selling activities and your proposal to favorably influence the decision maker or decision makers.

### Selection criteria

As part of its decision-making process, a buyer probably uses selection criteria to evaluate competing products and vendors. In some cases, the buyer has a written list of well-defined criteria. Other buyers have an informal set of criteria. At some companies, the decision makers may not even realize that they're using certain criteria.

Some of the questions a buyer asks in a request for proposal (RFP) are the buyer's selection criteria.

Unless you're responding to an RFP, don't expect to be given a list of the buyer's selection criteria. But you can ask some important questions during your sales process to find out what the buyer wants from a product and vendor. For example, you can ask whether having customer references is important to the decision.

Some selection criteria are extremely generic and common:

- The seller's reputation
- Whether the seller has other clients of a similar size and type as the buyer
- Whether the seller has references that can be verified from companies that have bought the product

Do you think that your proposals should include these three pieces of information? Of course they should! If you were a buyer, wouldn't you want this information about the seller?

On the other hand, some buyers have very specific selection criteria. For example, a company may want to select a CPA firm that is 1) a local accounting firm with 2) international tax experience.

These two selection criteria would quickly narrow the field. If you were a sales professional for a CPA firm that didn't have international tax experience, you'd have two choices: either move on to your next prospect or ask more questions about the buyer's international tax accounting needs. Perhaps your firm has an affiliation with a foreign accounting firm that can provide the necessary tax accounting expertise and services.

### Ranking selection criteria

Knowing a buyer's selection criteria gives you valuable insight into how it plans to pick the winning product and vendor. The criteria help you understand what the buyer really thinks is important. But what if the buyer has a long list of selection criteria? Wouldn't it be helpful to know which ones are the most important?

## Selection criteria warm-up

Try this exercise before you begin designing and writing your next sales proposal. Take a few minutes to identify the selection criteria that you think most of your customers use. Try to list as many as possible. Then decide how your company meets or satisfies each one.

Ranking the buyer's selection criteria may sound a little complicated, but it may be easier than you think. This information should come out as you talk with your contact person. If you can rank order a buyer's selection criteria, you can focus your sales activities and write a proposal that addresses the buyer's most important concerns.

For example, say that the top three *vendor* selection criteria (as opposed to *product* selection criteria) for a bank that's evaluating call center software vendors are

- ✔ Customer service and support
- ✔ Continuing software enhancements
- ✔ Product quality

The proposal could include the following subsections to address the buyer's selection criteria:

- ✔ A mission statement to show the company's commitment for serving its customers

- ✔ A chronological summary of software releases and added functionality to show that the company has ongoing programs to enhance its software products

- ✔ An overview of the company's software development process to show the methodology for ensuring that the company's product design and development meets quality standards

A sales professional could also address the selection criteria during the sales process. A trip to the software vendor's corporate offices to meet key customer service personnel and the company's product development staff may convince the buyer that the software company is dedicated to customer service and product quality. However, the sales proposal is still a great opportunity to show how the company meets the selection criteria.

If you can identify and rank a buyer's selection criteria, you can identify where your company has advantages and disadvantages over the competition. Knowing where your company has a competitive edge immensely helps your sales efforts.

# Following the 80/20 Rule for Proposals

All this buyer information I've been talking about probably represents 20 percent of the information you need to put in a winning proposal. The remaining 80 percent of your proposals can contain the same stuff for every buyer. Your proposal should follow an 80/20 rule.

Most 80/20 rules state that 20 percent of something causes 80 percent of something else. Remember the 80/20 rule used to define a company's key accounts: Twenty percent of the customers provide 80 percent of the company's revenue.

Your proposals should follow this 80/20 rule:

> 80 percent of the wording in a company's sales proposal is the same for most customers; the remaining 20 percent is specific to the buyer.

If your company sells two or three products, it may need a proposal model for each product. If your company offers one service, and one service only, it may only need one proposal model.

If 80 percent of your proposal's wording is the same for most buyers, guess what makes up the other 20 percent? You've got it: the information contained in the five buyer information categories I write about in this chapter.

The 80/20 "rule" is really just a generalization. Don't feel like you must have exactly 80 percent general information and 20 percent buyer-specific information. The numbers are somewhat flexible, depending on the nature of your business.

You can take advantage of the 80/20 rule by using proposal models and application worksheets. *Proposal models* are typically built to reflect the 80/20 rule. A proposal model is a proposal that's 80 percent complete. Twenty percent of its wording is missing. It has some critical information gaps. These gaps provide places to insert the buyer-specific information that's needed to make the model a finished proposal. You can't write a proposal using a proposal model unless you get all the appropriate customer information first. As such, the proposal model fits quite nicely with the whole notion of consultative selling.

Don't confuse a proposal model with a boilerplate proposal. A boilerplate proposal varies little from one buyer to the next; usually, only the buyer's name and the price are different.

Use an *application worksheet* to fill out your proposal model. The worksheet contains the questions you need to ask in order to get the information that you need to customize a proposal model for each buyer.

You can create both a proposal model and an application worksheet by following these steps:

1. **Finish reading this book (at least complete Part II) to learn more about the structure and content of a winning proposal.**

2. **Write a sample sales proposal, ideally using information from one of your real customers. You should end up with a proposal that is 100 percent complete.**

3. **Go through each section of your completed proposal and identify the standard wording (the 80 percent) and the buyer variables (the 20 percent).**

   Buyer variables are things that change from one buyer to the next — the improvement opportunity, needs and objectives, application, price, implementation schedule, and so on.

4. **Develop your application worksheet by writing a question or phrase that can prompt you to gather the information needed for each buyer variable in the proposal. You may end up with a list of questions to ask or you may create a table that needs to be filled in, among other possibilities.**

5. **Finally, turn the completed proposal into a proposal model by deleting the buyer variable information. Doing so leaves blanks and empty lines. The information you gather with your application worksheet should find a home in one of these blanks or empty lines.**

This sounds easier than it really is. Plan on spending one or two hours per page writing your proposal model. It should take you several more hours to develop the application worksheet. But you get a big payoff. The proposal model and application worksheet make writing winning proposals a lot faster and a lot easier.

Chapter 15 discusses how to use proposal models and application worksheets.

# Chapter 3

# Deciding What Goes into a Very Good Proposal

*In This Chapter*

▶ Knowing the purpose of a proposal

▶ Writing business proposals, not technical treatises

▶ Avoiding proposal pitfalls

▶ Using commonsense proposal guidelines

▶ Giving your proposal structure

*Y*our sales proposal is a personal conversation with the buyer's decision makers. It tells them about an important improvement opportunity that you see in their business and describes how your product or service can carry out that improvement. And your proposal provides all the critical information that the buyer needs to make an informed buying decision.

If you don't send the buyer a proposal, you create big problems. In the worst case, the buyer may not know exactly what you're selling. In the best case, neglecting the proposal makes you appear uninterested.

Using a one-size-fits-all, *boilerplate* proposal is better than not sending any proposal, but it doesn't work very well. Neither does using a *so-what* proposal — a proposal that doesn't provide the buyer with any financial justifications for making a change.

Buyers are looking for detailed information that's addressed specifically to them. In this chapter, I take you inside a proposal so that you can see exactly where its power comes from and so that you can avoid some common proposal mistakes.

# Understanding Your Proposal's Purpose

I believe in selling like a consultant, and I write about the consultative sales process throughout this book. (For an introduction to consultative sales, check out Chapter 1.) The consultative sales process and your proposal go hand in hand; they each affect the other.

The functions of your proposal include

- ✔ Documenting your consultative sales activities
- ✔ Matching the buyer's needs and objectives to your product's features and the resulting benefits.
- ✔ Providing an accurate and compelling financial justification for buying your product
- ✔ Giving the buyer confidence in your know-how, capabilities, and capacity to deliver
- ✔ Becoming the basis for continuing sales opportunities with the buyer

In the sections that follow, I explain each of these functions. I explain how making sure that your proposal meets all of these functions can create a favorable buying decision. I also introduce my five-section proposal structure.

## Documenting the sales process

Much of the work of creating a sales proposal occurs during the sales process. As you work with the buyer to identify its improvement opportunity, you determine

- ✔ How the application of your product will help the buyer reduce or avoid costs or increase revenues
- ✔ How much the product will cost the buyer
- ✔ How you plan to install or implement the product and who will do so

Keep in mind that most of your contact with the buyer occurs through a contact person. That contact person may not be the decision maker. Everything that you work out with the contact person needs to be put in writing for the decision makers to review. In fact, documenting the sales process is probably the most important function of a sales proposal.

The more complex and expensive your product is, the more important it is to document the findings of your sales process.

# Matching what the buyer needs with what you're selling

Differentiating between a buyer's needs and objectives can help you sell consultatively and write winning proposals. To help you keep needs and objectives straight, think of a buyer's needs as an immediate or short-term requirement — something that helps to implement a tactic. Think of objectives as strategic or long-term — something that helps to achieve a strategic plan.

At the end of the consultative sales process, you know exactly how your product can benefit the buyer. Describe, in your sales proposal, the precise benefits that the buyer will reap if it buys the product from you. Your proposal should

✔ Describe the needs and objectives that are created by the buyer's improvement opportunity.

✔ Describe the application of your proposed product in the buyer's business.

✔ Show how your product's features satisfy the buyer's needs and objectives.

Your proposal lets the buyer know you understand it and its unique business situation. The proposal shows that you know about the buyer's improvement opportunity and the needs and objectives that correspond to the improvement opportunity. It then presents the solution that you're offering.

# Providing financial justification

Describing how your product will reduce or avoid costs or increase revenues for the buyer is another important purpose for your proposal. In other words, your proposal identifies and explains the money-saving or moneymaking benefits the buyer will realize by installing your product.

Your proposal's financial benefit analyses and calculations help the buyer make the decision to purchase your product. You can make the decision even easier if you use easy-to-understand and accurate financial benefits analysis. Use the buyer's key performance indicators (its numbers) as the basis for your calculations. Using the buyer's numbers saves you from making mindless, general statements like:

✔ Installing the Acme Ace Widget reduces your production costs!

✔ Adding the XYZ Extraction Service increases your service revenues!

✔ Training with our Super Software improves productivity!

A winning proposal shows *exactly* how much value your product adds to the buyer's operation.

## *Reducing the buyer's risk*

Most buyers face a risk when making a change. Putting a new system into service, hiring a new (and unknown) consulting firm, or installing a new piece of equipment are all decisions that carry a large risk factor. Companies aren't eager to jeopardize their success, so risk makes a difference in the buyer's decision process.

To reduce the buyer's perceived risk, your proposal should present some information about your company's capabilities — your ability to deliver on the contract. In other words, the proposal can assure the buyer that your company knows what it's doing and has lots of experience doing it.

During the sales process, you can identify many of the buyer's concerns that may prevent it from making the proposed change. You do want to note the buyer's concerns and, if possible, make sure that your proposal adequately addresses each. If you follow a consultative sales process and build rapport and a relationship with your buyer contact, you learn what concerns the buyer has about making a change.

For example, a sales professional for a large software vendor learned that the buyer's last systems installation was a disaster. The installation created tremendous customer service problems that took months to resolve. Just considering another systems installation brought back some bad memories for the buyer. As a result, the buyer probably felt any systems conversion was more risky than it really is.

The software vendor responded to those worries by explaining how his company minimized any business disruptions. He included a detailed description of its conversion process in his proposal.

In many ways, your sales proposal itself can assure a buyer of your capabilities. Your proposal's general appearance and quality send subtle messages to the buyer. Its structure, content, format, paper quality, binding, and writing style tell the buyer about your company. If your proposal looks good, it makes you look good and it gives the buyer some assurances that your company may be the right choice.

Chapter 9 has lots of ideas on how to assure the buyer that your company knows what it's doing, and Chapter 12 offers tips on presenting your proposal.

## Becoming the basis for future sales

Here's a moneymaking idea that you can take to the bank — have a permanent goal to always sell more to your customers. But don't worry about improving your business with your customer. Worry about improving your customer's business. Looking for ways to help your customers thrive — and making a sale by doing so — is part of a successful consultative sales process. Remember that your customers should think of you as a business consultant or partner — not just a salesperson trying to make a buck. Here's an example to illustrate the point.

A software company used the consultative process to sell a large police department a property and evidence room management system (PRMS). During installation, the software firm learned that the police department also wanted to automate its auto impound operation. So the account executive submitted a proposal — and won. As that second engagement was proceeding, the software company realized the police department also needed to add a continuous video monitoring system to its property room to improve the security of its cash vault operations. So the company submitted a proposal for that purpose, it was accepted, and so on to a more and more profitable and satisfying seller-buyer relationship.

# Writing Business versus Technical Proposals

Your sales proposal must focus primarily on your buyer's key business issues rather than on its technical issues. Even if technology applications are an important part of the buyer's improvement opportunity, explaining the technology should never take precedence over explaining how your proposed product can help reduce the buyer's costs or increase its revenues.

Here's why. Usually, a buyer's senior management's number one goal is making or saving more money so the company can make a larger profit. A buyer's senior management isn't as interested in the details about a new technology as they're interested in how it can help the company reach its profit goal. Typically, senior decision makers rely on their subordinates or other employees to evaluate any new technology being proposed. If they're reading the proposal, the technology has probably already gotten a thumbs-up from the tech experts within the company. If the decision makers don't have faith in the technology, why would they be wasting their time reading a proposal?

## Techies talking to techies = no sale

In 1992, a leading telecommunications company proposed that a regional telephone carrier replace its existing telephone lines with fiber-optic cables. The fiber-optic cable was a new technology for the buyer. It represented a huge investment and strategic business decision for the regional carrier. The seller's proposal was nearly 200 pages long. It did a spectacular job of presenting the company's leading-edge fiber-optic technology, including some potential applications for the regional company.

The proposal wasn't accepted, even though the telephone company's top management liked the idea of fiber-optic cable. The primary reason for declining the proposal was that it didn't present any buyer-specific business improvement opportunities. In other words, the seller proposed that the telephone company spend millions of dollars installing fiber-optic cable, but didn't show it how it could make or save money using the technology. The huge proposal did little more than communicate technical information from the seller's techies to the buyer's techies.

You do want to make sure your proposal contains the technical information needed to support and justify the proposed business solution. However, you want to present the buyer with a proposal that focuses on the business solution rather than the technical solution for its improvement opportunity.

Consider putting the most of the technical details of your product in an appendix. Keep in mind that the main body of your proposal should always contain more business information than technical information. Your proposal is more likely to succeed if it addresses how the buyer can reduce costs or increase revenues at length and only mentions the technology as an adjunct to the improvement opportunity.

Chapter 11 gives you the details on using appendices.

If your company's sales proposals focus more on technical issues than on business issues, your company may have one of these problems:

- ✔ Your sales professionals may lack the consultative skills needed to analyze the buyer's operation, identify improvement opportunities, and present business solutions.

- ✔ Your company may have too many tech experts and too few consultative sales professionals and business people helping to write sales proposals.

- ✔ The market for your company's technology exists — your company has a technical solution for which no viable business need exists.

# Avoiding the Pitfalls: No Proposal, Boilerplate, and So-What Proposals

To better understand the purpose of your proposal and its importance as a product of your consultative sales process, you need to learn what can happen if you:

✔ Don't write proposals.

✔ Write *boilerplate* proposals.

✔ Write *so-what* proposals.

## No proposal! An invitation to the dreaded "internal" document

Here are some occasions when you may be tempted to not write a proposal:

✔ Your contact at the buyer tells you that he can get the deal approved without a proposal — the bigger the deal, the less likely it can get approved without a written proposal.

✔ You've demonstrated your product to the ultimate decision makers and they were really impressed. No one asked for a proposal and you didn't ask if you needed to present one. Before this deal heads south, ask the buyer what's the next step in its decision process and if it needs a proposal from your company.

✔ You know it's going to take you two days to write a proposal and you just don't have the time. You think your contact has enough information from you and knows enough about your product to get the deal approved. Will you have enough time to save this deal if the buyer decides to talk with your competitors before making a decision?

What if you just don't write a proposal? What's the worst that can happen? The worst, I think, is that your inaction gives your competition an opportunity to move in. Here's how that works. If your prospective buyer really thinks your product makes sense, someone in the buyer's company may decide to write an *internal sales proposal*. This internal sales proposal is intended to give the buyer's decision makers the information that you should have put in your sales proposal in the first place — the information needed to make an informed buying decision. However, an internal sales proposal often lists some other sources the buyer has for buying your product — your competition. (See Chapter 17 for more information on the internal sales proposal.)

Without question, you put your sale at risk if you force a buyer to write an internal sales proposal. You can quickly lose control of the sale and of the sales message. When compared to a well-written sales proposal, an internal proposal often doesn't have an in-depth presentation of your product's application and the resulting benefits. And the internal proposal may even compare the advantages and disadvantages of your product with those of your competitors — uh-oh.

Most buyers don't have the in-depth product knowledge that you have. As a result, they probably can't develop the compelling financial justifications needed to support a buying decision. Internal proposals suffer from a lack of knowledge.

## Beating up on boilerplate proposals

A *boilerplate* proposal is a proposal where most of the wording is the same for all buyers. The only difference from one of the seller's proposals to the next is usually the buyer's name and the price. Boilerplate proposals send several bad messages to a buyer:

- ✔ **All buyers are the same.** The seller doesn't care that buyers have different business operations or unique business needs and objectives.

- ✔ **The buyer is not a key account.** The buyer's business isn't that big of a deal for the seller.

- ✔ **The seller has untrained or perhaps inexperienced sales people.** The sales people don't follow a consultative sale process or they've never been trained to sell consultatively.

- ✔ **The seller is selling a commodity.** The seller's product is a commodity and the buyer should only care about price and availability.

### Why companies use boilerplate proposals

Believe it or not, some companies that sell very complex products only use boilerplate proposals. These sellers have reasons for doing so and they usually include one or more of the following. They want to:

- ✔ Deliver a standard sales message to every buyer. Perhaps they want to make sure all their sales professionals correctly describe generic product features or service capabilities.

- ✔ Make sure that each proposal contains some standardized wording that's needed to satisfy a legal or regulatory issue.

- ✔ Make it very easy for their sales professionals to get a proposal in the hands of a buyer. These sellers don't expect their sales professionals to follow a consultative sales process.

## Leaky boiler

Here's a classic boilerplate situation. It's real and it concerns a large truck leasing company that used nothing but boilerplate proposals. Its excuse for this primitive practice was that it wanted to make sure that all of its proposals completely described how it did business. Except for the buyer's name appearing wherever the word-processing system found the *[customer name]* field, the leasing company's proposals were really little more than long, boring brochures. And they weren't very well written. The proposals forced prospective buyers to figure out, on their own, how the leasing company's services and systems could improve the buyer's operations and reduce truck acquisition and operating costs.

The real irony is that this truck leasing company had one of the best and most sophisticated truck leasing services available — maybe the best in the country. But the company's president said he wanted his sales professionals to rely on *relationship selling* — schmoozing with customers. He didn't care if their sales professionals were consultative and he really didn't put much value in the need for a buyer-focused sales proposal. He didn't seem to care that their boilerplate

proposals failed to define a buyer-specific application and the resulting benefits. He felt the only thing his company's customers really cared about was price. Well, the boilerplate proposals really helped buyers focus on that!

It's not surprising that this leasing company closed only about 25 percent of their sales proposals. This meant its competitors, probably with lesser services and equivalent prices, won 75 percent of the time. It appears as though relationship selling wasn't enough to close more business. If relationship selling was as important as the president thought, then 75 percent of the company's prospects actually liked the other sales professionals better!

You may be thinking, "But if they can submit more proposals than other companies, they don't need to have a real high success rate." True, but submitting more means the sales force has to make more calls and schmooze more prospects. The cost for making sales calls continues to rise, and many companies are trying to cut travel budgets. So, the numbers game doesn't work too well in a complex sales situation.

Boilerplate proposals just don't give a buyer any compelling reasons to make a change because they don't contain any buyer-specific information.

Maybe the bottom line reason for any company to use boilerplate proposals is the old numbers game. These sellers think the more proposals their sales people can get in the hands of potential buyers, the more deals the company will close. How does this fit with a company that follows a consultative sales process? It doesn't.

A fancy brochure and a price quote serve the same purpose as a boilerplate proposal.

### Boilerplate proposals create problems

If a buyer thinks your proposed product deserves a further look and you give it a boilerplate proposal, you force it to do some work that it may not be prepared to do. The buyer wants to understand how your product can work in its unique business (the *application* of your product). It wants to identify the resulting financial and non-financial benefits. So if you give a buyer a boilerplate proposal, you probably aren't giving it all the information it needs.

To put it another way, a boilerplate proposal can force the buyer to do things that are really your responsibility. That's not good, and what's even worse is that your boilerplate proposal may cause the buyer to analyze the situation in more detail. What if your buyer's analysis convinces it that the generic improvement opportunity in your boilerplate proposal does apply to it? What if it decides to send *Requests for Proposals* (RFPs) to other companies that it thinks can provide the same product at a lower price? Now your boilerplate proposal has caused you to lose of control of the sales process. Your buyer is now going to get lots of help identifying, selecting, and evaluating other options from your competition.

What's the bottom line? Writing sales proposals that your buyer can use to make an informed buying decision is a lot more productive than writing boilerplate proposals.

## Avoiding so-what proposals

A *so-what* proposal isn't much more effective than a boilerplate proposal. A so-what proposal doesn't give your buyer the financial justification that it needs to make a buy decision because your value proposition is deficient. (*Value proposition* is simply a fancy way of saying the reasons that they buyer has to buy your product — the value that your product brings.)

To determine if you're writing so-what proposals, ask your buyers what they think. Get their reactions to your proposals. If a buyer says something like, "Your product seems like a good idea, but I just don't know what it'll do for our bottom line," you're writing so-what proposals. In most cases, a person who says he doesn't understand how your product can benefit his business is also admitting that he doesn't have the time or the knowledge to calculate the financial benefits.

Because a so-what proposal lacks the financial justifications that your buyer's top management needs to make the buy decision, the buyer may try to develop financial justifications to support your proposal. Who do you think is better able to analyze the financial benefits of your product, you or the buyer? You had better know more about the financial benefits of your product than a prospective customer! So you should be the one to calculate these benefits. Further, if your buyer has to calculate its financial benefits, you're not following a consultative sales process.

Just like what can happen with boilerplate proposals, a so-what proposal can cause you to lose control of the sale. So avoid writing them. Leave nothing to chance or a buyer's miscalculation. Make sure you always control the proposal process and the numbers — the analyses of the buyer's improvement opportunity and the financial benefit calculations of your product.

# Following Commonsense Guidelines for Your Proposals

Don't forget to use common sense as you write your sales proposals. Consider this section as a reminder of all the "obvious" things that you should keep in mind while writing. The tips I give you here are the basis for the five-part proposal I show you later in this chapter and much of the other content in this book.

## Writing it from the buyer's viewpoint

When you write a proposal, try to put yourself on the buyer's side of the desk; pretend you're one of the buyer's decision makers. Look at your proposal from that viewpoint. If you had to make the buying decision, what would you:

- Expect the seller to know about your business?
- Need to know about the seller's proposed product?
- Want to know about the seller's company and how it does business?

If you're having trouble looking at things from the buyer's viewpoint, pretend that you own the buyer's company and it's your money. Pretend that you set a goal for your company and for yourself: If the company makes more than a 20 percent pretax profit margin, you get to buy a new Corvette convertible. Whenever a proposal crosses your desk, you look at it to see if it can help you hit the goals that you've set.

Writing your proposals from the buyer's viewpoint may be the most important guideline I offer you. Putting yourself in the reader's mind will quickly put your sales proposals at the head of the pack.

## Giving it order and making it flow

Your proposal should have a logical flow of information and ideas. For example, your proposal should include a description of the custom application of your product and then present the resulting features and benefits. Another example: Your proposal should *not* present your proposed engagement schedule and then present the buyer background — that sequence makes no sense.

Your proposal also should group similar types of information. One main section of your proposal should contain all the information about your company, for example. In other words, you present all the things a buyer may want to know about your company and how you do business — your mission statement, company history, research and development programs, and so on — in one section.

This is commonsense stuff. Don't worry about designing your proposal's structure and content right now. Part II of this book gives you lots of help.

## Educating the reader

Try to write every proposal as if one of your buyer's decision makers had little or no knowledge about the specific business function or operation being discussed. For whatever reason, he doesn't know anything about this particular part of the buyer's business and the related improvement opportunity. In other words, don't assume that all of the decision makers have the same knowledge level. You write a better proposal when you assume one decision maker doesn't know anything. Your proposal should give all its readers all the information they need to make an informed buying decision.

## Controlling length

Everyone wonders about proposal length. Here are some of the most frequently asked questions on that subject:

- ✔ Can a proposal be too long?
- ✔ Should a $500,000 proposal be ten times longer than a $50,000 proposal?
- ✔ Will a buyer think that something's missing in a proposal if it's shorter than other proposals?

Part of the answer is that a complex product or improvement opportunity probably dictates a proposal that needs to be fairly lengthy. The cost of your proposed product also may affect a proposal's length (although a $500,000 proposal definitely does not need to be ten times longer than a $50,000 proposal). Another factor that affects your proposal's length is the amount of information it includes about your company to help a buyer decide if it wants to do business with you. If you include a detailed description of your company's history or your R&D process, you add a page or two to your proposal's length. Even issues like font size and page margins affect length.

I'm tempted to give you advice about the length of your proposal — how many pages is too short, how many pages is too long — but there are just too many variables. If you follow the guidelines in Part II of this book, your proposals will be better designed and probably more precise than if you obsess over length.

The best answer to any question about how long or short a proposal should be may be this: Your proposal should be long enough to get a signed contract, but short enough to hold the reader's attention. (Hey, that sounds like an answer from a politician!)

Use these two guidelines if you're still wondering about your proposal's length:

- ✔ Ask your buyer what it expects. Some companies don't like to receive and may not accept lengthy proposals. They may expect that the main body of the proposal will be 10 to15 pages long — but they may not have limits on the number and length of appendices.

- ✔ Try to limit the amount of detail in the main body of the proposal. Remember that a well-written sales proposal won't bore the reader (too much). Therefore, avoid lengthy product descriptions, specifications, or implementation task lists in the main body. Instead, summarize this stuff and put the details in appendices.

# Structuring Your Proposals

The next few pages give you an overview of the five-section proposal that I advocate. As you read about each section's contents, think about how the structure creates a logical flow of information and ideas. You can find out all the details in Part II of this book, Chapters 4 through 10. The section titles I use in these figures and tables are generic. Part II shows you how to use specific titles.

Note that the first section of the proposal is background information about the *buyer,* not the seller. (Raise your hand if the last proposal you wrote started with background information about your company.) Your proposals should document the results of your consultative sales process. If you sell consultatively, you focus on your buyer and your proposals should have the same focus.

Table 3-1 introduces the proposal sections that I recommend and briefly describes the contents of each.

| Table 3-1 | Five-Section Proposal Structure | |
|---|---|---|
| *Section* | *Generic Title* | *Contents* |
| One | Background Information | Everything you learned about your customer during your sales process. This section *sets the stage* for your proposed product. |
| Two | Proposed Solution | Everything your customer needs to know about your proposed product: description, application, features, and benefits. |
| Three | Implementation | The who, how, and when about implementing your product. |
| Four | Seller Profile | Things your customer wants to know about your company. |
| Five | Business Issues | All the boring but necessary business stuff. |

Here's the logic for using these five sections in this order:

First the buyer want to know that you know about its company and have identified a viable improvement opportunity. Section 1.

Next, the buyer wants to learn about your proposed product, its application in the buyer's company, and the financial and non-financial benefits the buyer can expect. Section 2.

If the buyer buys into the proposed product section of the proposal, it then wants to learn about how you plan to deliver on the contract. Section 3.

If your proposal accomplishes the above three things, the buyer probably asks the following question: "Hey, who are these guys?" So, you next need to give the buyer some info about your company. Section 4.

Finally, the buyer is ready to look at all the boring business stuff associated with the deal. Section 5.

Your proposals require more than the five main sections to be complete, however. Table 3-2 lists some other important elements that you should include in your proposals. Chapter 11 explains each element in detail.

| Table 3-2 | Other Important Proposal Elements |
|---|---|
| *Element* | *Comments* |
| Title Page | The cover page to your proposal that, if titled correctly, can help focus the reader's attention. |
| Executive Summary | A concise synopsis of the entire proposal; a proposal in miniature. |
| Table of Contents | A listing of the proposal's main sections and subsections with page numbers. |
| Appendices | Brochures, detailed schedules, preprinted materials, and so on that are used to support information summarized or referenced in the main proposal sections. |

Figure 3-1 illustrates the five-section proposal structure. A version of this illustration appears in most of the chapters in Part II. The recommended subsections are slowly added to the figure as you work your way through Part II.

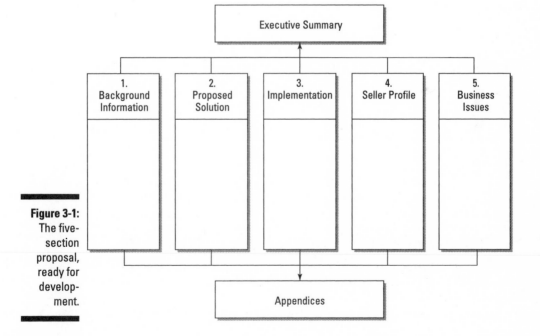

**Figure 3-1:** The five-section proposal, ready for development.

Table 3-3 lists the five recommended proposal sections and the chapters in which I show you how to write them.

| Table 3-3 | Proposal Sections and Book Chapters |
|---|---|
| *Proposal Section* | *Chapter* |
| Background Information | 4 and 5 |
| Proposed Solution | 6 and 7 |
| Implementation | 8 |
| Seller Profile | 9 |
| Business Issues | 10 |

# Part II
# Making the Parts of a Great Sales Proposal

The 5th Wave    By Rich Tennant

CONFERENCE ROOM 4E

"New rule — the next time we want to create buzz with a sales proposal, we use wasps whose stingers have been removed."

## In this part . . .

A winning sales proposal is focused on the buyer and presents ideas and information in a logical sequence for the reader. In this part, I present my proven five-section proposal structure. Using the structure, you first write about the buyer, then about your product, then about how you plan to implement your product, and only after all of that do you provide information about your company. The last section of the proposal covers business issues.

# Chapter 4

# Writing First about the Buyer — Grabbing Interest from Page One

∙∙∙∙∙∙∙∙∙∙∙∙∙∙∙∙∙∙∙∙∙∙∙∙∙∙∙∙∙∙∙∙∙∙∙∙∙∙∙∙∙∙∙∙∙∙∙∙∙∙∙∙

*In This Chapter*

▶ Appealing to the buyer's self-interest

▶ Bringing some readers up to speed

▶ Playing it straight — just the facts

▶ Including the right subsections

∙∙∙∙∙∙∙∙∙∙∙∙∙∙∙∙∙∙∙∙∙∙∙∙∙∙∙∙∙∙∙∙∙∙∙∙∙∙∙∙∙∙∙∙∙∙∙∙∙∙∙∙

Many salespeople who use the consultative sales process start their proposals with a background information section about their company. What happened to putting the customer first? Some possible reasons for this flip-flop include

✔ The salesperson gets blank-page syndrome when she starts to write the proposal. Rather than stare at a white computer screen, she writes about a subject she knows very well — her company. After a while, the creative juices start to flow and she includes some stuff about the buyer, but she buries it deep in her proposal.

✔ The salesperson really thinks the buyer wants and needs to know a lot about her company (how big it is, how many offices it has, and so on) before getting into the real meat of the proposal, which is the buyer's business improvement opportunity and how much money the buyer can make or save.

✔ The salesperson's company has always written proposals this way.

Your proposal does need to include information about your company. But first focus your proposal on the buyer. Show the buyer that you understand the situation. This chapter tells you how to get your proposal off to a great start. It should be read in conjunction with Chapter 5, which also contains information about writing the first section of your proposal.

# Showing that You Know Your Prospect

The first section of your sales proposal:

- ✔ Documents your in-depth understanding of your buyer's business and improvement opportunity — those things you learned while you were face to face with the buyer's contact person, surfing the Internet, reading your buyer's annual report, and analyzing what you found.

- ✔ Provides detailed background information, including the key performance indicators that measure the buyer's improvement opportunity. Some proposal recipients don't know as much as you may think they do about their own business.

- ✔ Sets the stage for the second section of the proposal, in which you roll out your product or service.

You can't fake knowledge, and you obviously can't use a boilerplate from other proposals while writing this section. It must demonstrate your thorough understanding of the buyer's business, particularly those functions that are relevant to the buyer's improvement opportunity.

# Educating the Reader — Some May Need Help

Use the background information section to educate the readers — the buyer's decision makers — by providing them the pertinent information about the improvement opportunity that their organization has. Give them the knowledge foundation on which to base their buying decision and make sure that all the buyer's decision makers have the same level of knowledge. Try and delight the readers with how much you know about their company. After reading this section, the buyer may start to think you're more a business consultant than a salesperson.

Say that you're the senior vice president of human resources for a Fortune 500 company. You sit on the company's executive committee, which makes strategic buying decisions. Your company is currently evaluating electronic bill presentment and payment (EBPP) options and has several proposals on the table. You have limited involvement with the company's billing and accounts receivable process. Actually, all you know about this function is that the company sends its customers paper bills every month and most customers send the company checks to pay their bills.

You don't know anything about EBPP, other than that it seems to be one of those newfangled Internet thingies. You didn't even know what *EBPP* meant until it was defined in one of the proposals you're reading. You realize that other members of the executive committee seem to know a lot more about EBPP than you do. Many seem to think this e-commerce application is critical for the company's future operations. You're looking for help so that you don't appear ignorant to your peers. You need some background information about EBPP and you need it now. You hope that one of the proposals you're reading will give you that information, rather than simply hyping the vendor and its product's features.

You're wishing that just one of these EBPP sales professionals could put himself in your position. If he were in your position, he'd quickly realize that his proposal needs to educate some of its readers. Instead of assuming that everyone in the buyer's organization has the same level of knowledge, he'd provide all the information anyone would need to make a buying decision. His proposal would have to relate the background on EBPP to the buyer's current billing process. He'd also probably know that he should include some information on what companies similar to yours are doing with EBPP.

You should constantly ask one question when writing a buyer background section for your proposal:

"If I had to approve this purchase, does this section provide me with enough background information about the current situation to understand the need for a change?"

Decision makers want to know that you really understand their business. They also want to know that you've identified and clearly defined a viable improvement opportunity for their company.

If your proposal fails to effectively define the buyer's current situation or reflect a thorough understanding of its improvement opportunity, the buyer may delay making a choice until your provide more information. A buying delay, rather than an outright rejection, may appear to signal that the buyer likes your proposed product. But it may also mean that the buyer wants to start looking at what your competitors have to offer. The delay can only complicate and endanger your sale.

Get all the decision makers' knowledge levels to the point where they understand the current situation and the improvement opportunity that you've identified for their company. Always give them sufficient information about the causes and effects so that they feel confident making a critical buying decision.

## Even the big guys can miss the point

Several years ago, a major CPA firm gave me two proposals that it wanted me to evaluate using my Proposal RATER (see Chapter 16). It told me that one of the two proposals won and the other lost. They wanted to see if I could pick the winner and loser.

In one of the proposals, the CPA firm proposed a $750,000 consulting engagement that would improve a defense contractor's manufacturing process by reducing its raw materials inventory levels. The proposal contained little information about the company's current manufacturing process and no quantitative data (key performance indicators) about the procurement process or its current inventory levels. The lack of customer information in the proposal gave me the impression that the CPA firm really didn't understand the problem. It seemed that either the CPA firm was unable to analyze the defense contractor's unique business situation or the CPA firm was proposing a major consulting engagement to correct a problem that it really didn't understand. Maybe it thought that its consultants would figure the problem out on the fly.

This proposal was the loser. I suspect the manufacturing company's decision makers viewed the proposal much like I did. If the CPA firm had spent more time analyzing the defense contractor's situation, it may have been able to write a proposal that had some depth to it. The proposal needed a lot more background information about the defense contractor's procurement and manufacturing processes and current key performance indicators, including inventory volumes and costs. It also needed a clear improvement opportunity statement. With a bit more work, the CPA firm may have signed a nice, juicy, $750,000 consulting contract.

One thing that I'll always remember about this proposal was the appendix that contained ten or so biographical resumes of the partners and consultants who would be assigned to work on the project. Every resume was one-page long, except one, which was two pages. The two-pager was much more expansive than the others. I asked my contact at the CPA firm if the person in charge of writing the proposal also had the inflated resume. Indeed he did. Interestingly, that person wasn't the partner-in-charge or even one of the managers.

# *Providing Unbiased Analyses: Just the Facts*

Your proposal's first section can't be your interpretation of the buyer's past bad decisions or poor management. Further, this section can't make it appear that the buyer isn't aware of some recent improvements or innovations in its industry.

One of the decision makers, or his or her boss, subordinate, or close friend could be responsible for a current operational problem. You don't want to put something in your proposal that criticizes or embarrasses anyone reading your proposal. You don't want to force a decision maker to defend his or her company's current situation (the problem). When someone has to defend the current situation, he will probably oppose any change or buying decision that would improve the situation. Further, if a decision maker feels he has to defend the current situation because of something you put in your proposal, it could result in resentment towards you and your company. Therefore, always adhere to the just-the-facts approach when you write the customer background section.

# Picking a Title for the First Section

Picking a good title for your proposal's first main section is important. You can use one of these generic titles for section one:

- ✔ Current Situation
- ✔ Present Operations
- ✔ Proposal Background
- ✔ Improvement Opportunity
- ✔ Statement of the Problem
- ✔ Statement of the Opportunity

If possible, try to select a section title that helps identify the profit or operations improvement opportunity available to your buyer. For example, rather than using the bland title "Current Situation," some sales professionals use these types of titles in their proposals:

- ✔ Current Equipment Maintenance Program Opportunities
- ✔ Customer Billing and EBPP Opportunities
- ✔ Data Processing Costs and Considerations

You also can include the buyer's name in the section title to focus the reader's attention. Some examples:

- ✔ Acme Manufacturing: Current Equipment Maintenance Program Opportunities
- ✔ 1st National Bank: Internet Banking Opportunities

# Deciding What Subsections to Include

Buyers and buying situations are unique; therefore, you must carefully decide what to include in the opening section of your sales proposal. I recommend the following parts, and I list them in the order that I think makes best sense:

Industry Background (optional)

Buyer Background

Current Operations or Functions

Improvement Opportunity: Definition, Analysis, and Plans

Needs and Objectives

Purpose of This Proposal

I cover the last three subsections in Chapter Five; I cover the first three in this chapter.

# Titling the Subsections

Always try to select titles that clearly describe the subsection's content and focus the reader's attention. Rather than titling a subsection "Industry Background," a sales professional used "Employee Preselection Testing in Retail Sales." If you were a decision maker working in the field of retail sales, you'd probably be much more interested in reading a subsection that specifically mentioned retail sales.

Table 4-1 provides some examples of subsection titles used by a software company selling electronic bill presentment and payment (EBPP) software.

| Table 4-1 | Examples of Generic and Specific Subsection Titles |
|---|---|
| *Generic Title* | *Customer- or Buyer-Specific Title* |
| Industry Background | EBPP Trends in the Insurance Industry |
| Buyer Background | ABC Insurance Company: Background Information |
| Current Operations (or Functions) | Current Insurance Premium Billing Processes |
| Needs and Objectives | ABC Insurance Company: EBPP Needs and Objectives |
| Purpose of This Proposal | Purpose of This EBPP Proposal to ABC Insurance |

# Writing about the Industry Background

In certain sales situations, you may want or need to include an industry information subsection in the first main proposal section. This subsection describes the _seller's_ industry.

The industry background subsection can be critical when you're selling a new product. For example, if an EBPP software vendor is trying to convince an insurance company to make EBPP available to its policyholders, it should include EBPP industry background in its proposal. In other words, the seller needs to update the buyer on the seller's industry because EBPP is a relatively new innovation.

Here's another example: The computer-based training industry has gone through major changes in its delivery medium, from CDs to Web-enabled delivery directly over the Internet. This recent industry innovation should be explained in the first subsection of section one.

An industry background subsection should give proposal recipients a better understanding of current trends, innovators, and innovations in the seller's industry as they relate to the readers' business. With today's rapid technological innovation, staying up-to-date with all that's happening is difficult for anyone. Think of this subsection as a summary of all the articles, white papers, and press releases you wish the decision makers had read.

## Paging all buyers

One of my clients, a wireless software vendor, wanted to sell its latest software product to a paging company for use in alphanumeric paging services. We included an industry background subsection titled "Alphanumeric Paging and Wireless Innovations" in the proposal to educate the paging company's decision makers. This subsection presented recent trends in the rapidly growing wireless and alphanumeric paging business. It also contained background information about alphanumeric paging: its history, major service providers, types of applications that were popular, growth projections, and the demographics of wireless and alphanumeric subscribers in the United States. The subsection also identified recent applications of the seller's alphanumeric paging software by other wireless and paging companies.

This background information educated the paging company's decision makers about the business opportunity being proposed by the software company. It also helped position the seller as a leading software vendor in the industry.

# Writing about the Buyer Background

The customer background subsection in your proposal provides a brief overview of your buyer's business. Include general buyer information in this subsection — the type of information found in most annual reports or on a company's Web site. I'm talking about information like the number of employees, annual revenues, and the number of locations. Putting information like this in your proposal assures the buyer that you understand its business.

You can also use this subsection to include the detailed information that's relevant to the buyer's improvement opportunity and to your proposed product. For example, if you're trying to sell the buyer technical training for desktop applications, you probably should include which desktop applications the buyer currently uses and how many employees use them.

The following buyer background subsection examples can give you some ideas about how much detail to include in your buyer information subsection. Take a close look at the third example and *avoid* duplicating it.

In the following example, the sales professional found most of the information she needed in the buyer's annual report. If the president of the company is involved in the decision process and reads the proposal, he would be flattered to see that he was quoted in the seller's proposal. Everyone has an ego.

### Company Background: Pacific Bookstores

### Our Understanding of Pacific Bookstores

Pacific Bookstores owns and operates world-class retail outlets in the western United States. Pacific Bookstores feature a vast inventory of books, music, and videos, and hosts in-store appearances by authors, musicians, and artists. Most stores also offer a casual espresso cafe.

Pacific Bookstores:

- Employs 2,500 Associates

- Operates 55 stores

- Generated revenues over $800 million in 1999

William F. Fisher, Pacific Bookstores President, stated in the annual report:

"Change, innovation, and growth describe the dynamic and challenging environment in which Pacific Bookstores operates. In a year characterized by constant challenges, we never faltered in our push to create productivity while we grew our business by more than 15%, to $800 million".

This shows evidence of a dynamic company, searching for ways to improve.

Writing a buyer background section is easy. I wrote the following insurance example by taking information right from a Web site. Searching the Internet took me less than five minutes. I've changed the company name and some of the information to protect the innocent.

### AIS Background Information

The American Insurance Service Companies (AIS) have served the insurance, pension and risk management needs of individuals and businesses for more than 120 years. Nearly 750 member cooperatives and associations own AIS's fiscal agent and parent company, American Insurance Service Cooperative. The AIS Companies include

- American Service Cooperative

- American Service Casualty Insurance Company

- American Service Life Insurance Company

- AIS Service Insurance Company

- AIS Insurance Company

- AIS Insurance Foundation

- American Pension Solutions, Inc.

AIS has nearly 1,000 employees and exclusive sales representatives supporting the following core businesses:

- Commercial Insurance & Risk Management

- Personal Insurance & Risk Management

- Personal and Corporate Pension Solutions

Whatever you do, don't write a buyer background subsection that reads anything like this:

**Background Information: [Company Name]**

**[Company Name]** is a successful leader in the **[Industry Name]** industry. Because of this success, its sales force has grown over the last several years. Further, its primary product, **[Customer Product Name]**, has extensive product features and benefits which must be persuasively positioned in the company's sales proposals.

Buyers spot this type of fill-in-the-blanks model immediately. It may save you a few minutes, but it could cost you a sale. If you follow a consultative sales process, writing a paragraph or two about the buyer's business shouldn't be difficult. At the very least, go to the buyer's Web site and get some general background information to include in your proposal.

# Writing about the Current Operations

Your proposal must clearly define the buyer's current operations as they relate to the improvement opportunity. In other words, write about that part of the buyer's business that can be changed by your proposed product. This subsection does the most to educate those decision makers who may have limited knowledge about one particular function in a large company. Remember that a winning sales proposal provides its readers with sufficient information about some aspect of the buyer's current situation to enable them to make an educated decision.

This is where you really use the key performance indicators that represent the variables that you and your buyer agree to use for measuring the buyer's current costs and revenues. I show you how to identify and define the buyer's key performance indicators in Chapter 2.

Before you can calculate the financial benefits of your product for a buyer, you need to measure the *current* costs and revenues associated with its improvement opportunity. Use key performance indicators to do the measuring. When you calculate the *future* financial effects of your proposed product, use these same key performance indicators as a basis for your calculations.

Say that you're proposing that a manufacturing company engage your executive recruiting firm for all its recruiting needs related to employees at the middle-manager level and above. Your proposal needs to include information about the company's current management recruiting program. You may include

✔ The number of mid-level and senior managers in the company

✔ Current mid-level and senior manager recruiting practices

✔ Average annual turnover rate for mid-level and senior managers

✔ The number of mid-level and senior managers hired each year

✔ Average salaries for mid-level and senior managers

✔ Average relocation costs for mid-level and senior managers

All of the items in the list are key performance indicators but the second. The other items can be used to *measure* the costs of recruiting, hiring, and relocating a manager.

This subsection of your proposal should educate the buyer's decision makers about their company's current recruiting programs and challenges. More importantly, your proposal should reflect your in-depth understanding of the buyer's current mid-level and senior manager recruiting program. Do you think the buyer's decision makers will feel more comfortable with your executive recruiting firm's capabilities when they see that your proposal presents this information?

See how the sales and proposal processes are integrated? Your consultative selling activities help you identify and gather the buyer information needed to write your winning sales proposals. You can't write a winning sales proposal for a complex sale or to a key account without being consultative.

Do you think learning lots about your buyer's current operations and including this knowledge in your sales proposal can elevate your status in the buyer's eyes? It can't hurt. Besides, knowing lots about a buyer's current operations and identifying a viable improvement opportunity can make you seem less like another vendor and more like a business consultant. More importantly, knowing lots about how the buyer's operation works makes it easier to describe how your product will work in the buyer's business.

Your executive recruiting proposal may not contain buyer-specific information for two possible reasons:

✔ You knew the information but just didn't put it in the proposal.

✔ You didn't know the information because your sales process wasn't consultative — you were just another peddler.

Neither excuse is a good one!

Think about this logic when you're selling and writing a proposal: If, after reading your proposal, the decision makers don't understand their current situation, they probably won't understand the improvement opportunity available to their company. And, if they don't understand their improvement opportunity, they probably won't buy your proposed solution.

In the following example, the seller is a software company selling an electronic bill presentment and payment system (through which customer bills are presented and paid on the Internet). The software company uses the current operations section of its proposal to educate decision makers about the current cost of the buyer's paper-based billing operations.

As you read this example, keep track of the key performance indicators that the software company is using.

### Current Operations

The City of Centerville Public Utilities Department sends customer bills each month to residential, commercial, and industrial customers for water and sewer services. The following statistics define the scope and magnitude of the billing operation:

| | |
|---|---|
| Total commercial customers: | 22,000 |
| Total residential customers: | 108,000 |
| Total number of customers: | 130,000 |
| Number of customers on auto draft: | 5,000 |

The City of Centerville currently uses an IBM AS 400e RISC 9406-730 computer for its Customer Information System (CIS) and Cashiering System (CR). These systems are licensed from MuniSystems of Plano, Texas. The system is a DB2 proprietary database with SQL calls. Information can be exchanged using TCP/IP protocol.

BillDocs in Dallas, Texas provides paper bill production and mailing services for the City of Centerville. BillDocs charges the city $0.425 for each bill mailed. This includes the cost for paper, envelopes, printing, and bulk mailing.

Centerville National Bank provides a retail lockbox service for the city. The bank receives and processes all payments sent by mail (approximately 96 percent of all bills). For each payment it processes, the bank charges the city $0.11. The bank provides payment information in machine-readable format, which is transmitted to the city on a daily basis.

If you were a decision maker reading this proposal, your interest would probably be piqued after you see exactly how much you're currently paying to have your bills processed.

# Chapter 5

# Discovering the Buyer's Improvement Opportunities

● ● ● ● ● ● ● ● ● ● ● ● ● ● ● ● ● ● ● ● ● ● ● ● ● ● ● ● ● ● ● ● ● ● ● ● ● ● ● ● ● ●

*In This Chapter*

▶ Telling the buyer how to improve its business

▶ Giving the buyer credit for the good work it has already done

▶ Clarifying the needs and objectives

▶ Explaining the purpose of your proposal

● ● ● ● ● ● ● ● ● ● ● ● ● ● ● ● ● ● ● ● ● ● ● ● ● ● ● ● ● ● ● ● ● ● ● ● ● ● ● ● ● ●

*I*n Chapter Four, I show you how to get started on the first section of your proposal. In this chapter, I show you how to finish the first section of the proposal by determining the buyer's improvement opportunity, explaining the buyer's needs and objectives, and explaining the purpose of the proposal.

Figure 5-1 depicts the proposal in its entirety and also lists subsections in the first main section.

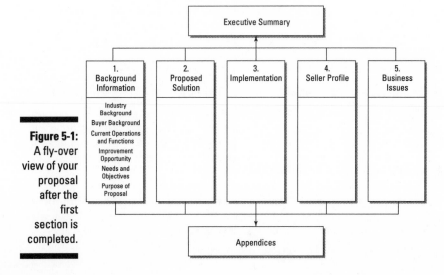

**Figure 5-1:**
A fly-over view of your proposal after the first section is completed.

# *Writing about the Improvement Opportunity*

The *improvement opportunity* is simply the chance that the buyer has to make or save money. You must accurately define the improvement opportunity for the buyer and explain the costs that are now incurred that your product could cut or the new revenues that your product could help the company earn.

The buyer must agree with you about the existence of the improvement opportunity and the validity of the financial measurements you use. You can't manufacture or engineer an improvement opportunity for the buyer just to make a sale. If you do, you'll really seem like just another peddler to the buyer — doing whatever you have to in order to make a sale and beat this month's quota. Not only will you not make the sale, but your credibility will be shot.

Make sure that the buyer's decision makers can easily understand that their company has an opportunity to reduce or avoid costs or increase revenues. Keep the decision makers in mind as you write this section of the proposal.

If you've been methodical and thorough in gathering current operations data from the buyer, some aspect of the buyer's current operations will probably pop up like a big red flag marking an improvement opportunity. I don't think that finding an improvement opportunity is that difficult. The key is knowing how your product can work in the buyer's business. Keep in mind that if you're selling a product that you know pretty well and have seen businesses use to benefit their bottom line, you have a head start in identifying improvement opportunities.

For example, say that you're selling data processing services to Centran Manufacturing, a company that currently buys data processing services from a service bureau. You've listened carefully, taken good notes, and found that the $350,000 Centran is spending every year for data processing:

- ✔ Is 20 percent higher than what similar companies spend
- ✔ Represents 18 percent of Centran's "Other Expenses" — a big chunk
- ✔ Reduces the companies earnings per share by 4.3 cents

The numbers in the list are *key performance indicators.* Key performance indicators are the variables that you and your buyer agree to use for measuring the buyer's current costs and revenues.

If you were proposing to sell Centran Manufacturing an in-house data processing system, you certainly should use these key performance indicators in the improvement opportunity subsection of your proposal. And you can and should use these numbers in the next main section of your proposal — the second section, in which you describe your proposed solution — to show how your solution will reduce the company's data processing costs and thereby increase earnings.

The improvement opportunity subsection of the first section is tied to the second section, in which you present your proposed solution. In this example, if you were the sales professional for the in-house data processing vendor, your proposal needs to measure the financial benefits of your system based on Centran's key performance indicators — the Other Expenses and Earnings per Share measures. To do this, your proposal should include these key performance indicators in the first section and then should use them in the second section as a basis to calculate the financial benefits of your system.

Using this example, here's how your proposal should be designed so that the first section sets the stage for the second section.

| *If section one identifies the company's data processing cost . . .* | *Then section two should show how an in-house data processing system can . . .* |
|---|---|
| Totals $350,000 | Reduce that annual cost to less than $350,000 |
| Is 20 percent higher than similar companies | Make this cost comparable to companies of similar size and type |
| Represents 18 percent of its Other Expenses budget line | Reduce data processing costs to less than 18 percent of the company's Other Expenses |
| Lowers its earnings per share by 4.3 cents | Lower earnings per share by less than 4.3 cents |

When you analyze the financial benefits of your product in your sales proposal, keep in mind that most senior managers of corporations also own stock in the company. In the Centran example, assume the decision makers own lots of stock in the company. Do you think they get excited when someone shows them how to reduce the impact of data processing costs on the company's earnings per share? You bet they do, because it's money in their pockets. Using earnings per share as a key performance indicator sets the stage for a financial benefit calculation that shows how your proposed product can increase the buyer's earnings per share.

The public sector is just as interested in reducing operating costs as the private sector is. Figure 5-2 shows how ElectroBill presented a cost reduction opportunity to the City of Centerville — a potential $86,000 reduction in utility billing costs.

**City of Centerville: EBPP Needs and Objectives**

We identified the following electronic bill presentment and payment (EBPP) processing and systems needs for the City of Centerville during our analysis of their current utility billing operations:

- Acquire an EBPP system or EBPP services to provide a dynamic, new service to utility customers and reduce paper-based utility billing costs.
- Begin offering EBPP services to Centerville utility customers during the second quarter of 2001.
- Allow utility customers to self-activate the EBPP services.
- Allow utility customers to make payments by either debiting their checking accounts or charging their credit cards.
- Provide EBPP customers with a 12-month rolling history of past bills and payments.

We also identified several long-term EBPP objectives for the City of Centerville:

- Expand EBPP processing to other city services, e.g. property taxes, building permits, parking, and traffic tickets.
- Establish city-owned Internet terminal kiosks so utility customers without Internet access at home can participate in EBPP.

**Figure 5-2:**
Making a clear statement about an improvement opportunity.

# *Moving Forward if the Buyer Has Identified the Improvement Opportunity*

Sometimes the buyer is way ahead of you. Someone in the buying company may already have identified the improvement opportunity and developed plans for achieving it. If this is the case, the improvement opportunity subsection of your proposal should mention the buyer's plans. This subsection should also discuss any project the buyer has underway to address the improvement opportunity.

If the buyer has identified the improvement opportunity, I think the proposal should acknowledge the work of someone in the buyer's organization. It never hurts to give someone from the buyer's organization credit for his or her efforts, especially if the decision makers aren't aware of the efforts or aren't familiar with the person. Doing so makes you look classy and wins support.

Here are examples of proposal language that acknowledge plans a buyer may already have to address an improvement opportunity:

In October 2000, the City of Centerville established a task force to evaluate the viability of offering electronic bill presentment and payment services to the city's commercial and residential water and sewer utility customers.

To improve the company's cash management function, Acme Food Stores started a project to provide cash concentration processing for its 145 stores.

In most situations where the buyer has developed a plan for achieving its improvement opportunity, your proposed product can be complementary and supportive. Your product can fit into the buyer's plans. In fact, your proposal can help the decision makers view your proposed product as a key ingredient of their plan.

When your proposed product fits the buyer's plan, the buyer may take ownership of your proposed solution. In other words, the decision makers will think that buying your product was their idea. They may even be right, as they probably identified the improvement opportunity and formulated the plan before you got there. Your chances of securing a signed contract are greatly increased when the decision makers feel that your product is just helping them enact their idea.

# Writing about the Needs and Objectives

Your buyers have needs and objectives that are outgrowths of their improvement opportunities. Use these definitions to help you understand the difference between a need and an objective:

- ✔ **Need:** The fact or condition of not having enough; shortage; deficiency. A buyer's needs are usually immediate and short term.

- ✔ **Objective:** Something aimed at or striven for. A buyer's objectives often have a strategic or long-term purpose.

Buyers' decision makers must understand their company's available improvement opportunity and the financial and non-financial benefits provided by your product. Identifying the buyer's short-term needs and long-term objectives helps decision makers see the improvement opportunity and the financial benefits that are available. Most salespeople, when they write a proposal, like to separate the short-term stuff and the long-term stuff, and this division works quite well. See Figure 5-2 for an example of some needs and objectives. If you're still having a hard time with needs and objectives, just ask yourself what has to follow logically from the improvement opportunity.

Your improvement opportunity subsection begins to set the stage for introducing your product (the proposed solution) in the second section, and the needs and objectives subsection continues to set the stage. You first must clearly identify the buyer's *confirmed* needs and objectives. Just like you can't fabricate a buyer's improvement opportunity, you can't fabricate its needs and objectives. The buyer would perceive any fabrication as manipulative and not very reflective of a consultative selling process (although it does work very well for used cars). You need to work closely with the buyer to help it define its needs and objectives. Your behavior should reflect your customer-focused consultative sales process.

Plan to spend some time working with your buyer to get its needs and objectives right. Be consultative. If you can understand and confirm the buyer's unique needs and objectives, you can use this knowledge to develop a custom application of your product. And your custom application can become the basis for converting your product's features into buyer-specific benefits — your *value proposition* for the buyer. (See the next chapter for more on value propositions.)

Identifying and defining the buyer's needs and objectives is really beneficial. Try this logic:

If you can identify the buyer's needs and objectives, you can then define a unique product application for the buyer.

By defining a unique application, you present product features and resulting benefits that perfectly match (and satisfy) the buyer's needs and objectives.

Then, your proposal really can convince the decision makers that buying your product makes perfect sense.

## Fat cats have needs and objectives too

A couple had $1,200,000 in their investment and retirement accounts (a nice little nest egg!). Over the last three years, their total annual returns were less than 5.0 percent, while the S&P average was higher than 12.5 percent each year. The couple recognized the *need* for professional investment management services to improve their portfolio's performance. During the sales process, a trust company sales professional also identified two long-term investment *objectives:* 1) retire at age 60 and 2) generate $150,000 in annual earnings from their investments.

The trust company's sales professional identified and confirmed these needs and objectives with the couple before including the needs and objectives in her proposal. The first proposal section listed these needs and objectives to set the stage for the trust company's services, which were presented in the second section. By letting the clients know that she really understood their needs and objectives, the sales professional showed that her company provided custom, personalized service.

Doesn't it seem obvious that putting the buyer's needs and objectives in your proposal lets you close more business?

This subsection example continues with the City of Centerville case study and follows along with the background information and improvement opportunity subsection examples found in Chapter 4 and in this chapter.

Figure 5-3 presents the needs and objectives the sales professional identified while working (selling consultatively) with representatives from the City of Centerville. In this example, Centerville's improvement opportunity is to offer EBPP to its customers. The improvement opportunity results in these short-term needs and long-term objectives.

Figure 5-3 shows how a proposal can contain some very specific buyer needs and objectives. Do you think the seller (the EBPP software vendor) has a program that will help the City of Centerville achieve each need and objective? You bet — and it will be presented in the second section of the proposal. If you were a decision maker for the City of Centerville, would you be ready to see what the seller is going to propose?

---

**Electronic Bill Presentment and Payment Opportunities**

Measuring the opportunities to reduce paper-based billing costs by using electronic bill presentment and payment (EBPP) is an easy calculation assuming that City of Centerville's demographics follow national averages.

| | |
|---|---|
| • Total number of residential customers | 108,000 |
| • Percentage of residential customers with Internet access | 30% |
| • Residential customers with Internet access: | 32,400 |
| • Total number of commercial customers | 22,000 |
| • Percentage of commercial customers with Internet access | 60% |
| • Commercial customers with Internet access: | 13,200 |
| • Total customers with Internet access | 45,600 |

Annual costs of paper-based billing and payment processing costs for utility customers with Internet access can be calculated as follows:

45,600 customers x ($0.425 per paper bill + $0.11 per payment) x 12 months = $292,752

If the City of Centerville demographics reflect national averages, then 25% or 8,100 of its residential customers and 40% or 5,280 of its commercial customers will convert from paper-based bills to EBPP in the first year. This could reduce paper-based billing costs by nearly $86,000 annually. In the second year, another 25% of customers with Internet access will probably convert to EBPP. However, more customers will have Internet access in the second year which will further increase the opportunity to reduce paper-based billing costs.

**Figure 5-3:**
An example of a needs and objectives subsection.

# Wrapping Up the First Section by Explaining the Proposal's Purpose

You may think that if your first section effectively defines the buyer's improvement opportunity, any reader will know why you're proposing a change. You may think that you don't need to explain the purpose of the proposal. Nevertheless, that's what I suggest you do at the end of the background information section — before you move on to propose a way to capitalize on what you have described as the buyer's improvement opportunity.

If you're seriously considering ignoring my advice, all I can say is this: Never overlook an opportunity to make sure that your proposal keeps the reader focused. This subsection is especially worthwhile if any of your buyer's decision makers have limited knowledge about the operation affected by the improvement opportunity.

You can fill that gap in knowledge very simply. ElectroBill shows how when it summarizes the advantages to the City of Centerville of adopting electronic billing (EBPP):

- ✔ Provide a new service to the city's utility customers.
- ✔ Reduce total billing costs.
- ✔ Extend the EBPP system to billing and receiving payments for other city services.

The proposal also will present ElectroBill's proposed application of its EBPP system for Centerville and describe the resulting non-financial and financial benefits.

# Looking at Section One from the Buyer's Viewpoint

Decision makers carefully read the first proposal section to decide if you really understand their business and have accurately identified a valid improvement opportunity for their company. Your buyer background information, particularly the buyer's key performance indicators, must be accurate and up to date. The defined improvement opportunity must be legitimate and the associated needs and objectives must reflect those identified and confirmed with your contact person during your consultative sales process.

If you skip steps or take shortcuts in your consultative sales process, your lack of in-depth buyer knowledge can be very obvious in the first section of the proposal. You may find that as you write this section, some of the critical buyer information you need is missing. As a result, your proposal will lack depth. You can expect that most readers will immediately spot these deficiencies and may discount the rest of your proposal. The readers may think that if you can't make the effort to learn about their company and understand their unique situation, how can you possibly propose a product that can work for them?

The less customer-specific information that you put in this section, the more it reads like a boilerplate proposal. When your proposal contains little information about the buyer, you're perceived as another tell-and-sell peddler rather than as a valuable business consultant.

# Chapter 6

# Proposing Business Solutions to Your Customer: Hey, We've Got a Perfect Match!

........................................................

........................................................

The toughest writing in any sales proposal is in the second section, where you tell your prospect how it can solve its business problems by purchasing your product. I don't mean solving *all* its problems, just the ones you spotted during your consultative selling activities — those improvement opportunities you have noted. If you want to convert those opportunities into sales, you have to describe in your proposal how your product can capitalize on the opportunity.

If you do a good job of writing about the proposed solution, you really set yourself apart from the competition. But you must provide the buyer's decision makers with a clear understanding of your proposed product, taking care to thoroughly describe how your product will help the buyer take advantage of the improvement opportunities that you've already identified in the first section of your proposal.

Remember that the first section of your proposal sets the stage for the proposed solution. In the second section, you explain the proposed solution by showing a realistic application of your product in the buyer's business. And yes, that puts you one step closer to hearing your cash register ring.

In this chapter and the next, I show you how to write a great solution section of your proposal. (See Figure 7-1, in the next chapter, for an illustration of how section two fits into the overall proposal.)

# Linking the First Section and the Second Section

As I discuss in Chapter 1, I believe strongly in *consultative selling*. Consultative selling requires that you really get to know the buyer's business — just like a consultant would. A thorough analysis of the buyer's situation is what distinguishes you from just another peddler. If you have the right information and accurate information about the buyer's business and operations in section one of your proposal, you have a strong foundation for writing a winning section two. These two sections link together and help the buyer make an informed buying decision. Specifically, your proposal's first and second sections link

- ✔ The buyer's improvement opportunity with the application of your product
- ✔ The buyer's needs and objectives to your product's features and the resulting benefits

To show you how a buyer's improvement opportunity, needs, and objectives link to a seller's product application, features, and benefits, take a look at Figure 6-1. It shows the notes a salesperson from Electronic Payroll Services made after calling on Western Data Services. The data services company is in the market for an electronic payroll service, and that's what the salesperson is selling.

What do you think? Is Electronic Payroll Services going to be able to make neat connections between its product and the buyer's improvement opportunity and the resulting needs and objectives? Because the salesperson has done such a good job of getting to know the buyer, the odds are pretty good that the proposal will make these connections.

**Notes by Electronic Payroll Services concerning
a forthcoming proposal to Western Data Services**

Western Data Services employs 350 people at four locations in
California. The company is experiencing severe problems processing
its payroll. They have outgrown their current system and need to
streamline this function. This is an <u>improvement opportunity</u>!!
We have identified the following needs and objectives for WDS:

- Lower payroll processing costs.
- Integrate the payroll system with the company's job reporting system.
- Provide online input from its main office and three remote sites.
- Satisfy all tax and regulatory reporting requirements.
- Offer direct deposit of payroll checks as an employee option.

Western Data expects to outsource its payroll processing to a firm
specializing in that service. It will only select a payroll processor
that allows payroll clerks in the company's four locations to submit
data and information using some type of online input.

<u>**Important:**</u> Being able to input payroll information from the
company's main office and three remote locations represents one of
Western Data's needs for outsourcing it payroll system. I think this
is also one of the company's <u>selection criteria</u>. WDS probably will
not consider any vendor that doesn't offer remote.

When we write our proposal to Western Data, we can list our service
capabilities and benefits that specifically satisfy WDS's needs and
objectives. We must be sure to say that our service "allows online
input of payroll information from Western Data Service's four
locations."

**Figure 6-1:**
The sales-
person's
notes after
calling on a
prospective
buyer.

# *Picking a Title for the Second Section*

What title do you tack onto the part of your proposal where you present proposed solutions to the buyer's needs? Here are some plain-vanilla choices:

- ✔ Proposed Services
- ✔ Proposed Project

✔ Proposed Improvement Project

✔ Proposed Consulting Engagement

✔ Proposed Strategy

You're probably better off if you can come up with a section two title that mentions the name of the proposed solution or describes the solution. For example, a trust company may title the second section *Proposed Personal Trust Services.* A software company could use the name of its proposed system in the section title, such as *Proposed PowerMfg System.*

# Deciding What Subsections to Include

I recommend four subsections for section two:

Product description

Product application

Non-financial (qualitative) benefits

Financial (quantitative) benefits

Remember that in this book I use *product* to mean either a product or a service. If you are selling a service, your first two sections would cover the service description and the service application.

***Note:*** I list non-financial benefits before financial, but you can change the order if you want. Some companies like to present financial benefits first. Others reverse the order. If you can't decide, ask your contact person which he or she prefers.

If all this section and subsection stuff is getting confusing, check out the figure on the cheat sheet in the front of the book for an overall view of the proposal and its contents.

# Titling the Subsections

You can also use subsection titles that include the name of the proposed product. For example, Electronic Payroll Services sells PayDay, a payroll processing service. The seller can apply the title as shown in Table 6-1. Using the buyer's name in the subsection titles makes it pretty obvious to the reader that the subsection describes the application of the payroll service in the reader's company.

| Table 6-1 | Customizing Your Subsection Titles |
|---|---|
| *Generic Title* | *Buyer-Specific Title* |
| Product Description | PayDay: Overview |
| Product Application | PayDay for Western Data Services |
| Non-Financial Benefits | PayDay: Non-Financial Benefits |
| Financial Benefits | PayDay: Financial Benefits |

# Describing Your Product

The product description subsection must give the buyer a general idea of what your product is all about. So write a good one! Follow these guidelines:

✔ **Tell the buyer exactly what you want it to do with your product.** There's nothing wrong with making sure the buyer's decision makers are on the same wavelength that you are. Here's an example:

"Electronic Payroll Services (EPS) proposes that Western Data Services convert its internal payroll processing and systems to the EPS PayDay payroll service."

This one sentence leaves absolutely no doubt about what the seller wants the buyer to do.

✔ **Describe the product.**

✔ **Describe optional product components.**

## Describing the standard product

Give the buyer a crisp, concise description of your proposed product. Writing this description should be easy. You can probably get most of the information you need from one of your own brochures or right off your company's Web site. Include information that you would want to know if you had to make the buying decision. Your description can include such things as operating specifications, capacities, service levels, service frequency, deliverables, and so on.

Decision makers want to know something about what you're trying to sell, but they don't need a user's manual. Resist the temptation to load up this part of the proposal with your boilerplate materials. Remember that you can always put a brochure in an appendix if you want the readers to have more information.

## Describing the options

If your product has options, tell the buyer about them even if those options are not part of the proposed application. Identifying options lets the buyer know that they're available.

Some of my clients don't want to include any information about options in their product description subsections. They worry that listing options can confuse the buyer, and that's a valid concern. But if you think of this part of your proposal as a brochure, you can use it to let the buyer know about everything that's available with your product. I also think listing options can lead to future sales. Hey — maybe one of the decision makers will see an option she likes and add it to the deal! See Figure 6-2 for an example of a product description subsection.

Pretend you're a decision maker at Western Data. Does the service description you see in Figure 6-2 give you enough information to help you understand EPS's payroll processing services?

The description of your product should be no longer than is necessary to deal with the complexity of your product. Keep in mind that you're writing a business proposal, not a technical proposal. Make sure that the technical content of this subsection doesn't overshadow the business aspects of your proposed solution. Where possible, summarize the technical information and use a supporting appendix for the details.

Most decision makers are more interested in the *value proposition* — how your product can improve their operations — than in the details of your product. They already accept that the proposed product can work for their company. They just want a brief explanation of how.

**EPS PayDay™ Services**

Electronic Payroll Services (EPS) proposes that Western Data
Services convert its internal payroll processing and systems to the
EPS PayDay™ payroll service.

EPS provides payroll-processing functions that range from simply
calculating employee payroll and tax obligations, producing checks,
and preparing management reports to optional services such as filing
payroll taxes and preparing W-2s. EPS PayDay™ services include:

- Training Western Data Service's payroll specialists to perform
  payroll-related responsibilities
- Calculating payroll from wage and hour input
- Calculating federal and state tax liabilities
- Posting payroll data to general ledger
- Monitoring payroll tax deposit due dates
- Monitoring changes in federal and state payroll taxes
- Preparing and filing payroll tax returns

EPS offers these options:

- **PayDay Connect:** EPS' proprietary PC-based software that offers
  your payroll specialists a convenient, easy, and accurate way to
  complete basic functions like payroll entry, adding and changing
  employee information, and comprehensive reports. Information is
  transmitted to EPS using a standard modem.

- **Internet PayDay:** Your Payroll specialists enter employee hours,
  earnings and other payroll data quickly and easily from any PC that has
  Internet access. They simple complete the time sheet online and
  submit it to EPS for processing.

- **Tax Payment:** The Tax Payment service offers automatic tax filing and
  payment, preparation and submission of federal, state, and local tax
  returns, and the deposit of funds with tax authorities.

- **Direct PayCheck:** EPS uses the Federal Reserve Automated Clearing
  House to connect with over 13,000 financial institutions. EPS transfers
  employee wages their checking or savings accounts, Last year EPS
  transferred over $20.5 billion in employee payments.

**Figure 6-2:**
A product
description
subsection
— the first
subsection
in the
second
section.

# Covering the Application Details

Always use the second section in section two to describe the buyer-specific application of your proposed product. Give the readers a very specific explanation of how your product can work in their business. Keep in mind that if your product description subsection (which comes right before this subsection) is well written, writing this subsection should be easy. Consider following these guidelines when you write an application subsection:

- ✔ Start by telling the buyer what's going to happen.
- ✔ Continue by explaining how your product can work in the buyer's business, including how any proposed options can work.

## Telling them what's going to happen

In one or two paragraphs, explain how you plan to install or implement the proposed product in the buyer's business. This explanation doesn't need to describe your implementation methods or schedule in detail (you can do that in the next proposal section — the third section). Rather, tell the buyer more about how and when you're going to install, convert, deliver, or implement the product.

Here is a very good short explanation of how a product will be applied to a buyer's business:

> The American Institute on Substance Abuse in the Workplace (ISAW) will implement its OnAlert program at all Pacific Food System locations starting on October 1, 2002. ISAW staff will conduct all management training and employee rollout sessions. OnAlert will be fully operational throughout PFS by December 15.

## Explaining the application

Tell readers exactly how your product can work for them. Remember that the proposal recipient has just finished reading a description of your product in the previous subsection. So, you don't need to repeat product description information in the application subsection. Simply tell the buyer how your product can work in its unique business environment by:

✔ Highlighting key product components and briefly describing how each works

✔ Explaining in very general terms who will be doing what

✔ Describing which product options will be used and how they will work

Earlier in this chapter, you met Electronic Payroll Services and its products. Figure 6-3 shows how those services can be applied in the prospective buyer's business.

**EPS PayDay™ Services
for Western Data Services**

EPS will convert payroll records from Western Data Service's in-house payroll system to the PayDay system. As part of the conversion process, EPS will develop automated interfaces from the PayDay system to Western Data's general ledger and job tracking and costing systems.

Starting on the first day of the month in which service will begin, Western Data payroll specialists will input payroll information to the PayDay system. EPS will calculate and generate the first biweekly payroll for Western Data. Some important aspects of the proposed PayDay payroll service for Western Data include the following:

- **Input:** Acme payroll specialists at the main office will input payroll information using PayDay Connect; payroll specialists at Western Data's three remote locations will use Internet PayDay for input.

- **Download Reports:** Western Data payroll specialists will download all payroll reports directly using a secure EPS direct connection.

- **Tax Deposits:** EPS will calculate, prepare, and make Western Data's payroll tax deposits.

- **Tax Reports:** EPS will generate all federal, state, and local tax reports for Western Data's review. Upon approval, EPS will file the tax reports for Western Data.

- **W-2 Processing:** At year-end, EPS will generate W-2s for Western Data and mail them directly to employees. Upon approval, EPS will file all summary and detail reports to the appropriate regulatory agencies for Western Data.

- **Direct Deposit:** Western Data employees can signup for the Direct PayCheck option at anytime. EPS will transmit the direct deposit transactions directly to Western Data's bank for entry into the Federal Reserve Automated Clearing House system. Note: EPS will provide Direct PayCheck brochures, signup forms, and announcement materials.

## Advantages of separating description and application

You may think that combining the description and application subsections would be easy. Doing so can certainly cut a few pages out of your proposal, which means the buyer has less to read. In some situations and for some products, combining these two subsections makes sense. So, if you think doing so can work for your company, give it a try. However, having separate description and application subsections has some real advantages.

You only have to write the description subsection one time and you only have to rewrite it when your product offering changes. Otherwise, you can treat it as part of your proposal model's standard wording — it's part of the 80 percent. (See Chapter 2 for more on the 80/20 rule.)

A separate description subsection gives you the opportunity to identify optional product components. As previously mentioned, putting product options in your proposals lets the buyer know what options are available (the application subsection tells the buyer which options have been selected for it).

A separate application subsection is shorter than a subsection that combines the description and application. A separate application subsection is also easier for you to write and easier for the buyer to read than a combined section.

If you ever plan to automate proposal production, doing so is much easier if you use separate product description and application subsections. The description subsection will be part of your proposal model, the 80 percent that's the same for all buyers. The application subsection will vary from buyer to buyer — part of the 20 percent that changes.

## Shortcomings of boilerplate when it comes to application

A sales proposal that doesn't define the application leaves the buyer in the dark. A buyer's decision makers simply won't understand how the seller's proposed product can work for them. The more complex the seller's product, the bigger the knowledge gap a boilerplate proposal creates for a buyer. The buyer just doesn't have the critical information needed to make an informed buying decision if you submit a boilerplate proposal.

A boilerplate proposal usually contains a generic description of the product's application. This generic description forces the readers to take a shot at defining the application for their company — something totally inappropriate in a consultative sales process. More importantly, not all buyers will be able to define the application, especially for complex products. Boilerplate proposals jeopardize the sale because they: 1) don't document buyer-specific applications and 2) send the wrong message about the selling organization and its sales force.

# Chapter 7

# Answering the Buyer's Question: "What's In It for Us?"

*I*n addition to describing your product and explaining its application (see Chapter 6), the second section of your sales proposal shows how your product benefits the prospective buyer. (See Figure 7-1 for a view of the proposal in its entirety, with the subsections filled in for section one and section two.)

Benefits can be either *non-financial* or *financial:*

✔ **Non-financial** (or *qualitative*) benefits are hard to measure in dollars and cents (I guess that explains the name). These benefits represent *soft value* rather than the *hard value* provided by financial benefits. "Gives students real-time feedback to measure progress" is a non-financial benefit of computer-based training (CBT). The buyer and the seller know this is a very real benefit of CBT, but trying to measure this benefit in dollars and cents makes no sense.

✔ **Financial** (or *quantitative*) benefits represent the reduced or avoided costs or increased revenues provided by your product. Financial benefits represent *hard value* to the buyer. Your proposal should calculate the buyer's financial benefits in dollars and cents using the buyer's key performance indicators as a basis for the calculation. For example, "Eliminates student travel costs" is a financial benefit of computer-based training (CBT). If you were selling CBT, one of the financial benefits in your proposal would calculate exactly how much money the buyer can save by not sending students (in this case, the buyer's employees) out of town for training.

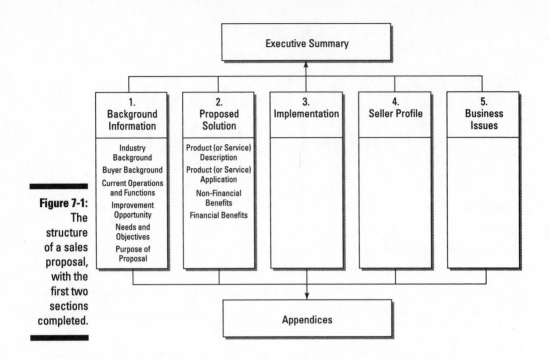

**Figure 7-1:**
The
structure
of a sales
proposal,
with the
first two
sections
completed.

# Delivering Value through Benefits

As you can imagine, the non-financial and financial benefits of your product are important to the buyer. They represent the *value proposition*. Some consultative selling methodologies use the terms *value-adding* or *value justification*.

Your ability to define buyer-specific benefits is directly related to how well you sell like a consultant. The benefits subsections of your proposal are much more convincing if you've done your job as a sales professional. To develop buyer-specific benefits — the value proposition — you must

- ✔ Identify the buyer's key performance indicators, needs, and objectives.
- ✔ Figure out how your proposed product can work in the buyer's unique environment — the application.

These consultative, buyer-focused sales activities typically present the greatest challenges in complex sales situations. (See Chapters 4, 5, and 6 for more information.) The good news is that if you do a thorough job of selling and write the first parts of your proposal well, coming up with the value proposition should be fairly simple.

## Using benefits to duplicate success

PrintPro, a printing and duplication company, wanted to provide printing and outsourcing services to Andrews University, a private university in southern Wisconsin. To develop buyer-specific non-financial and financial benefits, a PrintPro sales professional and proposal team analyzed the university's printing and duplication functions. They looked at such things as current costs, staffing and equipment, job types, volumes, and future projections. They also identified the university's printing and duplication needs and objectives. Of course, these were the consultative selling activities that were vital to writing the buyer background section of PrintPro's proposal.

After PrintPro understood the university's situation, the company easily formulated a unique outsourcing service plan. The custom application made defining buyer-specific financial and non-financial benefits easy. And these benefits were compelling reasons for the university to outsource its printing and duplication services. To the decision makers at Andrews University, the application and benefits subsection in the proposal made it seem as if PrintPro had designed its outsourcing services just for the university.

The more you learn about writing winning proposals, the more you realize that there're no substitute for having lots of information about the buyer and solid product application knowledge.

# Writing about Soft Value — the Non-Financial Benefits

The non-financial benefits subsection describes how your product adds soft value to the buyer's business. Non-financial benefits are the benefits that don't easily lend themselves to dollar and cents measures. These are the features that the buyer knows can improve its business operations, but it also knows that putting a number on the value of the benefit is really tough.

## Users like non-financial benefits more than decision makers do

The end-users of your product are probably more interested in its non-financial benefits than the decision makers are. End-users are much closer to the real action and they're the ones who actually use your proposed product. They more clearly understand how your product can improve operations. The decision makers, of course, are usually more interested in the direct monetary benefit — probably because their fat bonuses are tied to how much money the company makes.

Write the non-financial benefits subsection as if you were explaining the product's features to a new employee in the department that will use the product. Explain the how and why of some important pieces of the operation and explain how the proposed product makes the department work better.

## Generic statements are less effective than specific ones

A winning proposal must go beyond generic benefits statements. Here's a generic statement: "Automated document assembly can save your staff valuable time." That statement has little meaning to end-users or decision makers. These end-users and decision makers may not understand which company documents need to be automated and how automating assembly can save time.

You can make that generic statement into a buyer-specific one: "Automated document assembly of all annuity plan agreements will eliminate clerical errors." This statement means something to a user who manages the clerical staff who physically produce the annuity plan agreements for the company. This benefit is also meaningful to a decision maker who may be thinking that the company can cut clerical staff if, by implementing the system, the company will have fewer errors assembling annuity plan agreements. (See how those decision makers are always thinking about money!)

Buyer-specific benefit statements help the buyer understand the soft value provided by your product.

Expect to use a combination of generic and buyer-specific benefit statements in your proposals — *don't only use generic statements.* Spend some time trying to figure out exactly how your product features convert into buyer-specific benefits. Work with the buyer and be consultative.

## Benefits grow out of your product's features

Barbara Schenck, the author of *Small Business Marketing For Dummies,* explains the relationship between features and benefits this way:

Every time you describe a *feature* of your product or service, you're talking to yourself. Every time you describe the *benefit* that your product or service delivers, you're talking to your prospect, because consumers don't buy the feature — they buy what the feature does for them.

Here are some examples:

- Consumers don't buy V-8 engines. They buy speed.

- They don't buy shock-absorbing shoes. They buy walking comfort.

- They don't buy the lightest laptop computer. They buy the freedom to work wherever they want.

Follow these steps to translate features into benefits:

1. **State your product or business feature.**

2. **Add the phrase "which means."**

3. **Complete the sentence and you are forced to state the benefit.**

*The feature + "which means" = the benefit*

For example, Electronic Payroll Services (EPS) sells payroll processing systems to small to medium-sized organizations. EPS developed generic non-financial benefits based on two capabilities: remote data entry and direct deposit of paychecks to employee accounts. Table 7-1 shows how an EPS sales professional used these generic benefits to develop buyer-specific non-financial benefits for Western Data Services (WDS).

The column on the left is standard product-feature language — the kind of language you expect to see in sales literature. The middle column moves a big step closer to the buyer by introducing the human element, and the column on the right tells exactly how *this* buyer will benefit.

| Table 7-1 | Feature to Benefit Conversion Examples | |
| --- | --- | --- |
| *Feature (Capability)* | *Generic Benefit* | *Buyer-Specific Benefit* |
| Remote data entry of payroll information via secure Internet connection. | Allows data entry clerks with Internet access to input payroll information from any location. | WDS payroll clerks can input payroll information from its headquarters and three California locations. |
| | | WDS does not have to modify the desktop personal computers in its payroll offices to input to the EPS system. |

*(continued)*

**Table 7-1 *(continued)***

| Feature (Capability) | Generic Benefit | Buyer-Specific Benefit |
|---|---|---|
| Direct PayCheck provides direct deposit of payroll checks. | Employees simply need a checking or savings account at any financial institution to use direct deposit. | WDS can add direct deposit to its employee benefits program — nationally, 85 percent of U.S. employees use direct deposit of their payroll checks. |
| | | Direct PayCheck will significantly reduce the amount of time needed to reconcile the WDS payroll account. |

The custom benefits in Table 7-1 apply specifically to Western Data Service's unique situation. The EPS sales professional couldn't have developed these buyer-specific qualitative benefits if she didn't have an in-depth knowledge of Western Data's current data processing situation and a concise understanding of the proposed EPS payroll service application at Western Data.

Consider using a table format to make reading and understanding the non-financial benefits provided by your product as easy as possible. You may also find that the table format makes it easier to organize your thoughts.

# Writing about Hard Value — the Financial Benefits

To a buyer, a financial benefit means either less cost or more revenue (or both). Financial benefits represent the *hard value* part of your value proposition because you can measure financial benefits in dollars and cents. You use the financial benefits subsection of your proposal to show how your product or service reduces costs or increases revenues — in other words, how it lets the company take advantage of its improvement opportunity.

Make the financial benefits realistic and accurate and support them with an easy-to-understand, unquestionable financial analysis. Obviously, the content and accuracy of your financial benefits subsection is dependent on what you know about the buyer's business, including the buyer's key performance indicators (that you identified in section one of your proposal — see Chapters 2 and 5 for more information).

Understanding key performance indicators is crucial to writing an effective financial benefits section. Remember that you use the buyer's key performance indicators to measure the buyer's current costs, revenues, profitability, margins, productivity, or proficiency levels.

Why does measuring a buyer's financial benefits using its key performance indicators as a basis for your calculations make sense? Because the buyer's decision makers know and understand their company's key performance indicators — they use these indicators to measure how well their business is doing. Using the buyer's key performance indicators adds validity to your financial benefits calculations and helps the decision makers understand the hard value of your proposed product.

Here's an extended example of the financial benefits developed by a company that sells employee profile testing systems. The example shows the financial benefits a bank would realize if it could lower the employee turnover rate of its customer service representatives.

Precision Staffing Systems (PSS), a company that develops employee profile testing systems, worked with First National Bank (FNB) representatives to do an extensive analysis of a high customer service representative (CSR) turnover situation. They determined that 50 percent of CSR turnover problems were the result of employee-job mismatches.

Table 7-2 lists:

✔ Key performance indicators a PSS sales professional would need to develop the financial benefits subsection for FNB

✔ Questions she may ask representatives from FNB to get values for the key performance indicators

✔ Answers FNB representative may give the PSS sales professional

| Table 7-2 | Determining Key Performance Indicators | |
|---|---|---|
| *If This Is a Key Performance Indicator for FNB* | *The PSS Sales Professional May Ask the Buyer This Question* | *The Buyer at FNB May Give This Answer to the PSS Sales Professional* |
| Number of CSRs | How many CSRs work for FNB? | 300 |
| Annual turnover rate | What's your annual turnover rate? | 55 percent; 165 new CSRs are hired and trained each year. |
| | How does that compare to other companies like yours? | Our turnover rate is 75 percent higher than the national average for similar companies. |

*(continued)*

**Table 7-2 *(continued)***

| If This Is a Key Performance Indicator for FNB | The PSS Sales Professional May Ask the Buyer This Question | The Buyer at FNB May Give This Answer to the PSS Sales Professional |
| --- | --- | --- |
| | What do you think is the primary cause for your high turnover rate? | We're not sure. Many new CSRs quit in 3 or 4 months. They say that they're just not happy doing that type of work. |
| Recruiting and hiring costs | How much does it cost to recruit and hire a CSR? | $1,500 |
| Training costs | How much does it cost to train a new CSR? | $2,000 and it takes two weeks of intensive training. |
| | Does the $2,000 dollars include lost production time? | No, the $2,000 is the cost to run a CSR through our training program. It doesn't include the cost of not having the CSR working. |

The PSS sales professional would include the information shown in the table in section one of her proposal (the buyer's background information). She would put the key performance indicators in the current operations subsection of section one to help her set the stage for introducing her solution, the PSS employee profile testing system.

By getting these key performance indicators, the sales professional is also able to develop solid financial benefits for FNB in the second section of the proposal. The financial benefits cost-justify the implementation of the bank purchasing the testing service.

Using past experiences with similar clients, PSS estimated that its employee profiling system would reduce FNB's CSR employee-job mismatches by 90 percent (from 82 to 8). This seems like a big reduction, but PSS has several customers who experienced this significant of a drop. Reducing CSR turnovers caused by job mismatches can cut the bank's turnover rate to around 30 percent. This turnover rate is more in line with industry averages.

PSS licenses its Employee Profiling System for $95,000 and charges 15 percent (or $14,250) for annual maintenance after the first year. Additionally, PSS charged the bank $20,000 to customize the system for the bank's CSRs. FNB's implementation costs totaled $105,000.

Figure 7-2 shows how the PSS financial benefits section turned out in its proposal to FNB.

Do you think this financial analysis gives the bank's decision makers some good information on which to make an informed buying decision? The first-year savings of $154,000 is hard value for FNB because it represents net, real dollar savings for the bank. By using FNB's key performance indicators (annual turnover rate, recruiting costs, and hiring and training costs), PSS added lots of validity to its service's financial benefits. The buyer-specific financial benefits should make a buying decision easier for FNB's decision makers.

**PSS Employee Profiling System:**
**Financial Benefits**

By licensing the PSS Employee Profiling System, First National Bank (FNB) can reduce the CSR turnover rate from 55% to 30% by reducing employee-job mismatches by 90%. The resulting financial benefits are calculated as follows:

| | |
|---|---|
| Recruiting and hiring costs | $1,500 |
| CSR training costs | $2,000 |
| Total | $3,500 |
| Number of new CSRs per year | 165 |
| Total annual new CSR costs | $577,500 |
| Total annual new CSR costs attributed to mismatches (82 x (1,500 + 2,000)) | $287,000 |
| | |
| New CSR recruiting and hiring and training costs | $3,500 |
| Number of CSR mismatches each year | 82 |
| Number of CSR mismatches eliminated through PSS' employee profiling system (90% x 82) | 74 |
| 1st year CSR recruiting and hiring and training costs using the PSS employee profiling system | $259,000 |
| 1st year PSS fees | $105,000 |
| 1st year ASC cost savings | $154,000 |
| Return on investment ($154,000/$105,000) | 147% |

**Figure 7-2:**
An example
of a
financial
benefits
section.

# Understanding that Hard and Soft Dollars Create Hard Value

Depending on the type of product you sell, you may have to work with soft dollars and hard dollars to calculate the buyer's financial benefits. Not all the dollars in a financial benefits calculation may be created equal — some may be worth more than others because some dollars provide direct savings or revenue increases and other dollars only provide indirect savings or revenue increases.

- ✔ *Hard dollars* result in *direct* savings or revenue increases.
- ✔ *Soft dollars* result in *indirect* savings or revenue increases.

You need to understand that your financial benefits calculations may be measuring hard and soft dollars. Think of it this way: hard dollars are real money and soft dollars are almost real money.

Yes, this is a bit confusing — but keep reading.

## Hard dollars = real money

Hard dollars represent real money because they result in *direct* cost savings or revenue increases for the buyer. In other words, buyers will see the benefits of the product directly on their bottom line. The following items are examples of hard dollar benefits:

- ✔ A building owner will get hard dollar benefits by installing a more energy efficient heating and cooling system because the system reduces energy costs — energy bills will be quantifiably lower.
- ✔ A retail store will get hard dollar benefits by offering a private label credit card (meaning a credit card with the store's name on it). Customers spend more per purchase and make more purchases when they use the store's private label credit card.

## Soft dollars = almost real money

Soft dollars represent almost real money. Soft dollars are *indirect* cost savings or revenue increases for the buyer. Your financial benefits calculation can show soft dollar cost savings or revenue increases, but you and the buyer know that soft dollar savings or increases do not show up dollar for dollar on the buyer's bottom line. You and the buyer may agree to convert soft dollars to hard dollars, which is a topic I cover later.

The next example includes hard and soft dollar benefits for the buyer (the financial benefits are printed in boldface type for your convenience). The company gets *soft dollar* benefits by using computer-based training (CBT) rather than classroom training. The soft dollar savings are the result of the company's employees spending less training time using CBT than they would need to spend in a classroom to get the same level of instruction. Because CBT takes less time away from production work, the company should *indirectly* make more money — because the company's employees are producing and not in training.

The company won't see the increased revenues on its bottom line. Rather, the company knows that this is a soft dollar benefit of CBT. The company's decision makers know that with CBT their employees will be away from work less and therefore have time to produce more. But having additional production time doesn't necessarily mean that the added time will result in higher production.

Table 7-3 shows the basis for a financial benefits calculation by identifying the current training costs (hard and soft dollars) for ABC Company.

| Table 7-3 | Current Training Costs |
|---|---|
| ABC Company gross revenue | $8,000,000 |
| Total number of employees | 100 |
| Average annual employee contribution (gross revenue/total number of employees) | $80,000 |
| Employee contribution per hour (average annual employee contribution/2000 hours per year) | $40 |
| Percentage of employees needing training | 70 percent |
| Number of employees needing training | 70 |
| Estimated duration of training required for each employee in classroom hours | 24 |
| Estimated cost of a one-day classroom training program (8 hours of training) | $100 |
| Total **hard dollar** cost to purchase classroom training for all employees | $21,000 |
| Total **soft dollar** revenue lost to send employees to classroom training (estimated duration of classroom training required for each employee × employee contribution per hour × number of employees needing training) | $67,200 |
| Average estimated classroom training cost per employee | **$1,260** |
| Estimated total **hard** and **soft dollar** cost of classroom training | $88,200 |

To this point, the financial benefit analysis shows it costs ABC Company $88,200 to send its employees to classroom training.

✔ $21,000 of *hard dollar* costs that ABC Company has to pay some training vendor for classroom training.

✔ $67,200 in *soft dollar* costs, which in this case represent lost revenue because the employees aren't working.

Now, the financial benefits calculation in the proposal needs to show how computer-based training is more cost-effective, as seen in Table 7-4.

| Table 7-4 | The Financial Benefits of CBT |
|---|---|
| CBT efficiency ratio (computer-based training hour) equivalent to one classroom | 0.60 |
| Estimated duration of training required for each employee in CBT hours (classroom hours × CBT efficiency ratio) | 14 |
| Annual **soft dollar** revenue lost to train employees using CBT (estimated duration of CBT required for each employee × employee contribution per hour × number of employees needing training) | $40,320 |
| Average per student cost for CBT program | $175 |
| **Hard dollar** cost of proposed CBT Solution | $12,250 |
| Average estimated CBT **soft** and **hard dollar** cost per employee | **$751** |
| Total estimated **hard** and **soft dollar** cost of CBT: | $52,570 |

The financial benefits analysis shows that ABC Company can spend $52,570 using computer-based training (CBT) to provide the same level of training that classroom training has been providing.

✔ $40,320 in soft dollar costs, which represents lost revenue because the employees take CBT courses instead of working.

✔ $12,250 to purchase the CBT program ($175 × 70 employees).

The analysis then moves on to show hard and soft dollar savings and a total of both, as shown in Table 7-5.

| Table 7-5 | Hard and Soft Dollar Benefits |
|---|---|
| Out-of-pocket (**hard dollar**) savings with CBT versus classroom training | $8,750 |
| **Soft dollar** benefits with CBT versus classroom training | $26,880 |
| Total **hard** and **soft dollar** benefits with CBT versus classroom training | $35,630 |

At the end, the financial benefits analysis calculates total soft dollar and hard dollar savings of $35,630 for ABC Company.

- ✔ $8,750 of hard dollar savings because it's cheaper to buy CBT courses than it is to send employees to classroom training ($21,000 – $12,250).

- ✔ $26,880 of soft dollar savings (in this case, higher revenue contributions) because employees are away from work for less time with CBT ($67,200 – $40,320).

## Converting soft dollars to hard dollars

Some of your buyers may want to convert soft dollars to hard dollars so that they can get closer to the actual bottom line impact of your proposed product. But they don't convert soft dollars to hard dollars on a one-for-one basis. For example, some buyers may treat three soft dollars as one hard dollar, although there's no fixed conversion standard.

In the previous example, lost soft dollars were $67,200 for classroom training and $40,320 for CBT. The $26,880 soft dollar difference can probably help the decision makers choose CBT over classroom training. But what if they want to convert these soft dollars to hard dollars to get closer to total hard dollar savings? For this example, assume the buyer agrees that three soft dollars equal one hard dollar — a 3:1 conversion ratio of soft to hard dollars. $26,800 soft dollars would equal $8,960 hard dollars. The training company can use this calculation in its proposal to show the true hard dollar benefits of CBT over classroom training. In the sales proposal, it would be written something like this:

Out-of-pocket (**hard dollar**) savings with CBT versus classroom training: $8,750

**Soft dollar** benefits with CBT versus classroom training converted into hard dollars ($26,880/3): $8,960

Total savings: **$17,710**

$17,710 is the hard dollar difference between CBT and classroom instruction. It's hard dollar savings because $8,750 is the actual out-of-pocket cost difference between CBT and classroom training and $8,960 is probably close to actual lost production revenues (it's certainly a lot closer to actual lost production revenues than the $26,880 soft dollar figure).

*Note:* This example uses an arbitrary 3:1 soft to hard dollar conversion ratio. The ratios you use may be higher or lower. If you plan to convert soft dollars to hard dollars in your proposal's financial benefits calculation, ask buyers what conversion ratio works for them. If the buyer doesn't have any ideas, always remember that using a lower soft to hard dollar conversion ratio makes cost-justifying your product easier.

# *Using Common Financial Benefit Calculations*

Your sales proposal should calculate financial benefits using a method that the buyer's decision makers understand — probably a financial calculation that they normally use to make buying decisions. Ask the buyer how it wants to see financial benefits calculated in your proposal.

Two commonly used calculations for measuring the financial benefits of an investment are:

- Return on investment (ROI)
- The payback method

ROI is a very common investment performance measurement. It's calculated as follows:

Income (or savings) ÷ invested capital = return on investment

Here's the ROI calculation using the numbers from the First National Bank (FNB) and Precision Staffing Systems (PSS) example that I introduce earlier in this chapter. In the first year, FNB would save $154,000 in recruiting, hiring, and training costs by investing $105,000 in PSS software and services. Its first year return on investment would be 147 percent.

$154,000 ÷ $105,000 = 147 percent

The payback method calculates the period needed for the after-tax cash inflows from the product to accumulate to an amount equal to the capital invested in the product. In other words, it calculates how much time the product needs to pay for itself.

Invested capital ÷ annual after-tax cash inflow = payback period

Again using the numbers from the FNB and PSS example, the payback calculations are as follows, using a 20 percent tax rate for FNB. FNB would invest $105,000 in PSS software and services to reduce its recruiting, hiring, and training costs by $154,000. Since the $154,000 is a before tax number, the sales professional needs to reduce it by the 20 percent tax rate (by a total of $30,800) to get a true payback period.

So, $105,000 is the invested capital, which is divided by ($154,000 – $30,800), which is the after-tax cash inflow for the first year. This calculation results in a payback period of 0.85 years (10.2 months).

## Uncommon financial benefits calculations — you may need help!

The buyer may want you to use an uncommon method to measure financial benefits. The two methods I briefly explain in this sidebar are more difficult than the ROI and payback methods. Unless you have solid accounting experience, you may want some help. If you have an accounting department in your company, ask someone from it to help you with these calculations. One of the accountants can probably give you a quick lesson in accounting and point out what key performance indicator information you need to get from the buyer.

**Net present value (NPV)**

To calculate net present value, follow these steps:

1. Identify the cash flows for each year of the proposed investment.

2. Using a discount rate, calculate the present value of each cash flow.

3. The sum of the present values is the net present value.

The buyer will probably consider the proposed investment if the NPV is positive.

**Earnings per share (EPS)**

A buyer's senior managers (who happen to be the decision makers) often own shares of common stock in the corporation. They know that their decisions can directly affect the corporation's earnings, which are measured in earnings per share (EPS). EPS represents one of the variables investors use to set the price that they pay for a corporation's stock. So, some decision makers want to see what impact their buying decision has on the company's EPS. They're really asking how much your proposed product will increase the corporation's bottom line.

*Net income available to common shareholders ÷ weighted average number of shares of outstanding common stock = earnings per share*

# *Writing about Financial Benefits That Aren't Apparent*

Yes, this is the real world. No, you can't always calculate the financial benefits of a product. Two possible reasons why this could happen (and what to do about it) are:

- ✔ **The buyer can't or doesn't want to measure the financial impact of its improvement opportunity.** In this situation, you don't have the buyer's financial performance indicators to use as the basis for your financial benefits calculations. You can still have a financial benefits subsection in your proposal. You include general financial benefit statements focused on the buyer's business. For example, "By outsourcing its payroll processing functions, Western Data Systems will eliminate the costs associated with the maintenance and operation of its in-house payroll system."

- ✔ **Your product or service just doesn't lend itself to measuring financial benefits.** You may be selling something that the buyer absolutely needs, so calculating its financial benefit is pointless. For example, many public accounting firms write proposals to secure tax service engagements. Calculating the financial benefits of the tax service is almost impossible. Sure, a sales professional from a CPA firm could compare the cost of the service to what would happen if the company didn't submit a tax return or the cost that the company would incur for preparing the return internally. But both calculations would be a waste of time and seem pretty ridiculous.

If measuring the financial benefits of your product is very difficult, forget about having a financial benefits subsection. Instead, include a general subsection on benefits that focuses on the non-financial benefits.

# Chapter 8

# The Implementation Plan: Raising the Buyer's Comfort Level

*M*idpoint in the sales proposal process, a buyer who has not worked before with a certain seller may start thinking: "Hey, this proposal really makes good sense. We can really help our bottom line with this company's proposed solution." Long pause. "But can these guys deliver?"

Questions like that take the wind out of your sales — pun intended. So far you have done all the right stuff. You have identified a wonderful improvement opportunity and you have explained how your product or service is the best way to capitalize on that opportunity, topics I cover in Chapters 5 and 6.

Suppose that the buyer really likes your proposal up to this point. But now the buyer senses some potential risks attached to choosing *you*. So, when and how do you sidestep those risks and raise the buyer's comfort level?

The time and place where you take the initiative is the middle section of your sales proposal — part three of the five-part proposal that I recommend in this book. (Figure 8-1 shows your proposal after the middle section is completed.) And what you do is carefully explain how you intend to implement the proposed project. This chapter shows how.

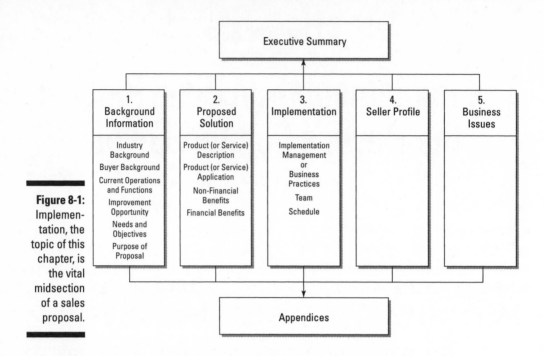

**Figure 8-1:** Implementation, the topic of this chapter, is the vital midsection of a sales proposal.

# Easing the Buyer's Uncertain Feelings about You

One of the functions of the third section in your proposal is to reassure the buyer. When a company decides to make a change by buying your product, the decision makers feel some risk. Pretend you're the CFO of a large manufacturing company and your company has decided to implement an integrated purchasing/inventory control/accounts payable system. Implementing an integrated system that controls these three key functions is a big deal for any company. As you review the proposals from the system vendors, you start to feel the risk associated with this critical decision. You feel two types of risk:

✔ **Business risk.** If you make the wrong choice, you create operational problems for the company, which can result in lost revenues or higher production costs. Profits could head south. You know that if profits are down, the board of directors will start pressuring the president. And the president will probably want to try another reorganization to deflect the heat.

✔ **Personal risk.** A wrong decision reflects on you personally. Since you're the CFO, the other decision makers think you know lots about purchasing/inventory control/accounts payable systems. So they look to you to really study the options and recommend an integrated system that makes the most sense for the company. If you pick the wrong system, your name will be tied to any problems that result from the choice. You know that if the integration bombs, it's *your* system.

So what can you do as a salesperson to reduce the risk that the CFO in the integrated purchasing/inventory control/accounts payable example feels? First, you can reassure the CFO that you've thoroughly studied the company's operations. You do this in section one of the proposal. Then, you define how your system can work in the CFO's company — section two of your proposal. In the third section, you convince the CFO that your company can really deliver by presenting the implementation plan.

*Note:* You also use customer references to reassure the buyer, as I write about in Chapter 9.

# Using the Implementation Section to Show You've Been There, Done That!

This section of your proposal should describe your company's standard implementation methods, project management techniques, or business practices. It should define the steps, phases, and activities that your company normally follows. It should identify the resources your company will use to implement your proposed product. It can also include an estimated schedule for completing the implementation.

## How we beat the big guys

In the late 1980s, I was a partner in a professional services firm that developed computer-based training programs to customer specifications. To put a price on a proposal, we had to work closely with the buyer to define the instructional objectives, curriculum design, and estimated course length by module or unit. We plugged all these estimates into a project planning system, and the system generated a price and a timeline for completion, which we put in our proposals. We also included the actual computer-generated report in an appendix to the proposal.

We closed a lot of business. Once, when we beat a big consulting group for a large project for an automobile manufacturer, one of the buyer's staff commented, "We know you guys are a small company, but you really seem to have a handle on how to do business."

He was referring to the implementation section in our winning proposal, and I guess he was saying, in effect, "We know you guys have been there and done that, so we think you can do it for us, too."

Use this section to send the buyer one strong signal about your company's ability to deliver on the contract — *been there, done that!* In other words, after reading your proposal's implementation section, the buyer should realize that your company has experience in successfully implementing its products. If your company is brand new or if this is your first project as an independent consultant, you can still give the buyer the impression that you have experience with this type of project — probably because you do have the experience, even if its not with your current company or as an independent consultant.

If you haven't included been-there-done-that information in your proposal before, you may be pleasantly surprised at how easy it is to design and write this section.

Start by talking to the people in your company who actually implement your products. Your company's operational staff probably can give you everything you need for your proposal. But don't be surprised if they question your motives. Operational staff members always blame the sales guys for promising the world to customers, and now you're asking for their help. But you can win them over because they'll like the idea that they have some input into the implementation schedule. (At some companies, this exchange of information with the operational staff is standard operating procedure for writing proposals.)

To give you some realistic estimates on the resources and time needed to complete the implementation, your operational staff probably needs to know something about the prospective buyer. They need to know things like background information about the buyer's business, how your proposed product can work in the buyer's company, and what benefits the buyer expects to receive.

---

## What if you haven't been there and done that before?

If you're just starting out in business and haven't developed standard implementation methods, project management techniques, or business practices, you need to develop them right now. Start by using the books and Web resources listed in Appendix A.

# Coming Up with a Title for the Implementation Section

Some generic section titles you can use for section three are listed below. Of course, you'll have to choose an appropriate title based on what you're selling.

- ✔ System Implementation
- ✔ Product Installation
- ✔ Project Management
- ✔ Engagement Management
- ✔ Business Practices

Although a generic title is an option, consider customizing the section title. Because this section really discusses elements of *your* business, some logical titles can include your company's name:

- ✔ FSCS: Conversion Management
- ✔ McDonald Technologies Project Management Overview
- ✔ Mueller & Jones: Engagement Practices

Optionally, you also can use the section title to focus the reader's attention on your proposed project:

- ✔ Custom Systems Development: ELS Protect System
- ✔ Audit Services Transition and Engagement Practices for XYZ Systems
- ✔ Central Expressway Plaza Project: Construction Management

# Deciding What Subsections to Include

To make a decision, a buyer needs to know how, with whom, and when you plan to implement your product. You address that need in the implementation section through the three standard subsections:

Methods

Team

Schedule

You address the what and the how in the methods subsection, the who in the team subsection, and the when in the schedule subsection.

Table 8-1 shows how you can either use generic or custom titles for these subsections. The table shows how adding the seller's name or the product's name, and for some subsections the buyer's name, makes a proposal appear more customized.

| Table 8-1 | Examples of Subsection Titles |
|---|---|
| *Generic Titles* | *Example Custom Titles* |
| Implementation | FSCS Implementation Plan |
| or | |
| Implementation Plan | FSCS Implementation Plan for 1st National Bank |
| or | |
| Project Management | McAndrew and Paine Consulting Practices |
| or | |
| Engagement Practices | McAndrew and Paine Project Management |
| Team | FSCS System Implementation Team |
| or | |
| Project Team | 1st National Bank & FSCS Project Team |
| or | |
| Implementation Team | |
| Schedule | EnviroControl III Installation Schedule |
| or | |
| Project Schedule | FSCS Project Schedule |
| or | |
| Implementation Schedule | McAndrew and Paine Implementation Schedule |

Keep your eye on the prize as you write the third section. Your objective is to:

✔ Clearly differentiate your company and its proposal from the competition.

✔ Assure the buyer that your company has implementation management capabilities and experience.

✔ Present your company's standard approach for doing business.

# Deciding What to Say about Implementation Management

For any size project, whether it takes less than a month to complete or lasts more than a year, your proposal needs to assure the buyer that your company can manage the implementation team, resources, logistics, and activities. The implementation management subsection should include the following information:

✔ Major project activities or phases

✔ Deliverables or end products by phase

✔ Buyer review and approval points within each phase

You don't want to put too much detail into this section. Only include the major phases and important activities. Identify the significant deliverables or outputs that the buyer can review and approve. For example, if you're designing a system, you can include the functional design document and detail design documents in this section.

Don't worry about the project schedule for now. After you describe your major phases and activities, you can create a schedule that's easy to understand.

The simple plan shown in Figure 8-2 illustrates how a public accounting firm can present its engagement practices in one of its proposals.

| Phase | Activities |
|---|---|
| **Planning** | • Meet with client to review problems and concerns<br>• Meet with client to review internal audit procedures<br>• Document accounting systems<br>• Identify major areas of audit focus<br>• Coordinate audit process with client |
| **Interim Fieldwork: Audit Procedures** | • Review internal controls<br>• Audit property and equipment additions and depreciation calculations<br>• Review operations<br>• Meet with client representatives and the Audit Committee to discuss any areas of concern |
| **Post Year Audit Fieldwork** | • Update work performed during interim phase<br>• Perform additional audit procedures<br>• Review yearend statements<br>• Prepare audit report<br>• Write Letter to Management |
| **Communicate Audit Findings** | The following activities are completed with the client's management and Audit Committee:<br>• Discuss audit process followed<br>• Present audit report<br>• Present Letter to Management<br>• Discuss corrective actions needed if any and next steps |

**Figure 8-2:**
An example of a simple implementation plan.

Figure 8-3 presents a complex project plan for a software company. Notice how the table format makes the plan easy to read.

| Phase | Activities | Deliverables |
|---|---|---|
| **1. Implementation Planning** | • Define team roles and responsibilities<br>• Plan implementation<br>• Order hardware (turnkey system only)<br>• Order telecommunications facilities<br>• Plan marketing program | • Implementation Plan and Schedule<br>• Electronic bill specifications<br>• Alpha and Pilot Test Plans<br>• Marketing Plan |
| **2. Software Customization** | • Develop interfaces to the City of Centerville's CIS and CR systems<br>• Develop formatted electronic bill<br>• Develop Web site<br>• Customize EBPP system<br>• Install EBPP hardware and software (turnkey system only) | • Installed and tested CIS and CR interfaces<br>• Installed and tested software and hardware (turnkey system only) |
| **3. Alpha Testing** | • Test systems and interfaces<br>• Develop operational procedures | • Completed Alpha Test<br>• EBPP System Operational Procedures |
| **4. Systems Operations Training** | • Train Administrators and customer support staff<br>• Validate Operational Procedures | • Trained EBPP system operators and customer support staff<br>• Approved Operational Procedures |
| **5. Pilot (Acceptance) Testing** | • Select test customers<br>• Conduct Pilot Test and review results | • Tested hardware, software, and procedures<br>• EBPP system operational |
| **6. Initial Customer Rollout/Signup** | • Market EBPP program to all customers<br>• Customer signup | • Bill presentment customers<br>• Electronic bills and payments |
| **7. EBPP Operations** | • Daily EBPP processing<br>• Customer support activities<br>• ElectroBill system support | • Ongoing EBPP operations |

**Figure 8-3:**
A complex project plan for a software firm.

# Writing about the Team

Your implementation management subsection tells a buyer what your company does and how it does it, and then the team subsection lets the buyer know who's going to do it. Most buyers like to see that a team is involved, especially when your proposed solution requires a complex or long implementation. Buyers also like the idea of a team if your company is providing ongoing service. Maybe the vision of a bunch of people working towards a common goal reduces some of the buyer's perceived risk. Who knows, maybe when a decision maker sees the word *team* he thinks of his favorite football team that just won the big game.

Just remember that including a team subsection sends a strong message that your company knows what resources are needed to deliver on its obligations. A well-designed team subsection also demonstrates your company's willingness to commit your resources to help the buyer take advantage of its improvement opportunity.

## Including basic team information

In many situations, the team consists of people from the buyer's organization and yours. For example, a software company usually needs someone from the buyer's company to help it develop conversion program specifications to convert data from an old system to the new system. The software company may also need some buyer representatives to help it define processing options for the new system. Include the following information for each team member, whether the team member works for your organization or for the buyer:

- ✔ Organization name
- ✔ First and last name of the team member
- ✔ Corporate or functional title of the team member

Also include the telephone numbers of team members who are a part of your organization.

## Defining team roles and responsibilities

You can use the team subsection of your proposal to do two things:

- ✔ Impress the buyer's decision makers. A well-designed team subsection clearly identifies the critical team resources that are needed.
- ✔ Make sure that the buyer understands its responsibilities in the implementation by including the roles and responsibilities of the buyer's team members.

Writing a team subsection for every proposal may seem like a lot of work. But if your company uses a standard implementation management approach or follows standard business practices, team member roles and responsibilities don't change that much from one proposal to the next.

As you write, keep in mind the 80/20 rule that states 80 percent of the information in your proposal remains the same for most buyers and 20 percent changes from one buyer (or project) to the next. You may find that the 80/20 rule applies to the team member information in your team subsection.

## Including team member resumes

Certified public accounting, consulting, and systems development firms, among others, may include biographical resumes of the people they plan to assign to the project. When a company is buying intangible services, their decision makers are probably interested in the education, experiences, and the past projects of the seller's staff. Think of this resume concept the next time you're sitting in a dentist's chair reading the dentist's diploma hanging on the wall. You know the root canal will hurt, but at least you know that the dentist has learned the proper way to create the pain.

If your company sells professional services, consider including a biographical resume of each team member in an appendix. Chapter 11 gives more information on this subject.

## Using a chart to introduce a team

Figure 8-4 shows how you can use a chart to explain who does what on a complex team that includes both seller and buyer staff members. For this example, I'm calling the buyer *1st National Bank* and the seller *Financial Services Control Systems*. The seller's task is to implement a new information system at the bank. Note the following features in the chart:

 ✔ Team members are grouped by buyer and seller organization.

 ✔ All team members have a specific role, which is printed in boldface.

 ✔ The names and titles for all the team members are included and the seller's team members also have their telephone numbers listed.

 ✔ All team members have their primary responsibilities clearly defined

**1st National Bank & FSCS Conversion Team**

A team comprised of staff member from 1st National Bank (FNB) and
Financial Services Control Systems (FSCS) will convert FNB from its current
system to FSCSystem 2000. The following table identifies the team members
and their roles and responsibilities.

| Organization | Team Role | Responsibilities |
|---|---|---|
| 1st National Bank | **Conversion Liaison**<br><br>Ann Gollen<br>VP & Cashier | • Primary customer contact for FSCS<br>• Coordinate on-site conversion activities<br>• Coordinate communications with FSCS<br>  and current data processor and ATM processor |
| | **Deposit Application Specialist**<br><br>Gene Sills<br>AVP & Deposit<br>Product Manager | • Define checking, money market, savings,<br>  and certificate of deposit processing requirements:<br>  product specifications, service charge routines,<br>  interest calculations, reporting, etc. |
| | **Loans Application Specialist**<br><br>Jack Denton<br>AVP & Loan Product<br>Manager | • Define Loan processing requirements: installment,<br>  commercial, and mortgage product specifications,<br>  reporting, etc. |
| | **Teller & Platform Application Specialist**<br><br>Julie Anderson<br>AVP & Personal<br>Banking Center<br>Manager | • Define Teller operations and processing requirements:<br>  journal and validation printing specifications, security<br>  requirements, reporting, forms, etc.<br>• Define Platform and Customer Information File (CIF)<br>  operations and processing requirements, e.g., new account<br>  processing specifications, printing specifications, forms,<br>  account relationships and structures, etc. |
| **Financial Services Control Systems** | **Conversion Leader**<br><br>John Fischer<br>Vice President<br>(972-404-7810) | • Coordinates and manages the entire conversion process<br>• Maintains adherence to FSCS' Conversion Management<br>  Methods<br>• Prepares weekly status report for Bank and FSCS<br>  management<br>• Resolves conversion issues<br>• Ensure conversion is on schedule, in balance, and fully<br>  operational in preparation for sign-off |
| | **Bank Liaison Representative**<br><br>**Angela Carter**<br>Senior Client<br>Representative<br>(972-404-7820) | • Assembles list of Bank's requirements and option<br>  preferences<br>• Coordinates Bank's pre-conversion activities<br>• Communicate conversion and parameter changes to<br>  FSCS technical personnel |
| | **Data Conversion Specialist**<br><br>**Ted Krause**<br>Senior Conversion<br>Analyst<br>(972-404-7830) | • Collects test data from the existing data processing<br>  resource<br>• Writes and tests data conversion programs<br>• Collects Bank data for live conversion<br>• Performs actual data conversion<br>• Remains at Bank through the first posting cycles |
| | **Customer Service Conversion Representative**<br><br>**Bill Gander**<br>Sr. Conversion<br>Representative<br>(972-404-7840) | • Approves pre-conversion test of Bank's data<br>• Delivers pre-conversion training<br>• Ensures Conversion Day and subsequent day balancing<br>• Delivers post-conversion training and support |
| | **Installation Specialist**<br><br>**Randy Lealand**<br>Sr. Technical Analyst<br>(972-404-7850) | • Assembles and tests Bank's custom FSCSystem Plus<br>  2000 equipment<br>• Coordinates Bank cabling with Bank's electrician<br>• Installs and tests equipment prior to conversion |

**Figure 8-4:**
Using a
table to
show the
members of
a team.

Do you think a buyer's decision makers will be impressed if a sales proposal contains a team subsection with this level of thoroughness? I think most decision makers will be very impressed. This type of team subsection leaves little doubt in a decision maker's mind that the seller has an abundance of implementation experience.

A table with this amount of detailed information can take you some time to develop. However, if your company uses the same implementation or project management plan for most sales, the biggest changes to this subsection will be the team members' names, titles, and telephone numbers. You don't have to create a totally new team subsection for every proposal.

# The Schedule: Showing When Things Get Done

Your proposal's implementation management subsection tells a buyer what you're going to do and how you're going to do it. Your team subsection lets the buyer know who's going to do it. And the schedule subsection gives the buyer information about when the implementation will happen. The information in this subsection is important to the buyer because it lets the buyer know when your proposed product will be installed.

*Note:* Remember that in this book I use *product* to mean either a product or a service. If you're selling a service, the schedule subsection indicates when the service will begin or be delivered.

Look at the 1st National Bank and FSCS conversion information presented in the previous implementation management and team subsection examples. The bank's decision makers need to know when the conversion can start and how long it will take FSCS to complete it. What if the FSCS proposal stated only that the conversion would be completed by the end of the second quarter of next year? A vague schedule like that would probably make some of the decision makers a bit nervous.

Your schedule subsection, if it's done well, assures the buyer that you've thought about everything that's needed to complete its implementation. This subsection can include the major phases or activities and realistic dates for completing the project. You can use high-level bar charts or tables that reference an appendix for more detail. Remember that your schedule subsection must coordinate with the project phases and activities that you define in your implementation management subsection.

You can present a schedule very simply in a table showing the phases and their start and stop dates, as shown in Figure 8-5, or you can get a little fancier, as in Figure 8-6.

| Project Phase | Start Date | Stop Date |
|---|---|---|
| Conversion Analysis and Planning | 7/01/03 | 07/14/03 |
| Preparation and Equipment Acquisition | 07/15/03 | 08/15/03 |
| System Testing and Validation | 08/01/03 | 08/31/03 |
| Installation and Training | 09/01/03 | 10/16/03 |
| System Conversion | 10/17/03 | 10/17/03 |
| Quality Assurance | 10/18/03 | Ongoing |

**Figure 8-5:**
A simple
schedule.

| Project Phase | Month | July | Aug | Sept | Oct |
|---|---|---|---|---|---|
| Conversion Analysis and Planning | | | | | |
| Preparation and Equipment Acquisition | | | | | |
| System Testing and Validation | | | | | |
| Installation and Training | | | | | |
| System Conversion (October 17, 2003) | | | | | |
| Quality Assurance (ongoing) | | | | | |

**Figure 8-6:**
A more
complex
schedule.

Do you think the chart in Figure 8-6 provides enough detail for the 1st National Bank's decision makers? It probably does provide enough information for the bank's senior decision makers (hey, some of the people probably don't know how to turn on a computer). This bar chart does provide enough detail if Appendix F in the FSCS proposal has the detail to back up the chart. But some of the bank's decision makers might like the next example more than this one.

Figure 8-7 is another bar chart. This bar chart provides more detail for the bank's decision makers. It also uses the 1st National Bank and FSCS conversion examples.

In Figure 8-7, changing the time scale from months to weeks gives the impression that FSCS has put a lot of work into scheduling the conversion.

## Keep those details under control!

Several years ago, I helped a financial information software company develop a proposal model for its sales force. The company licenses software to small to medium-sized financial institutions. Typically, its sales professionals sell to banks that either use a third-party data processing provider or have their own in-house system.

When I asked the company how it implements its system, it handed me a five-page list of 167 tasks — the company's installation checklist. It was thorough and quite impressive. But the five-page list was far too much for the proposal.

To solve the problem, we created six major implementation phases and five to ten major activities in each phase. Next, we assigned each of the 167 conversion tasks to one of the activities within the six phases. For each major phase, we also identified some deliverable or output that the buyer could review or approve. By organizing the details in this fashion, we created a useful part of a proposal. Some of the examples in this chapter are based on that plan.

**Figure 8-7:**
An even
more
complex
schedule.

| Project Phase | Week | 1 | 2 | 3 | 4 | 5 | 6 | 7 | 8 | 9 | 10 | 11 | 12 | 13 | 14 | 15 | 16 | 17 | 18 |
|---|---|---|---|---|---|---|---|---|---|---|---|---|---|---|---|---|---|---|---|
| Conversion Analysis and Planning | | ▓ | ▓ | | | | | | | | | | | | | | | | |
| Preparation and Equipment Acquisition | | | | ▓ | ▓ | ▓ | ▓ | | | | | | | | | | | | |
| System Testing and Validation | | | | | | | ▓ | ▓ | ▓ | | | | | | | | | | |
| Installation and Training | | | | | | | | | | ▓ | ▓ | ▓ | ▓ | ▓ | | | | | |
| System Conversion (October 17, 2003) | | | | | | | | | | | | | | | ▓ | | | | |
| Quality Assurance (ongoing) | | | | | | | | | | | | | | | | ▓ | ▓ | ▓ | ▓ |

# Using an All-Purpose Implementation Table

If your implementation or project management tasks aren't very complex, you can use a multipurpose table to do triple duty. You can use a multipurpose table to:

 ✔ Define your implementation or engagement tasks.

 ✔ Assign implementation or engagement responsibilities.

 ✔ Define the implementation or engagement schedule.

For example, a trust company may use the bar chart shown in Figure 8-8 in this subsection.

| Activity | Responsibility | Start Date | Stop Date |
|---|---|---|---|
| Draft Trust Agreement | MNB Trust Company (MTC) | 1-19-02 | 1-22-02 |
| Review Trust Agreement | Bill & Kathy Jones | 1-26-02 | 1-30-02 |
| Execute Trust Agreement | Bill & Kathy Jones / MTC | 2-03-02 | 2-07-02 |
| Transfer Assets to MTC | MTC | 2-10-02 | 2-28-02 |

# Using a Table to Show Team Commitment

You can include an optional table in your implementation section that shows team commitment by project phase. This table has one purpose: to show team member commitment levels for each phase of the implementation or project. The table also lets the buyer know how much of their team members' time you expect on the project. For smaller projects, identifying the buyer's team commitment levels may not be that big of an issue. But for long or complex projects where the seller needs expertise and cooperation from the buyer's organization, it makes a lot of sense to include this type of table in the implementation section of your proposal.

A team commitment by project phase table combines information from two subsections:

✔ It uses the project phases from the implementation management subsection.

✔ It includes the organization, team member, and team member role information from the team subsection.

Figure 8-9 is a team commitment by project phase table. It shows the percentage of each team member's work time that is needed to complete the project. This table is based on the 1st National Bank and FSCS example.

What do you think would happen if the bank's team members were unable to participate at the levels listed in this table? FSCS would probably have difficulties keeping on schedule because the bank's team members have the expertise and knowledge FSCS needs to convert the bank from its current system to the FSCS system.

| Organization | Name | Project Role | % Time Commitment by Phase | | | | | |
|---|---|---|---|---|---|---|---|---|
| | | | 1 | 2 | 3 | 4 | 5 | 6 |
| FNB | Ann Gollen | Conversion Liaison | 50 | 25 | 25 | 50 | 50 | 25 |
| | Gene Sills | Application Specialist | 35 | 10 | 25 | 40 | 50 | 10 |
| | Jack Denton | Application Specialist | 35 | 10 | 25 | 40 | 50 | 10 |
| | Julie Anderson | Customer Service Rep. | 35 | 10 | 25 | 40 | 50 | 10 |
| FSCS | John Fischer | Conversion Team Leader | 50 | 50 | 50 | 50 | 50 | 20 |
| | Angela Carter | Bank Liaison Rep. | 40 | 20 | 40 | 75 | 90 | 20 |
| | Ted Krause | Conversion Specialist | 90 | 90 | 90 | 50 | 50 | 0 |
| | Bill Gander | Customer Service Rep. | 50 | 50 | 25 | 75 | 90 | 10 |
| | Randy Lealand | Installation Specialist | 50 | 25 | 25 | 75 | 25 | 10 |

**Figure 8-9:**
A team
commitment
by project
phase table.

# Chapter 9

# Spotlighting the Seller (That's You!)

*T*he way I design sales proposals, the section describing the seller — the part featuring you or your company — does not come at the beginning. It doesn't even rate second billing. I reserve this part for quite late in the proposal, after you cover the number one topic so far as the buyer is concerned (namely the buyer), and after you explain your product and how you plan to install it. Figure 9-1 shows you the overall view of the proposal, with the subsections for section one through four filled in.

The logic for waiting until late in the proposal to introduce your company is as follows:

✔ First, the readers want to know that you know something about their company's unique business operations, that you have identified an improvement opportunity, and that you understand their company's needs and objectives.

✔ Next, the readers want to see if your product can really make a difference for their company. Can your product help the company achieve the improvement opportunity, and does it offer the company some financial and non-financial benefits?

✔ Then, if the readers think you understand their situation and like your proposed product, they need to be convinced that you're able to implement the product.

✔ After reading this far in your proposal — and being impressed — the readers ask, "Hey, who are these guys?"

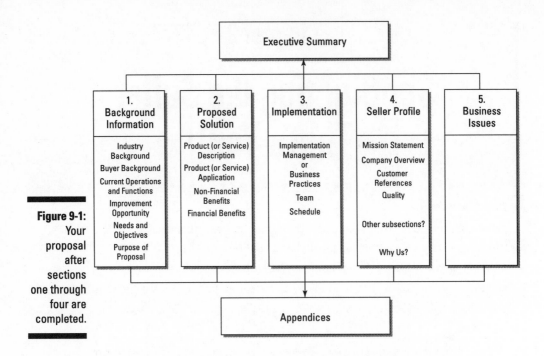

**Figure 9-1:**
Your
proposal
after
sections
one through
four are
completed.

As you can see in Figure 9-1, you write about yourself in the fourth main section of the proposal structure that I advocate. The fourth section's purpose is

✔ To reduce the buyer's risk in making a change or doing business with your company

✔ To give the buyer a synopsis of your company's qualifications and capabilities — information about your business, its employees, and its operations

✔ To tell the buyer how your company is very qualified to help it achieve its improvement opportunity

In this chapter, I show you how to cover all the bases.

## Risky business

In some ways, your implementation plan (see Chapter 8) and this section — all about you — have similar purposes: They both help reduce the buyer's risk. Both parts assure the buyer that you have the experience, capabilities, and resources to deliver on the contract. Remember that if your proposed solution represents a critical purchase, then the decision makers feel these two types of risk:

- **Business risk:** A wrong decision may adversely affect their company.

- **Personal risk:** They'll look bad or get blamed if they make a poor decision.

# Getting Off the Level Playing Field

Many buyers develop selection criteria to evaluate vendors in complex sales situations (see Chapter 2 for more information on selection criteria). Buyers quickly drop those sellers who don't meet the criteria. The remaining sellers make the buyer's shortlist. Consciously or unconsciously, the buyer may put all shortlist sellers on a level playing field. In other words, the buyer can think that all the shortlist sellers are equally qualified to deliver on the contract, so it doesn't spend additional time studying the sellers' qualifications.

You can't stop the buyer from using selection criteria to decide which vendors are on the short list — who's on the level playing field. But you can use section four of your sales proposal to rise above the crowd. A well-crafted seller profile can really help you differentiate your company, highlight your employees, and explain the way you do business. A well-crafted seller profile section in your proposal just may force the buyer into reevaluating its shortlist contenders.

# Selling the Buyer on Your Company

Your seller profile section gives the buyer a bunch of reasons why it should buy your products and do business with you instead of one of your competitors. This section gives a newer company a chance to really convince a buyer that, while it may be the new kid on the block, it's a really bright and industrious kid. A long client list may not impress the buyer as much as an innovative manufacturing process or a new approach to service delivery, for example.

Don't make the mistake many companies do in their proposals: Don't use this section just to impress the buyer with how big your company is or how many employees and locations it has. Being big doesn't immediately qualify your company as the best choice for the buyer. Instead, use this section to impress the buyer with your company's unique qualifications. For example, impress the buyer with your company's business philosophy, quality programs, or approach to customer service.

## Using standard wording but beating the boilerplate

This section contains the most standard wording. But that doesn't mean it's boilerplate (you don't ever want any part of your proposal to be boilerplate). Rather, this section's contents may require the fewest changes from one proposal to the next. If you're tempted to use a standard section four in all of your proposals, don't do it. Remember that you need to look at every proposal from the buyer's viewpoint. Go back and review your meetings and other conversations that you had with the buyer to get some clues to what it wants to know about your company.

You may even want to insert special subsections for specific buyers. For example, if a buyer is concerned with your company's disaster recovery plans, by all means include a subsection on disaster recovery. You may end up developing lots of special subsections that you can drop in depending on the buyer. I give you more information on optional subsections later in the chapter.

Just remember that section four isn't a boilerplate description of your company. You need to use this section to sell a buyer on your company. Each buyer is unique and has unique information needs — hot buttons that you have to push.

## Answering the buyer's twenty questions

Design and write section four like you're being interrogated by one of the buyer's decision makers. The decision maker is playing the old twenty questions game with you to find out everything that he wants to know about your company. Remember that each buyer has its list of twenty questions. Some of the twenty questions are very similar for all buyers, but others are unique. Part of your consultative sales process is determining what the buyer wants to know about your company — it may not be exactly twenty questions, but every buyer has a need to know something about your company.

As you wonder how to customize your seller profile section for each buyer, think about these questions:

- ✔ What kinds of questions has the buyer asked about your company during the sales process?
- ✔ What are the buyer's top three selection criteria?
- ✔ What really seem to be important issues or concerns in the buyer's company?

Here's another way to make designing and writing a buyer-specific section four easier. Pretend you're one of the buyer's decision makers. You've only read sections one through three of the proposal (buyer background, proposed solution, and implementation) and you're pretty impressed. You've been nominated to interview the sales representative to learn about the seller's company. Write down the questions that you want to ask the sales representative about his or her company. Use the questions you want to ask to decide what unique information (and perhaps subsections) to put in the seller profile section.

# Coming Up with a Section Title

Some generic section titles you can consider include

- ✔ About Our Company
- ✔ About Us
- ✔ Our Profile

However, since this section profiles the seller, including the seller's name makes sense. Here are some examples:

- ✔ ElectroBill Systems Profile
- ✔ Management Overview: Electronic Lending Systems
- ✔ Randall, Smith, and Hannaford: Business Profile

# Deciding What Subsections to Use

Every seller should consider using the following five subsections in the seller profile section of their sales proposals because these sections say a lot about how a company does business:

Mission or Business Philosophy Statement

Company or Corporate Overview

Customer References

Quality

Why Us?

However, you may also want to add optional subsections. Consider your buyer's information needs and your buyer's perceived risks to help you decide what other subsections you may want to include in your seller profile section. Your interactions with the buyer during the sales process can help you identify what information the buyer may want to see in this section. The seller's business type or profession also helps determine which subsections to include in the seller profile section of a proposal.

Table 9-1 lists just some suggested subsections for four major business and professional categories. See the section on selecting optional subsections, later in this chapter, for more information.

| Table 9-1 | Subsection Options by Business and Profession | | | |
|---|---|---|---|---|
| Subsection Options | Equipment and Manufacturing | Consulting and Professional Services | Data Processing and Business Services | Computer Hardware and Software |
| Project Status Meetings and Reporting | | X | X | |
| Engagement or Project Budget | | X | | |
| Research and Development | X | | X | X |
| Staff | X | X | X | X |
| Facilities and Equipment | X | | X | X |
| Production Capacities | X | | X | |
| Customer Service | X | | X | X |
| Systems Design and Development | | | X | X |

# Using the Five Recommended Subsections

The following pages contain detailed information and examples for the five recommended subsections for the seller profile section.

## Mission statement subsection

Putting your company's mission statement or business philosophy in your proposal represents one of the best ways to assure the buyer that your company can deliver on the contract. The content of the mission statement gives the buyer a good idea of what the company is all about. Most company mission statements are brief — one paragraph — and they can set the tone for the rest of your seller profile subsection. For these reasons alone, you may want to begin your fourth section with your mission statement.

## Company or corporate overview subsection

Use this subsection to give your buyer some insight and background on your company. You can use it to tout your company's annual revenues, number of employees, number of locations, and so on. However, always look for ways to keep this subsection (and the entire section four) as buyer specific as possible. Depending on the buyer's needs or selection criteria, you can find it advantageous to customize this apparently static subsection. For example, a buyer may prefer to work with a small firm. To help satisfy this selection criterion, a large firm can use the company overview subsection to emphasize its local office philosophy and the continuity of its office managers.

If your company has a marketing department, ask it for some help. Remember that the marketing department is responsible for customer communications. Tell it what you're doing and ask it to write a short (2 to 3 paragraph) company overview to use in the company's sales proposals. The department may be very helpful. If the marketing guys are helpful, talk to them about possibly writing different company overview subsections for each of the company's target markets or to address different buyer selection criteria.

If your company has a Web site, you can start developing this subsection by copying information directly from the "About Us" page on your site.

## Creating a mission statement

"Your company's mission statement has to draw a compelling picture of what your business is all about. We often refer to this picture as creating a *tangible image* of the company. This statement tells what the company does, whom it serves, and what sets it apart from its competitor."

That description of a mission statement is from *Business Plans For Dummies.* If your company doesn't have a mission statement, you may want to develop one. Here are some tips for developing a mission statement, also from *Business Plans For Dummies.* (You have a good start to answering some of these questions if you've written sections one and two of your proposal.)

"We know that creating a mission statement for your company can sound like an impossible task — the Mount Everest of business-planning chores. Some preparation upfront, however, can make the process a little easier. Ask yourself the following background questions as you get ready to work on your company's mission statement:

✔ Which customers or groups of customers does your company plan to serve?

✔ What products or services does your company plan to provide?

✔ What needs do you satisfy?

✔ How does your company's product differ from the competition's?

✔ What extra value or benefits do customers receive when they choose your company over the competition?

✔ How fast are these answers changing?"

These three company overview examples can give you some ideas how different types of companies may write this subsection. The first example is from one of my client's proposals with the names changed to protect the innocent and the numbers inflated to impress this book's readers. I developed the other two examples by using information from Web sites. See, it's pretty easy.

This company overview subsection uses a chronological history of the company to show buyers the company's important achievements and milestones.

### Corporate Overview: BTI

Bankman Technologies, Inc. (BTI) is one of the fastest growing financial service software companies in the United States. Revenues last year exceeded $15 million. Its corporate headquarters are in Scottsdale, Arizona; however, the company has sales and customer support staff in its Chicago and Philadelphia offices. Over 100 financial service, customer support, and data processing professionals work for BTI.

### Corporate History

7/97 — Bankman Technologies, Inc. (BTI) founded.

10/98 — IBM announces BTI as a National Business Partner.

2/99 — BTI introduces the BankSystem 2000 family of software at the American Bankers Association Annual Conference.

5/99 — BTI successfully installs the first BankSystem 2000 beta site.

2/00 — SCO, a leading UNIX software vendor, invites BTI to become a National Development Partner.

3/00 — BTI introduces the BankSystem Plus 2000 product line to the banking industry.

7/00 — BTI acquires Pegasus, Inc., a Denver-based platform automation company with over 200 clients.

10/00 — BTI acquires iBank, Inc., a Milwaukee-based Internet banking software company with 55 worldwide clients.

11/01 — BTI installs BankSystem Plus 2000 at the 40th customer site.

The following is an example of a company overview subsection for a professional services firm. I pulled data from a consulting firm's Web site to create this example subsection. I've changed the consulting company's name and some of the background information.

### Titan, LLC: Profile

Titan, LLC, a consulting firm, works with its clients' senior managers to develop high impact solutions that affect business strategy. Titan develops business solutions and rapidly implements systems to:

- Accelerate business growth

- Turn around underperforming business units or solve management problems

- Rapidly deploy e-business solutions

Titan specializes in developing high-value growth strategies at all corporate levels. Our senior consultants who have held CEO or senior management positions in Fortune 1000 companies lead all of our engagements.

Titan has offices in Los Angeles, Dallas, Atlanta, Boston, Paris, and Bonn.

The following company overview subsection is one for a manufacturing company. I used a company's Web site to get information and have changed names and some of the content.

### Company Overview: Daniels Engineering & Manufacturing Company

#### A leader in manufacturing solutions

Daniels Engineering & Manufacturing Company is a leader in providing manufacturing solutions for North and Latin American companies. Daniels has three plants in Denver, Colorado. The company has a 32-year heritage of providing reliable, innovative manufacturing solutions for aerospace markets.

Daniels develops customized manufacturing solutions for its customers by integrating modular control components. These components can be used to develop solutions that range from manual to fully automated manufacturing processes.

Daniels' breadth of product and application capabilities has enabled the company to develop a number of revolutionary manufacturing solutions that have become aerospace industry standards over the last two decades. Daniels also has complete research and development, design engineering, manufacturing, project management, and installation service capabilities to assure it customers that its manufacturing solutions are developed to specifications and delivered on time.

## Quality subsection

Everyone is aware of the importance of quality. You've heard phrases like:

✔ Quality is Job #1.

✔ Quality. It's a Way of Life.

✔ Quality Is Our Most Important Product.

Back in the 1980s, people became more aware of quality than ever before and demanded quality in the goods and services they purchased and how they were treated as customers. Many companies implemented Total Quality Management and ISO/9000 programs to achieve world-class quality levels. Many companies' goods and services vastly improved. Now most buyers just expect that whatever they buy will be top quality.

All the media hype surrounding quality has decreased, but you should still show in your sales proposal that you can satisfy your buyer's demand for quality. The quality subsection in section four provides a great place to present your product quality policies, ongoing quality programs, and any quality awards that your company has won. Several well-written paragraphs can give the buyer assurances and meet its expectations:

✔ **Service providers** can describe their quality customer service commitment.

✔ **Consulting firms or consultants** can discuss how they ensure quality during the engagement and quality's relationship to the engagement budget.

✔ **Manufacturers** can describe their quality assurance processes, programs, and standards.

This short quality subsection really says it all about the seller's concern for quality. I pulled it directly from a Web site and only changed a few words around.

### Quality at Daniels Engineering

At Daniels Engineering, we define quality in our objective and policy. Quality satisfies the continuously changing needs of our customers, vendors, and employees, with our manufacturing solutions and services. It emphasizes our ongoing commitment to satisfaction through our constant improvement, education, communication, and evaluation processes.

The following example ties the seller's quality message to the company's mission statement, the proposal's customer references, and the case studies contained in an appendix of the sales proposal. This quality subsection really makes it seem as if the company walks the walk.

ElectroBill Quality Commitment

ElectroBill maintains a steadfast commitment to excellence, as stated in its mission statement. ElectroBill operates with the highest degree of integrity, provides quality electronic bill presentment and payment (EBPP) systems and services. For any company that sends a high volume of recurring customer bills, quality must be present in four areas: software, hardware, customer service, and people. After reading to this point in our proposal, you know that ElectroBill certainly pays close attention to the first two areas. However, for anyone to effectively measure all four areas requires time and experience working with our company. Therefore, we invite you to contact any of our existing customers to gauge our commitment to quality.

See the next subsection, "Customer References," and "Appendix H: ElectroBill EBPP Case Studies" for more information.

## Customer reference subsection

Customer references do two things. They:

- ✔ Let the decision makers know that their company is not going to be the first to buy the seller's product.
- ✔ Make it easy for the decision makers to talk to someone who has experience with the seller's company.

The buyer may not even check out the references. What matters is the fact that you're confident enough to include references in your proposal. Customer references say a lot about your company. While reading your customer references, a decision maker may think, "ABC Company is one of their references; I know how tough those guys are!"

Make it easy for a buyer to check your customer references. Include the following information for each reference:

- ✔ Company name
- ✔ Company address (city, state, and zip code)
- ✔ Contact name and title
- ✔ Contact telephone number (and, optionally, e-mail address)

You can also choose to include other information to help the buyer decide if it wants to check a reference:

- ✔ Date implemented or installed or customer-since date
- ✔ Type of product installed
- ✔ Other information that can show a reference's size or other characteristics, like the number of customers, number of employees, transaction volumes, operating system, and so on.

Before you include a customer reference in you sales proposal, make sure that doing so is okay with the customer. Some companies don't want to be bothered with calls from your prospective customers. Other companies may have a policy that prohibits them from endorsing or appearing to endorse anyone's product.

You need to know the difference between customer references and a customer list. A customer list is just that: a list of customers. No contact information is provided. Some sellers like to include a customer list in their proposals, especially if their customer list is long and impressive. But remember that you're not making it very easy for the buyer to talk to someone at a company that's included on your customer list. If you decide to include customer references and a customer list, think about putting your customer references in a subsection of section four and putting your customer list in an appendix. You can direct the reader to the appendix with a simple sentence, "See 'Appendix G: Customer List' for a list of current ABC System software licensees."

The following customer reference example uses a table to efficiently display information.

### Customer References

We have selected the following BankSystems customer references for 1st National Bank because these customers have similar demographics and asset sizes as your company.

| Customer | Contact | Title | Telephone | Asset Size (in millions) | Date Converted |
|---|---|---|---|---|---|
| Western State Bank 123 Main Street, Oshkosh, WI 54901 | Russ Kamphaus | SVP | 414-456-7890 | $755 | 3/00 |
| First Commerce Bank, 789 South Park Avenue, Phoenix, AZ 85222 | Bill Gleason | VP & CIO | 802-123-9874 | $689 | 5/00 |
| Dallas Merchants Bank, 321 Northwest Highway, Dallas, TX 75311 | Bob Lunden | EVP | 214-403-7899 | $925 | 1/01 |

For a complete list of current BankSystems licensees, see Appendix F.

## Why us? subsection

Always make the why us? subsection the last subsection in the seller profile section. This subsection is intended to pull everything together for the reader. It actually finishes the real creative part of your proposal because the fifth and last section of the sales proposal only deals with business issues (pricing details, the payment schedule, warranties, and so on).

You use this subsection to actually tell the buyer why your company is the best choice. Many sellers never think about including a why us? subsection in their proposals. Maybe some sellers are too humble and think that this subsection is egocentric. (Although that doesn't sound like too many sales professionals whom I've met.)

By not including a why us? subsection, you miss a great opportunity to link critical components of your sale and proposal. A well-written why us? subsection can help the buyer's decision makers make some very clear connections. It can connect:

- ✔ The buyer's improvement opportunity with your proposed solution
- ✔ Your proposed product's features and benefits with the buyer's needs and objectives
- ✔ Your capacity to deliver on the contract with the buyer's key selection criteria

Many sellers assume that by the time a decision maker has read this far in the sales proposal, these connections should be obvious. But you know what happens when people start making assumptions. . . .

Especially if you're proposing a complex product, the decision makers can be a bit overwhelmed by all the information you include in your proposal. Even if they're clear on the improvement opportunity, sections two and three can become a jumble. This subsection gives you a chance to help the decision makers clarify everything they've read.

Read this subsection. Do you think it links the critical components of the sale and proposal?

### Why ElectroBill?

ElectroBill's EBPP system is the best option because it lets the City of Centerville:

- Select and integrate a multiple billing type application for its current and future EBPP needs.

- Use off-the-shelf, low-cost hardware to host its EBPP application.

- Reach high levels of customer acceptance through its direct EBPP model.

Through its proven implementation approach, ElectroBill can ensure a smooth implementation to an operational EBPP system.

# Selecting Optional Subsections

You need to consider some optional subsections for your seller profile section. As you design and write this section, think about how you can make it more buyer specific. Also think about what may be important to know about your company for companies like those in the buyer's industry or profession. Try to put yourself in the buyer's position. What would you want to know about a seller's business if it were your decision to make or money to spend?

Some optional seller profile subsections to consider include

- Status Meetings and Reporting
- Engagement or Project Budget
- Research and Development
- Staff
- Facilities and Equipment
- Production Capacities
- Customer Service
- Systems Design and Development

## Status meetings and reporting

Companies selling professional services and consultants can use a status meeting or reporting subsection to describe how they plan to keep the buyer informed about their progress. If you include this subsection, detail the purpose of the meetings, how often you plan to hold meetings, who usually attends the status meetings, and how you'll report project or engagement status to the buyer.

If status meetings and reporting are a real hot button with the buyer, consider including a sample project status report as an appendix in your proposal.

Make sure that the information in this subsection ties together with what you included in section three.

# Engagement or project budget

An engagement or project budget subsection can be closely related to a status meeting and reporting subsection. Professional service and consulting firms who work under the limits of the buyer's budget frequently use an engagement or project budget subsection in their sales proposals. If you opt to include it, use this subsection to explain your plans for working within the buyer's budget. If you're proposing a long project, perhaps you need to address how you estimated the resource needs and usage for the project. Or you may need to explain how you will deal with budget variances should they occur.

# Research and development

Technology is changing so rapidly that most people can't keep up with it. Depending upon your customers and your business or profession, keeping up with technology may be very important. If you're a certified public accountant (CPA), you probably don't have to think too long or hard about whether you should include a research and development (R&D) subsection in your proposal — there's no need to. But if your company sells networking hardware and software or builds automated machinery maintenance systems, then the buyer probably want to know about your company's R&D program. Your buyers probably want to know how much you spend each year on R&D and what part your R&D budget is of your company's total budget.

Include a chronological list of major technical developments in this subsection to show the buyer that your company is getting something from its R&D program.

# Staff

A subsection on staff can be an important part of your proposal, especially if your company is a professional service or consulting firm. For a professional service or consulting firm, the education, experience, and competency of the company's staff usually has some relationship to the quality of the service the firm provides. Use this subsection to write about the people who deliver service for your company. Include your staff's years of experience and education, your company's certification requirements for consultants or professionals, and your company's ongoing staff training programs. Remember that this subsection usually ties to the team subsection in section three.

If your company is not in professional services or consulting, a staff subsection still can be an important part of your proposal. For example, if technology or R&D is important to the buyer, then the staff who develops the technology or who does R&D work for your company is important to the buyer. Or if customer service is important to the buyer, you may want to include some information about how your company recruits and trains customer service representatives. Some companies compensate customer service representatives on how fast and accurately they fix customer problems — including this type of information in your staff subsection may impress buyers.

## Facilities and equipment

Having a facilities and equipment subsection in your proposal may be important, depending on what you sell. If your company sells data processing services, it's a more important subsection than if your company provides consulting services. You probably need to put a facilities and equipment subsection in your proposal if the reliability and dependability of your product is dependent upon your data center, factory, computers, automated assembly line, or anything else of the sort. Put yourself in the buyer's position. The buyer's decision makers wants to make sure that you can deliver on the contract so they want to know something about the facilities and equipment that your company uses to deliver on the contract.

## Production capacities

This subsection is related to the facilities and equipment subsection. Besides wanting to know what facilities and equipment your company uses, the buyer may want to know how quickly you can deliver. If your company manufactures custom commercial-grade windows and is submitting a proposal to do all the windows for a new 400-room hotel, the architect and building contractor probably are very interested in how long it will take your company to build the windows. Look at your company's production capacity from the buyer's perspective. If your company has the best product at a very competitive price, the buyer still needs to know if you can meet the production volume requirements of the contract.

## Customer service

This is a hot button in the information age and in an economy that is very service oriented. Many buyers want to know how your company provides customer service. Your proposal needs to give them some information about your company's customer service philosophy, people, training, facilities, hours, systems, and procedures. If you sell anything that involves any form of service or support for the customer, your proposal probably should include a customer service subsection.

## Systems design and development

If you sell software application systems, buyers may want to know how your company designs and develops its systems, especially if the buyer plans to use your systems to run a critical operation in its company. Some of the buyer's decision makers may want to know about the systems development methodology that your company follows. Some decision makers may want to learn about end-user involvement in functional and detail design specifications. Other decision makers may want to learn about your systems testing and quality assurance programs.

# Chapter 10

# Writing the Boring Stuff: Assumptions, Fees, Schedules

. . . . . . . . . . . . . . . . . . . . . . . . . . . . . . . . . . . . . . . . . . . . . . . . . . .

## *In This Chapter*

▶ Avoiding buyer and seller surprises after the sale

▶ Covering assumptions, fees, and billing schedules

▶ Deciding if optional subsections are needed

▶ Understanding how to identify and define critical assumptions

. . . . . . . . . . . . . . . . . . . . . . . . . . . . . . . . . . . . . . . . . . . . . . . . . . .

*T*his chapter is about the boring stuff you have to put into every sales proposal — the standard provisions about assumptions, fees, and schedules. In my five-part proposal plan (see Figure 10-1), I lump all of these items together as *business issues*.

You may get bored writing about business issues and the buyer may get bored reading your lifeless prose. But believe me, the business issues are a very important part of the deal.

This section answers basic questions like:

✔ What assumptions are you making about the timing and pricing of the project?

✔ What is the total fee or price to install the proposed product or implement the proposed service?

✔ What additional charges should the buyer expect?

✔ When will you bill the buyer and for how much?

One of the ways to think about the purpose of this section is that it gets you and the buyer on the same page. You may be that rare salesperson who's never had a misunderstanding about price or some other expense. I'm not so lucky! Suppose, just for example, that *you* thought the buyer understood that travel expenses were extra but the *buyer* thought they were part of your price. Does that sound like a train wreck is looming somewhere down the line? If you don't like confrontations with unhappy customers, pay close attention.

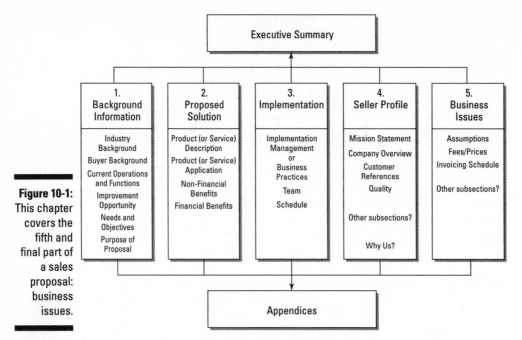

**Figure 10-1:** This chapter covers the fifth and final part of a sales proposal: business issues.

You can think of this section as an informal contract. Use it to cover business issues that you didn't present in a previous proposal section that are critical to your company's ability to maintain its profitability on the deal

Don't make the business issues section read like a legal document. Just write it to avoid surprises for everyone after the sale.

# Deciding What Subsections You Should Include

Three subsections are very common in the business issues part of a sales proposal. You should probably include these three subsections in every one of your proposals:

- ✔ Assumptions
- ✔ Fees/prices and other expenses
- ✔ Invoicing schedule

Depending on the type of business or profession that your company is in, you may want or need to include one or more of these optional subsections:

- ✔ Warranty and/or guarantee statements

- ✔ Environmental policies

- ✔ General service conditions (regarding how services will be performed; often used by professional services firms)

- ✔ Non-disclosure statement

- ✔ Regulatory statements, such as a statement defining the seller's compliance with equal employment opportunity regulations

Your legal department may take care of the wording for these optional subsections.

# *Writing about Assumptions*

As a seller, you can make some assumptions about certain aspects of the buyer's business to help establish your fees or prices, assign your resources, and schedule your installation, implementation, or engagement. You can usually base your assumptions on:

- ✔ Relevant aspects of the buyer's business and operations.

- ✔ Experiences you've had with similar engagements, projects, implementations, or production scenarios.

- ✔ Your estimates of the scope and magnitude of the proposed solution for the buyer's unique situation.

- ✔ Internal or external estimates of business and economic trends that may impact the buyer's business or your business. For example, fluctuations in the cost of a barrel of oil may affect your prices if you sell a product that's petroleum based.

Always keep the buyer in mind while writing this subsection. Your assumptions subsection should answer any remaining questions that the buyer's decision makers have about your proposed product after they've read the first four sections of the proposal.

Two rules to follow when developing assumptions for your sales proposals are:

- ✔ Include only critical assumptions, and not more than four or five of those.

- ✔ If you have too many assumptions, look at section two of your proposal (the proposed solution) or section three (the implementation) and ask yourself whether the assumptions you've saved for the end of the proposal really should be dealt with in these earlier sections.

# Identifying critical assumptions: The steps

As you write your proposal, especially the parts that deal with the price and your implementation schedule, follow these steps to identify your critical assumptions:

1. **Think about how you develop the price and schedule the implementation for the buyer.**

   Are you basing the price and schedule on everything going according to plan? How often does that happen?

2. **Think about what could happen to make the project cost more and reduce your profits.**

   At this point, your experience in the business can make a difference. Think about past deals that were similar. Did you have a problem with any of these deals? If so, what caused things to go wrong? If you're new to your company, ask a coworker for help. If everybody is new to the company (or if the company is new), hold a brainstorming session to figure out what could go wrong after the sale.

3. **Take the answers that you get when you ask yourself or a coworker what could go wrong or the ideas from the brainstorming session. Your assumptions are that none of these things will happen.**

   Say that you sell accounting services. From your past experiences, you know that things go terribly awry when the buyer doesn't have its various financial papers in decent shape when your accounting professionals show up. One of your assumptions, then, is that the buyer will have its papers in decent shape before your guys get there.

Here are some other examples of assumptions:

✔ To develop its implementation schedule, a software development firm assumed that the buyer would review and approve systems design documents within five business days of receipt.

   What would happen if the buyer took 20 business days to review and approve design documents? The project would take longer than planned, and the project delay would cost somebody money. Either the buyer would have to pay the consulting firm more because its consultants were tied up on the project, or, if the consulting firm doesn't make the buyer pay for the project delay, the consulting firm's internal costs will be higher and its profitability lower. The consulting firm will pay for the delay with lower profits.

✔ To maintain the equipment prices listed in the proposal over the term of the proposed agreement, a manufacturer assumed that its raw material costs would not increase by more than 5 percent during the scheduled production run.

   What would happen to the manufacturer's profitability if the cost of one of the key production materials jumped 15 percent during the agreement?

✔ When developing an audit fee quote, a CPA firm assumed that the client would provide workspace and administrative support for the firm's auditors during the audit.

What would happen if the client didn't give the auditors workspace and administrative support? Doing the audit would be a lot more difficult for the CPA firm. The audit would take more time to complete, and time is money (especially for bean counters doing audits).

If you were writing any of the proposals in the list, would you include these assumptions in the business issues section? Think about the consequences if you didn't and something went wrong after the sale. Think about who would get the biggest surprise if these assumptions weren't included in your proposals and something went awry.

## Avoiding too many assumptions

If you end up with a long list after you identify your critical assumptions, you have a problem: Your proposal is in *assumption overload*. Having too many assumptions in your proposal can be as bad as not having any assumptions. The buyer may not take any of the assumptions very seriously if you have too many. As a general rule, you don't want more than four or five assumptions in your assumptions subsection.

If your proposal has too many assumptions, you may have content problems elsewhere in your proposal. You need to take a hard look at the content and level of detail in two other sections: the proposed solution and the implementation (sections two and three). You may be using the assumptions subsection to make up for deficiencies in these sections.

✔ **Section two: description and application subsections.** Rather than clearly describing your product and then defining its application in the buyer's business in section two, you may be using the assumption subsection to define specifications. Or, you may be making assumptions to explain how your product will be installed. You can correct these problems by moving some assumptions to section two and including these assumptions in your product description or application definition.

✔ **Section three: implementation.** You may be using assumptions instead of defining team member's roles and responsibilities, project or engagement activities and deliverables, or the schedule. Check out Chapter 8, in which I show you how to write the implementation part of your proposal. By writing a better section three, you can cut down on the number of assumptions in your assumptions subsection.

Putting content in the assumptions subsection that really belongs elsewhere is easy. The following examples show some typical mistakes and how to correct them:

✔ A proposal for a training company that sells Internet-based training includes an assumption that the buyer will assign a training administrator to manage the training program for the buyer's employees. Assigning a training administrator is really one of the online training program's implementation and ongoing management issues. The need for the buyer to assign a training administrator belongs in the team subsection of section three. The seller should not include an assumption in its proposal that reads, "The buyer will assign a training administrator to manage the training program." Rather, the implementation section of the seller's proposal should list the training administrator as a member of the implementation team. The implementation subsection should also identify the training administrator's roles and responsibilities.

✔ A heavy equipment manufacturer's proposal makes an assumption that the buyer has a 12-inch-thick reinforced concrete floor at the installation site. The concrete floor is an installation requirement, not an assumption about the buyer's facilities. This information belongs in the product description subsection of section two or in an appendix.

✔ A software vendor's proposal includes an assumption that the buyer has Microsoft's Windows 2000 operating system installed on its personal computers. The Windows 2000 operating system represents a software product specification and not an assumption about the buyer's computer system configuration. This specification really belongs in the product description subsection of section two or in an appendix.

# Writing about Fees or Prices

Your proposal's readers, the buyer's decision makers, will have seen your fees or prices two times before they get to the price subsection of your proposal. Your prices are also in your proposal's executive summary and in the financial benefits subsection of section two. (Check out Figure 10-1 if you need a refresher on the overall structure of the proposal.)

The prices listed in the executive summary and financial benefits subsection are usually summary totals. You present detailed calculations and explanations in the price subsection in the business issues section of your proposal. You use this subsection to disclose and detail the buyer's total costs. Remember that the goal of the business issue section is to avoid buyer and seller surprises down the road. The more detail you include in the price subsection, the fewer surprises the buyer and you will have after the sale.

## Varying the price subsection

Different sellers put different price information in their proposals. Your price subsection's content can vary because of several factors, including:

✔ Your company's business type and accepted pricing practices

✔ The buyer's information needs and expectations

✔ The need to:

- Disclose fees or prices by project phase to support periodic invoices
- Disclose project-related expenses, such as freight, travel costs, duplication, and so on
- Show quantity, description, unit price, and extended price for products or product components

For example:

✔ A manufacturing company might list quantities, descriptions, unit prices, and extended prices for its product components. Additionally, its proposal may include applicable taxes and freight.

✔ A management consulting firm might list the hourly rates for each level or type of consultant, the estimated hours for each consultant to complete the engagement, and total estimated engagement fees. The firm probably would include estimated travel expenses, if any.

✔ A professional services firm might list fees by project phase with a grand total for the project. It also would include estimated travel expenses, if any.

## Including all other expenses

Follow this rule when deciding which expenses to include in your proposal:

**Include all expenses in your proposal.**

Remember that the primary goal of the business issues section is to avoid buyer and seller surprises after the sale. Make sure that your price subsection includes everything that you expect the buyer to pay for as part of the deal. This can include such things as:

✔ Freight, shipping, and handling

✔ Travel expenses (all travel expenses you that you pay and expect to get reimbursed for as part of the deal)

✔ Copying, printing, and postage

✔ Sales and other taxes

✔ Site preparation

✔ License fees (for required applications or operating systems)

✔ Equipment rental or lease payments (other than what you're selling or including in the deal)

✔ Anything else you can think of

Here's an example of a price subsection:

### Fees and Prices

### Installation Costs

TellComm Systems (TCS) will install cellular telephones and mobile facsimile machines in Mid-South Transportation (MST) trucks over a four (4) month period. The following table lists service startup costs by month based upon costs to begin service. The per truck startup costs are

| | |
|---|---|
| Equipment lease deposit | $180.00 |
| Advance lease payments (3 months) | $210.00 |
| Connect fee (one-time) | $50.00 |
| Total per truck | $ 440.00 |

The estimated schedule is as follows:

| Month | Number of Installations | Service Startup Costs |
|---|---|---|
| October | 40 | $17,600 |
| November | 60 | $24,600 |
| December | 60 | $24,600 |
| January | 60 | $24,600 |
| Total | | $96,800 |

### Monthly Fees

Monthly fees for the cellular phones and mobile facsimile machines are as follows:

|  | Intrastate Truck | Interstate Truck |
|---|---|---|
| Monthly cost for mobile fax machine (3-year lease) | $70.00 | $70.00 |
| Monthly cellular service fees: | | |
| Access fee | $30.00 | $50.00 |
| Estimated air time: 31 calls/month | $31.00 | $31.00 |
| Total monthly cost/truck | $131.00 | $151.00 |

Estimated monthly service fees during the implementation period are as follows:

### Cellular Equipped Trucks

| Month | Number of Installations | Intrastate Trucks | Interstate Trucks | Service Fees |
|---|---|---|---|---|
| October | 40 | 20 | 20 | $5,640 |
| November | 60 | 50 | 50 | $14,100 |
| December | 60 | 80 | 80 | $22,560 |
| January | 60 | 80 | 140 | $31,620 |

If you were a decision maker for MST, would you understand

✔ The costs and estimated timeframe for installing the cellular telephones and mobile facsimile machines in the trucks?

✔ How much your service fee will be during the installation period?

# Writing about the Invoicing Schedule

Your proposal should let the buyer know how and when you will invoice it for the proposed product. You want to make sure that the buyer never gets an unexpected invoice. Further, your proposal's invoicing schedule subsection can become very important if you link the timing of an invoice to the completion of a major project phase or deliverable. For example, a company that sells turnkey computer systems may send invoices to a buyer for:

✔ Fifty percent of the hardware costs when the buyer signs the contract

✔ Partial software costs at the end of each project phase

> ✔ The remainder of hardware costs upon completion of installation or acceptance testing
> ✔ Travel expenses for the company's implementation team members at the end of each month

Use the invoicing schedule subsection to clearly explain how you calculate the amount of your invoices and when you plan to send them.

You may want to include payment terms in this subsection. For example, include a statement like: *Terms: Net 30.*

In some situations, you may need to coordinate your invoices with the buyer's budget. As part of the proposal, you may agree not to send the first invoice until budgeted funds become available to the buyer. Timing invoices to hit when the budgeted funds become available usually happens at the end of a buyer's fiscal year. The buyer makes a commitment in the current fiscal year because the funds for the purchase are in next year's approved budget. Working around the buyer's next fiscal year and an approved budget allows you to start production or implementation activities in the current fiscal year. However, the buyer and you know that you won't send any invoices before an agreed-to date (usually next year).

Just make sure that everyone understands that the buyer is using next year's budgeted funds to approve your proposal and to authorize the project or implementation to start in the current fiscal year.

Here's an example of an invoicing schedule subsection:

### Invoicing Schedule

TellComm Systems (TCS) will invoice Mid-South Transportation (MST) for the proposed cellular telephone and mobile facsimile machine services as follows:

### Service Startup and Implementation Costs

We will invoice for service startup and equipment installations at the end of each month for installations completed during the month.

### Monthly Cellular Service Fees

We send invoices based on the previous month's actual air times on the first week of each month. Note that our invoices include transmission detail by telephone number (truck) and are available in machine-readable format.

All invoices are net 30 days.

# Part III
# Details, Details . . . and Presentation!

The 5th Wave                    By Rich Tennant

"Nothing serious. I'm still trying to use a pair of nun-chucks in my PowerPoint presentations."

# In this part . . .

A sales proposal must include certain elements to make it a complete business document. This part discusses those pieces of your proposal that probably aren't as difficult to write as the main body of the proposal, but that are equally crucial: the title page, the executive summary, the table of contents, the appendixes, and the transmittal letter.

This part also discusses a proposal's format and page layout. I write about the use of paper, color, and graphics in a proposal to make it easier to read and to differentiate it from the competition.

One chapter in this part presents the *letter proposal* — why, when, and how to write one.

# Chapter 11

# Adding Crucial Small Parts to Complete Your Proposal

*In This Chapter*

▶ Writing an effective transmittal letter

▶ Capturing the essence of your proposal in an executive summary

▶ Using a proposal title that will get the reader's attention

▶ Creating a table of contents

▶ Using appendixes to maintain the flow and control the detail

Decision makers live in a busy world, and your proposal just puts another demand on their busy schedules. Like it or not, some decision makers don't have the time to read every sentence of your carefully crafted masterpiece. They may only skim it, reading the portions that interest them. (They won't miss the price section, that's for sure!) But if you did a good job designing, writing, and producing your sales proposal, even the skimmers will notice its structure, layout, and overall appearance. They may sense that your proposal is top notch even if they don't read it carefully.

However, you can count on most decision makers to take the time to read your proposal. They're aware of the importance of your proposal to their company and they want to take the time to make a good decision.

You can help them use that time effectively by adding five additional parts to your proposal:

> Transmittal letter
>
> Executive summary
>
> Title page
>
> Table of contents
>
> Appendixes

This chapter shows you how to produce these small but crucial parts.

# Writing a Transmittal Letter and Executive Summary

The transmittal letter (which is basically a cover letter) and the executive summary frame the proposal by alerting readers to what's important — what you really want them to read and understand. These two components can work together as follows:

- ✔ **A transmittal letter** can help focus your proposal's readers because it:
  - • Gives your reasons for presenting the proposal to the buyer
  - • Highlights the critical issues concerning the buyer's improvement opportunity and your proposed solution
- ✔ **An executive summary** also can focus your proposal's readers because it captures the essence of your proposal by:
  - • Providing summary information on all the key points contained within the proposal
  - • Alerting readers to the critical information contained in the proposal's main sections

Some decision makers may only read your transmittal letter and the proposal's executive summary. They know from experience that these two proposal components, if well written, can provide them a heads up — a rundown of your entire proposal and valuable insight into the sales situation. They may rely entirely on these two proposal components to prepare for your presentation (if you get to make one). In these situations, your transmittal letter and executive summary play a critical role in positioning the reader for the sale.

In other instances, the heads-up provided by your transmittal letter and executive summary may convince a few readers that their improvement opportunity and your proposed product make some sense and need further study. These decision makers skimmed the proposal and only read the transmittal letter and executive summary. Now, they realize that they should either read your entire proposal or pass it down to a subordinate to review and report on. Of course, the subordinate can't skim your proposal. He or she is obligated to read the entire document and report to the boss. (See — somebody will read your every word!)

## Following transmittal letter content guidelines

You should always include a transmittal letter when sending or delivering your proposal. Including the letter with your proposal is good business etiquette.

Think of the transmittal letter as your proposal's cover letter. Address it to your primary contact or internal sponsor (or whoever requested the proposal) in the buyer's organization. Even though you address the letter to only one person, you may want to include a copy of the transmittal letter in every proposal so that all the decision makers have an opportunity to read it.

Your transmittal letter needs to cover a lot of ground in no more than one page. Use your transmittal letter to:

✔ Tell why you're submitting the proposal to the buyer (at the request of the buyer or in response to a request for proposal).

✔ Highlight the buyer's improvement opportunity and explain that implementing your proposed solution will reduce or avoid costs, increase revenues, or improve operations.

✔ Explain why your company is a good choice (a summary of your why us? subsection from section three).

✔ Include an offer to provide additional information or assistance if requested by the buyer.

✔ Thank your contact for his or her time and efforts in helping you gather the information needed to write the proposal.

Besides using your best writing skills while writing a transmittal letter, you need to follow three guidelines. Your transmittal letter should be

✔ **No more than one page long** because if it's longer, it's less likely to be read

✔ **Printed on company stationary** because it's a letter from your company

✔ **Signed by the sales professional** because that's who's responsible for the sale

## Don't let the boss pull rank

Occasionally, your sales manager, vice president of sales, or company president may want to sign your transmittal letters. I think this is inappropriate, especially if he or she hasn't met your contact in the buyer's organization or has had little direct involvement in the sale. This type of behavior does nothing to improve your chances, but it does tend to undermine your relationship with the buyer. It also sends the wrong message to the buyer — the sales professional is good enough to work with the buyer during the sales process, but when the buyer is ready to buy, one of the seller's big shots has to sign the transmittal letter.

Try not to let your boss or one of your company's big shots sign your transmittal letters. Show your boss or whoever wants to sign your transmittal letters this page in the book to support your position. Hey, if you let them sign your transmittal letters, the next thing you know, they'll want a piece of your commission checks.

Figure 11-1 is an example of a transmittal letter. It's from a high-tech data processing company to a financial institution; the seller is proposing that the buyer implement its systems.

**Bankman Technologies, Inc.**
171 Technology Drive
Scottsdale, Arizona 85055

August 28, 2002

Mr. Gordon Newsome
VP & Cashier
1st National Bank
2 Main Street
Plano, Texas 75022

Dear Mr. Newsome:

The enclosed proposal is a direct result of our Systems and Operations Audit that we completed for your bank. After our thorough review of 1st National Bank's operations, systems, and strategic objectives and at your request, we are submitting this proposal for your review and consideration.

In our audit review meeting, we agreed that the bank's data processing:

- Costs were significantly higher than its peer group of banks.
- Service provider was not offering many of the financial product options needed to compete in your highly competitive marketplace.

We think our BankSystem 2000 provides an excellent in-house system option for your bank. It will dramatically lower your data processing costs while providing tremendous processing flexibilities.

Bankman Technologies, Inc. (BTI) is one of the fastest growing financial service providers in the country. Our rapid growth clearly reflects two key reasons why we're the right choice for your bank: 1) our customers realize exceptional value from our family of BTI products and 2) our single server and open systems architecture approach provide a cost-effective platform for the rapid deployment of new systems and technologies.

The enclosed proposal provides a detailed description of our BankSystem 2000, the proposed turnkey system, and describes how we would implement it at 1st National Bank. It also discusses the resulting financial and non-financial benefits. Many are based on the findings of the audit.

Mr. Newsome, thank you again for working with our staff on the audit and for considering BTI. I am looking forward to our presentation to your Board of Directors on October 8. Please do not hesitate to call me if you have questions about this proposal or want to discuss the upcoming presentation.

Regards,

Leslie A. Wilson
Senior Account Manager

**Figure 11-1:**
An example
of a
transmittal
letter.

# *Writing an executive summary*

Your proposal's executive summary is a two to three page synopsis of your proposal. It's a proposal in miniature. Some decision makers may only read this part of your proposal.

Your proposal's executive summary is the first real component of your proposal. It follows immediately after the table of contents and precedes the first main proposal section. You can probably trace the executive summary's origins to the huge proposals prepared for the federal government by defense and other types of contractors. The length of these proposals forced the contractors to summarize the main points of the proposal's content so that decision makers could get an idea of what they were about to read. The executive summary provided a heads up to focus the proposal's recipients on the key points of the proposal. I'd guess that when most senior government officials received a proposal, they probably read the executive summary and passed it down the line for someone of lesser rank or grade to really study the details.

Some people dislike including an executive summary. They think an executive summary gives the buyer a way to avoid reading the entire proposal. Well, they're right. Some proposal recipients will use the executive summary for just that purpose. But what would these recipients do if there were no executive summary? Do you think they would feel obligated to read the entire proposal? I doubt it.

Your proposal's executive summary serves two critical purposes:

- ✔ It provides readers with a concise synopsis of your entire proposal. This alone probably makes the executive summary the single-most important component of your proposal. Your executive summary should bring out your best writing skills.

- ✔ Many experienced decision makers read your proposal's executive summary expecting that it identifies the key issues discussed in your proposal's main body. The executive summary gives these readers a heads up to the important issues presented in more detail in the main body of the sales proposal.

Think about it this way. An executive summary can be a *proposal in miniature*. It can capture the most important aspects of each of your proposal's five main sections and contain all the information that's needed by a buyer to make a buying decision.

I recommend you follow these guidelines when writing an executive summary:

- ✔ Write it last.
- ✔ Pretend that it's a miniature proposal.
- ✔ Keep it short.

### Writing it last

Your proposal's executive summary is a compact version of your proposal. Logically, you can't write it until you finish writing the sales proposal, right? Well, I know some salespeople who write the executive summary for their proposal first. They use the executive summary as a blueprint for writing the rest of the proposal. This really makes no sense to me. How can a writer summarize something before it's written? These salespeople probably don't follow a standard proposal structure, so they use the executive summary as a blueprint for their proposal design and writing process.

### Pretending that it's a miniature proposal

You may be asking yourself "How do I take all the information on 15 to 20 pages or more and boil it down to one or two pages? How can I possibly create a miniature proposal in the executive summary when everything in the proposal seems important?" Well, it can be easier than you think. If you wrote your proposal on a word-processing system, just follow these steps:

1. **Print a copy of your proposal.**

2. **Read each section and highlight or circle the critical information in each section.**

3. **Save a copy of your proposal in a new file titled *exec summary.***

4. **Using the new exec summary file, go through each section and delete everything except the critical information that you highlighted in the second step.**

   Condense, condense, and then condense some more until you summarize each section in a couple of paragraphs.

5. **Combine the paragraphs into your executive summary.**

6. **As an option, you may want to use the proposal's main section titles to create subsection titles in your executive summary.**

7. **Copy and paste the exec summary file into your proposal.**

You're done. If you follow these steps a few times, you'll get to the point where you can write a top-notch executive summary in less than an hour. Of course, that's assuming you start with a top-notch proposal.

### Keeping it short: Remember it's supposed to be a summary

If you could write a *perfect* executive summary, it would be one page long. However, writing a one page executive summary is tough. Expect that your executive summaries will be two or three pages (sometimes even four or more pages). The executive summary's page length is probably somewhat proportional to your proposal's page length. However, there are no hard and fast rules that say for every ten pages of a proposal, expect to generate one page in your executive summary.

Use the same page format and layout in your executive summary that you used in the rest of the proposal. If the main sections of your proposal use lots of white space, which makes them easy to read, then your executive summary can have lots of white space. Remember that you want to have an executive summary that's two, three, or four pages long and easy to read. Rather than trying to squeeze the executive summary on to one page by using tiny font, use nicely formatted pages of text that communicates your proposal's message.

Figure 11-2 is an executive summary from a cellular service provider to an interstate trucking company. Notice that it has five subsections, one for each of the proposal's main sections.

# Creating a Title Page

Think of your proposal's title page like it's the cover to a book. The title page conveys some basic information:

- ✔ Buyer's name
- ✔ Proposal's title
- ✔ Submission date
- ✔ Seller's name (and, as an option, address)

The title page is a good place to put your company's logo, if it has one.

## Be careful with the buyer's logo

You can include the buyer's logo on the title page of your proposal. But be careful. You need to get permission from the buyer before using its logo. Some organizations don't want anyone reproducing their logos.

In fact, you need to tread cautiously even if your contact with the buyer says that using the logo is okay. He may not be aware of some marketing department policy that restricts use of the company's logo. What do you think would happen if the vice president of marketing got a copy of your proposal? You certainly will not have made a good first impression. What if this vice president is one of the decision makers? Your proposal better have some very significant financial benefits.

**EXECUTIVE SUMMARY**

*Background Information*

Mid-Continent Motor Freight (MMF) offers interstate freight service between the West Coast and the Midwest. Most of MMF's customers are small to medium-sized businesses located within 100 miles of main east-west interstate highways. These customers normally do not ship full loads. Therefore, MMF is able to combine partial loads from several smaller customers and charge premium prices.

MMF requires its drivers to call dispatch once a day using an 800#. Dispatch can contact en route trucks only if they are able to reach drivers at a scheduled customer pickup or delivery point. A survey conducted by MMF and One Cell Corporation (OCC) staff found that MMF's total need for landline communications between dispatch personnel and en route drivers results in lost revenues and less than efficient routing -- MMF's average truckload capacity is 78%. Further, some MMF customers have to wait three to four days or more to get their freight picked up.

*Proposed OCC Cellular Solution*

After reviewing the company's operations and business communications needs, OCC proposes MMF install cellular telephones in its 200 interstate trucks. Having wireless communications capabilities will provide operational, employee, and customer service benefits for MMF:

  • Dispatch personnel will be able to easily make schedule and route changes -- better
    customer service.
  • The company will have immediate access to drivers in case of family emergencies.
  • Drivers will be able to get quick roadside assistance if they have an on-road breakdown.
  • Drivers will be able to advise dispatch of any travel delays due to inclement weather or
    equipment breakdowns.

Having wireless communications gives the company the ability to change the schedules and routes of en route trucks to maximize efficiency. This provides financial benefits for MMF:

It will cost $65,000 to equip 200 MMF trucks with cellular telephones.

| | |
|---|---|
| Reduced annual operating costs: | $ 200,000 |
| Estimated increased annual freight revenues: | 1,122,000 |
| Total | $ 1,322,000 |
| Estimated annual costs for cellular service and depreciation: | $980,000 |
| Estimated increased annual pre-tax profits: | $342,000 |
| The estimated return on investment (ROI): | 526% |

*Implementation*

Upon acceptance of this proposal, MMF staff and the OCC Wireless Team will establish an implementation team. This team will manage all equipment installations and dispatch and driver training activities. OCC will install and activate all cellular telephones within six weeks.

*One Cell Corporation Profile*

Amtel Communications Corporation is the parent company of OCC. Amtel is one of the world's largest telecommunications companies and OCC is the tenth largest U.S. cellular company. OCC has over 5,000 employees and revenues over $1.4 billion. It has been wireless communications industry leader since the industry's birth.

When MMF selects OCC it gains a Cellular Service Team. OCC's team members are experienced wireless communications professionals. They will:

  • Train all MMF employees
  • Develop wireless communications strategies for MMF
  • Ensure that MMF has leading-edge wireless services and equipment

OCC is unmatched in the industry for its depth of knowledge and commitment to providing top-notch service.

*Business Issues*

To start the implementation, MMF simply needs to provide OCC with a purchase order(s) that includes acquisition of the cellular equipment and provisions for a service agreement with a two-year term.

**Figure 11-2:**
An executive summary that echoes the proposal's five-part structure.

# What's in a title?

Spend some time thinking about your proposal's title. If you can, don't use a bland sales proposal title like everyone else does. If you're selling electric widgets, don't title your proposal "A Proposal for Electric Widgets." Be a bit creative. A more interesting title that can really focus the reader's attention might be "Increasing Employee Accuracy by Installing Electric Widgets." Without knowing anything about your proposal's content, this title does two things for the reader:

✔ It identifies the buyer's improvement opportunity — the need to raise employee accuracy levels.

✔ It identifies a key benefit of installing electric widgets — a way to increase employee accuracy.

Try this example. An employee-personality testing company can use either of these titles for its proposal:

> "Reducing Employee Turnover through Personality Profile Testing"
>
> "ProSelect Personality Profile Testing"

Both titles are appropriate. But which one do you think is more effective? See how titling your proposal can make a difference?

To create a great title for you proposal, just answer these two questions and then combine your answers into a title:

✔ What's the buyer's improvement opportunity?

✔ What's the primary benefit of installing your product?

If your answer to the first question is "reducing storage costs" and your answer to the second question is "our product allows the company to have less inventory on hand at any given time," then a good title would be "Reducing Storage Costs by Lowering Inventory Levels."

# Getting the buyer's and seller's names right

Put the buyer's name and your name on the title page. This isn't too difficult, but follow these rules:

✔ Use the full name of both the buying and selling companies.

✔ For individuals, use first names, middle initials, and last names.

✔ Don't use nicknames, abbreviations, or acronyms.

Here are several examples of correct and incorrect ways to include buyer's names on your proposal's title page.

| *Correct* | *Incorrect* |
|---|---|
| Electronic Lending Systems, Inc. | ELS |
| 1st Western Bank & Trust, N.A. | FWBT |
| McAndrew and Smith, LLP | M&S |
| William A. Jones & Mary L. Jones | Mr. & Mrs. Bill Jones |
| Anthony P. Church, III | Tony Church |

## Using the correct submission date

Use the date that you formally present your proposal to the buyer as the submission date. Follow two simple guidelines:

- ✔ The submission date on the title page and the date on your transmittal letter should be the same.
- ✔ Write out the month, day, and year; do not use a numerical date. For example, October 17, 2002, rather than 10/17/02 or 10-17-2002.

Figure 11-3 shows a correct title page. Note how the title identifies the buyer's improvement opportunity and a primary benefit of the seller's proposed product. You can bet the decision makers are anxious to read this proposal..

## Including a Table of Contents

Your proposal's table of contents can provide a roadmap or blueprint for the reader. A proposal's table of contents has two purposes:

- ✔ It shows readers how your proposal is organized.
- ✔ It helps the reader locate particular information in your proposal, which can be very helpful to the reader after he has read your proposal and wants to reread some section.

The table of contents should list the titles and page numbers for the five main sections and all the subsections. The table of contents also should list the title and page numbers of your appendixes.

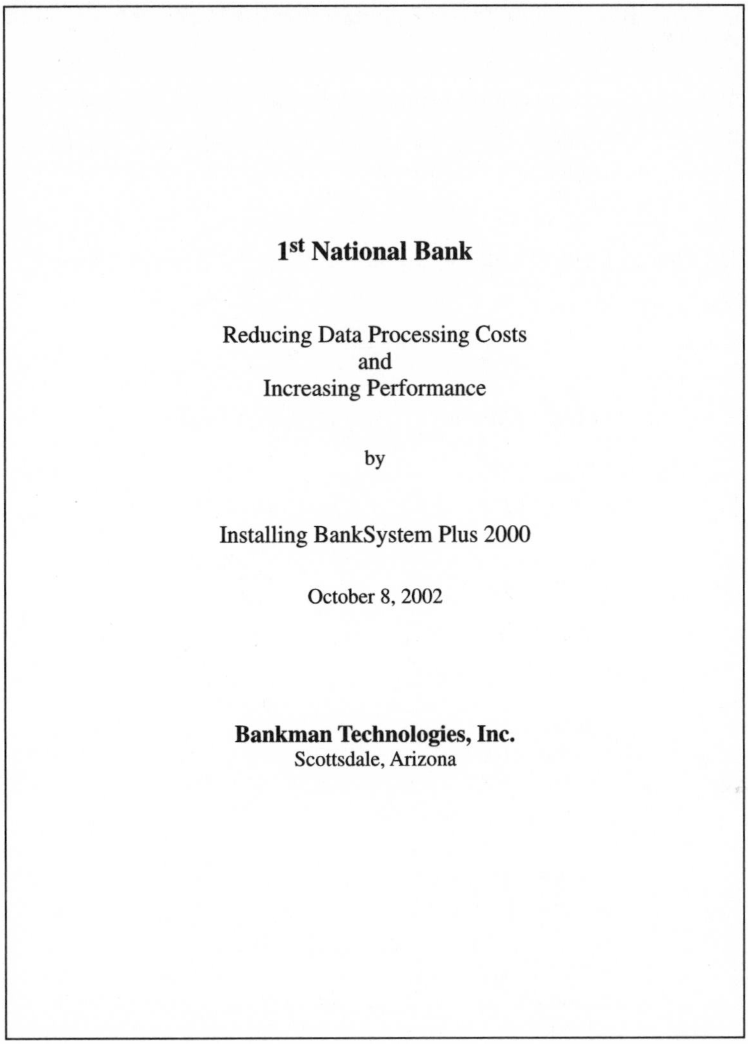

**1st National Bank**

Reducing Data Processing Costs
and
Increasing Performance

by

Installing BankSystem Plus 2000

October 8, 2002

**Bankman Technologies, Inc.**
Scottsdale, Arizona

**Figure 11-3:**
A well-done
title page.

Follow these simple rules when numbering pages in your proposal:

✔ All the pages in your proposal need a number except the title page.

✔ Use Roman numerals for the table of contents and the executive summary. The first page of the table of contents is page i.

✔ Number the pages in the five main sections one after the other; the first page of the first proposal section is page 1.

✔ You have two options for numbering the pages of your appendixes. You can

- Continue numbering from the proposal's main sections

- Use each appendix's alphabetic designation as part of the page number; the third page of Appendix C would be C-3. Do whichever is easier.

Figure 11-4 is an example of a table of contents with two levels: section titles and subsection titles.

**Figure 11-4:** A table of contents from a business selling EBPP technology.

## Automating your table of contents

If you're using a word processing system to write your proposal, you can probably automatically generate a table of contents. If you use Microsoft Word, you can automate your table of contents by following these simple steps:

✔ First, make sure that all the section titles are assigned the Heading 1 paragraph style.

✔ Then make sure that all the subsection titles are assigned the Heading 2 paragraph style.

✔ If you're using subheading within your subsections, make sure that they're assigned the Heading 3 paragraph style.

✔ Position the insertion point where you want the table of contents to appear in the proposal (immediately after the title page).

✔ Choose **Insert** then **Index and Tables.**

✔ Select the **Table of Contents** tab to display the table of contents options and select appropriate options.

✔ Finally, choose **Okay** and Word repaginates your proposal and compiles the table of contents.

For more information, check **Help** or a user guide for the word processing system that you're using. (I bet there's a *For Dummies* book that could help too, come to think of it.)

# Including Appendixes

Appendixes can make it easier for you to design and write your sales proposal by:

✔ Helping you maintain your proposal's flow of information and ideas by giving you a way to reduce the amount of detail in the main sections (which means you can control the length of the main sections).

✔ Offering a convenient way to include preprinted materials that you want or need to show the buyer. You can put brochures, product specifications, cost analyses, and so on in appendixes rather than in the main section of your proposal.

## Maintaining the flow

A well-written sales proposal should hold the reader's attention with its flow of information and ideas. You need to provide enough detail in the main sections to support key points; however, you never want to include too much or extraneous information because you risk overloading the reader. Too much information (or detail) can be confusing or dull. Too much detail may bore some readers to the point where they miss the critical reasons why their company needs to make a change.

## Putting preprinted materials in appendixes

You can ruin the professional appearance of your proposal by putting preprinted materials in the main body of your proposal. Putting preprinted materials in your proposal interrupts its flow of information and ideas. If you think there's a need to put something like a brochure or a specifications sheet in the middle of your proposal, you probably want the reader to read some critical information in the document. Give the reader a break. She will really appreciate it if you summarize the information on the preprinted material that you want her to read rather than sticking the complete brochure or spec sheet in your proposal. Write one or two paragraphs telling her what she needs to know and put the preprinted material in an appendix.

## Following two guidelines about appendixes

Use these two simple guidelines when developing appendixes for your proposals:

- ✔ **No dangling appendixes.** Don't put an appendix in the back of your proposal unless you reference it in one of the main proposal sections. If you have an appendix in your proposal that's not referenced in a main section, you're just wasting paper and probably confusing the readers — if they happen to read the dangling appendix, they may wonder why it's in the proposal.

- ✔ **Follow the order of reference.** Put your appendixes in the same order that they're referenced in the main proposal. For example, the first referenced appendix becomes Appendix A; the next referenced appendix becomes Appendix B, and so forth. This guideline is really just common sense.

## Using some common appendixes

Some appendixes are fairly common. In the list, I use the term *biographical resume*. A biographical resume lists work experience and education, but it omits phone numbers, addresses, and so on.

- ✔ **Cost Analysis.** Put an explanation of the critical assumptions you used in the analysis and the summarized numbers in a main section of the proposal. Put a complete copy of the supporting spreadsheet or analysis in an appendix.

✔ **Biographical Resumes.** Keep the main proposal short; only list names and titles in the proposal. Use a standard format for all biographical resumes; keep the length equal for all resumes.

✔ **Implementation or Project Methods.** Put major project or engagement phases, tasks or activities, and deliverables in the proposal. Use an appendix to provide detail or list subtasks and activities.

✔ **Installation Schedule.** Put the major project or engagement phases or tasks and their start and stop dates in the proposal. You may also want to use a bar chart in the proposal. Use an appendix to show a detailed project or engagement schedule or give a detailed bar chart.

✔ **Customer List.** Unless you really think it's important, don't put your entire list of customer or client names in the proposal. Use an appendix for a complete customer list.

Make sure that it's okay to include the customer or client name on the list.

Don't confuse your customer or client list with your customer references subsection in section four.

## Exiling excess info to an appendix

One of my clients used an implementation checklist when converting new customers to its system. The checklist contained 167 activities or tasks. My client included this long list in a main proposal section to show its prospects that it knew what it was doing and had experience. Certainly, this checklist contained essential information and assured the buyer that my client could handle the conversion. However, putting the list in a main proposal section overwhelmed (and bored) all but the most technical readers. To fix this information overload situation, we:

✔ Developed a six-phase conversion methodology.

✔ Put each of the 167 activities into one of the six conversion phases.

✔ Created a table that listed the six phases and their estimated start and stop dates and put the table in the proposal. Immediately following the table, we had a sentence that directed the reader to the appendix containing the 167 activities. Each activity was conveniently listed under one of the six conversion phases with their estimated start and stop dates.

# Chapter 12

# Packaging and Presenting Your Proposal

*O*ther chapters of this book cover the substance of your proposal. This chapter covers form — the physical look and feel of the proposal. Your goal in selecting font styles for headings and text, designing illustrations of various kinds, and choosing a binding method is simply to make your proposal attractive and engaging. Do this job right, and you can create a real *page turner,* as they say in book publishing. Your proposal may not be a thrill a minute, but it can be the next best thing: very persuasive.

## Making Sure It's the Right Font

Selecting the correct fonts for the narrative and headings of your proposal is important because the right font makes your proposal easy to read and gives it a professional appearance. ***Note:*** You may be more familiar with the terms *type* or *typeface* instead of *font.* All three terms are (more or less) interchangeable and refer to the way that letters and numbers look.

Ask for some help from others within your company if you're not sure what fonts look good or make sense. Start with the marketing department. You may find that it has selected the font for everyone in the company to use on all company documents. Or the folks in marketing may be surprised that you're asking for help. But once they realize why you're asking, they can probably show you exactly how to get a certain look in your sales proposals.

If your company doesn't have a marketing department, grab one of your company's latest brochures. Look at the different fonts used in the brochure and decide if the same fonts can work in your sales proposal. If your company doesn't have brochures, get a hold of as many brochures from other companies as you can. Pay close attention to how the brochures use and combine different fonts.

If you're still floundering around on font matters and your company doesn't have a company look that you can follow, pick one or two familiar fonts and stick with them. I suggest Times New Roman or Garamond for the text and Arial for headings (see examples in Figure 12-1).

Don't use some oddball font that only three people in the Western Hemisphere have ever seen. Doing so only distracts readers from your proposal's content.

You should probably know the difference between *serif* and *sans serif* fonts. Serifs are those tiny lines that cross the ending strokes of most characters (the font in this book has serifs). Serifs have an important job: They help the reader's eye move easily along the line, which makes reading easier and more efficient. Sans serif font — font without serifs — works well for titles and section and subsection names. Check any of the chapter titles in this book for an example of sans serif font. Figure 12-1 also has examples of serif and sans serif font styles.

One more thing about type is that a type's height determines its size. Type size is expressed in units called *points*. One point equals 1/72 inch. You probably want to use 10 to 12 point for proposal text, 12 to 14 point or larger for subsection names, and 14 to 16 point or larger for section names.

**Figure 12-1:**
Arial is a
sans serif
font. The
other type
styles in this
figure have
serifs.

# Arial Bold, 16 pt, for section headings
## *Arial Bold Italic, 14 pt, for subsections*
Times New Roman, 12 pt, book weight, for proposal text
Garamond, 12 pt, book weight, for proposal text
Times New Roman, 10 pt, book weight, for proposal text
Garamond, 10 pt, book weight, for proposal text

Look at the proposal templates on the CD to see how type can make a difference in a proposal's appearance and readability.

# *Laying Out the Pages*

Take some time to lay out your proposal so that its sections, subsections, tables, and other elements work together for easy reading. In particular:

✔ Don't use full text pages — just pages of text from top to bottom, because they make your proposal difficult to read; instead use bullets, tables, and white space (using white space means not filling the page with text).

✔ Don't use elaborate headers and footers because they distract from your proposal's message.

Figures 12-2 and 12-3 show how a little attention to formatting can help to reveal the content of a proposal.

Look at the proposal models on the CD to see how format and layout affect a proposal's appearance and readability.

Figure 12-2 is a very plain page. It correctly uses a serif type for text and a sans serif type for section and subsection headings. But put yourself in the reader's position. Does this page look inviting? It contains lots of information, but is it very easy to read?

Figure 12-3 contains the same information and uses the same types for text and headings. But this example uses bulleted lists to help the reader focus on important information. If you had to read an entire proposal and could pick its format and layout, would you pick the first or the second example? Which one looks more inviting?

---

## Check your word processing proficiency

How proficient are you with your word processing software? Some people use their computer like it's an electric typewriter and so they miss opportunities to make their lives easier and their proposals better. Here are some common functions and features that you should be using to improve the appearance of your sales proposals.

✔ Paragraph styles to create headings, subheadings, text, bulleted lists, and so on. (In Microsoft Word, styles controls type, color, and alignment of every paragraph.)

✔ Attractively formatted tables to present complex information.

✔ Automated page numbering so you don't have to manually number each page.

✔ Automated table of contents (by section and subsection) so it's easy to generate and update a two or three level table of contents for your proposal.

If you're shaking your head from side to side after reading this list and muttering that you just don't understand computers, experiment a bit with all the menus and buttons. You'll be surprised how quickly you can teach yourself some of the niftier word processing tricks.

---

**I. COMPANY BACKGROUND: GSFS**

**Our Understanding of GSFS**

Gulf States Food Systems, GSFS, a wholly owned subsidiary of GS Enterprises Inc., provides food distribution services to its franchise restaurants throughout the United States. GSFS has 5,000 associates, services 15,000 restaurants, and has distribution points scattered throughout the country. Its revenues in 2000 were over $3 billion. GFSF delivered 4.5 million pounds of food and restaurant products last years. Its trucks traveled over 40 million miles and made 1.5 million deliveries.

Richard F. Winfield, GSFS President, wrote in the company's annual report:

> GSFS operates in a challenging environment, but each year we never falter in our push to create productivity. Our business grew by more than 16% to over $3 billion; we serviced more than 15,000 franchise restaurant customers, but we traveled 4 million miles less on our service routes.

GSFS is obviously a company that constantly searches for ways to improve productivity and bottom-line profits.

**Substance Abuse at PFS**

Assuming GSFS's workplace demographics follow national averages, it's easy to measure the level and cost of alcohol or other drug (AOD) abuse in the company. Nationally, 10% of employees in similar business are substance abusers. This means 500 GSFS employees abuse AOD. Annual employer cost for each substance abuser is $10,000, so GSFS' estimated annual substance abuse cost is $5,000,000.

**Figure 12-2:**
Important facts are practically buried in dull paragraphs.

# Using Tables and Charts

If you're the least bit proficient with your word processing software, you can create some impressive tables and charts in your proposals. The nice thing is that you don't need to hire a graphic artist, buy a scanner, or do anything expensive or time consuming to create effective tables and charts. Tables and charts add to your proposal's readability and help you effectively and efficiently communicate complex information and ideas. Besides, tables and charts can make your proposal more interesting and enhance your message.

I. COMPANY BACKGROUND: GSFS

### Our Understanding of GSFS

Pacific Food Systems, PFS, a wholly owned
subsidiary of Pacific Enterprises, Inc., provides food
distribution services to independent restaurants.
PFS:
• Has 5,000 associates
• Services 15,000 franchise restaurants
• Has distribution points scattered throughout the country
• Had revenues over $3 billion in 2000 resulting from:
    – The delivery of 4.5 million pounds of food and
      restaurant products
    – Traveling of 40 million delivery miles
    – Making 1.5 million deliveries

Richard F. Winfield, GSFS President, wrote in the annual report,

*GSFS operates in a challenging environment*
*but each year we never falter in our push to*
*create productivity. Our business grew by more*
*than 16% to over $3 billion; we serviced more*
*than 15,000 franchise restaurant customers, but we*
*traveled 4 million miles less on our service routes.*

This shows evidence of a dynamic company, constantly searching
for ways to improve.

### Substance Abuse at GSFS

Assuming GSFS's workplace demographics follow national averages,
it's easy to measure the level and cost of alcohol or other drug (AOD)
abuse in the company.
• Percent of employees who abuse AOD in similar companies:    10%
• Employer cost for each substance abuser per year:    $10,000
• Estimated GSFS Associates who abuse AOD:    500
• GSFS estimated annual substance abuse costs:    $5,000,000

**Figure 12-3:**
Same facts
as Figure
12-2 —
formatting
brings them
to life.

## Put it in a table

Use tables in your proposals to display numbers and words in rows and
columns. Keep in mind that a table is normally too complicated for a reader
to just glance at in order to understand your message. Consider using tables
to condense and organize information so it's easier for readers to understand
and comprehend.

Figure 12-4 shows how a software vendor, BTI, proposes to convert a bank's data
processing system to a new system and gives the activities and deliverables in
each phase of the conversion.

| Project Phase | Phase Activities | Phase Deliverable |
|---|---|---|
| Project Analysis and Planning | • Form Conversion Project Team<br>• Perform site survey and define custom processing requirements<br>• Finalize preliminary equipment requirements and configuration | • Equipment and Site Preparation Requirements<br>• Telecommunications Requirements<br>• Application Conversion Specifications |
| Preparation and Equipment Acquisition | • BTI orders hardware<br>• BTI Conversion Team members order server and load Bank Systems 2000<br>• Western State Bank (WSB) Conversion Team members order telecommunications resources | • Hardware purchase orders<br>• BankSystems 2000 loaded on server |
| Systems Testing and Validation | • BTI Conversion Team members beta test BankSystems 2000<br>• WSB Conversion Team members validate and approve beta test results | • Validated and approved test results |
| Installation and Training | • BankSystems equipment installation and testing<br>• Initial WSB on-site staff education using conversion test files and on-site equipment | • Fully installed and tested hardware, completed initial WSB staff education |
| Conversion | • Final pre-conversion WSB staff education<br>• Convert and balance; WSB validation and approval<br>• Update and balance; WSB validation and approval<br>• Live operation | • Balanced and validated conversion<br>• Day 1 updated files<br>• Fully implemented BankSystems Plus 2000 |
| Quality Assurance | • Onsite BTI Customer Liaison monitors post-conversion activities<br>• Additional WSB staff education, as needed | • Quality Assurance Checklist |

**Figure 12-4:** Tables help to show how details fit into a big picture.

Do you think this table effectively and efficiently communicates how BTI plans to convert Western State Bank to the BankSystems Plus 2000? It doesn't contain all the conversion tasks and activities, but the level of detail in this table is probably more than adequate for most decision makers. Tables like this can reduce the risk some decision makers associate with making a change.

Use the preformatted tables from the proposal models on the CD to help you design tables for section three of your proposal (the implementation section).

# Charts

Use charts in your proposal to communicate relationships of parts to a whole, changes over time, and compare amounts. Charts also add visual interest to your proposal.

Remember how many pictures there were in your reading books when you first started reading? Charts appeal to the decision makers' inner child. You have to ask a psychologist if that will help you sell more, but it sure sounds pretty impressive in a book on sales proposals.

### Pie charts

Your readers can absorb the message in one glance if it's in a pie chart. Use pie charts to show the approximate relationship of the parts to a whole. For example, you can use a pie chart to show the types of investments in a customer's portfolio, the distribution of ages in a buyer's employee population, or illustrate market share within the buyer's industry. But if you want the reader to compare data or understand precise differences, use a bar chart or line chart.

### Line charts

Use a line chart to illustrate changes over time. The vertical axis represents quantity and the horizontal axis represents time. For example, if your proposal needs to show your buyer's increased costs over the last several years, you could use a line chart. The vertical axis on your table would represent costs and the horizontal axis would represent time.

### Bar charts

Use bar charts in your proposals if you want to compare amounts. You can use vertical or horizontal bars. You can also use bar charts to compare different things or to show changes over time. For example, you can use a bar chart in the implementation section to communicate your project's or engagement's planned schedule. Or you can use a bar chart to compare the number of customers you have to the number that your competitors have.

# Concerning Quality Reproduction

Printing your proposal shouldn't be an issue. Prices for laser and inkjet printers range from less than $100 to several thousand dollars for high-speed, high-resolution color printers. Even the least expensive laser or inkjet printer produces high-quality output. If you're still using a dot matrix printer, it's time to retire it. If you're under a tight budget and you have to use a dot matrix printer, at least put a new ribbon in it before you print your proposal.

## Adding some color

Your word processing system probably lets you add color to your sales proposals. Color enhances your proposal's appearance and readability. But color can do more than decorate pages; it can help communicate your message to the reader. You can use two, or possibly three, text colors for the sake of contrast. For example, you could use colored section and subsection titles to help the reader visually organize and categorize information. If possible, use color in your tables and charts to make them easier to understand.

# Even paper is important

One of the easiest and least costly ways to add to quality is by upgrading the paper you use for your proposals. Most printers and plain paper photocopiers can handle any grade, surface, or weight of paper, except for some high-gloss, coated papers. Think about getting special paper for your proposals.

Using the right paper is important. If this sidebar doesn't make any sense to you, go to a local copy store and ask the clerk to introduce you to the types of paper that are available.

Some paper considerations include

✔ **Size.** Your sales proposal is a business document, not a brochure or flyer. Use standard 8½-inch by 11-inch paper. If you want your proposal to stand out from the competition, be creative in packaging; don't use some oddball-size paper.

✔ **Coated.** Use a coated paper for your proposals if they contain pictures, graphics, and charts that use bright colors. Coated paper comes in different finishes: matte, dull, and gloss. Coated paper also offers better ink holdout than regular offset or bond paper. (*Ink holdout* refers to the extent ink dries on the surface rather than soaking into the paper.)

✔ **Offset.** Offset paper, also known as *uncoated book paper,* is available in several shades of white and light colors and in several finishes and weights. Quality #1 is the smoothest and brightest; Quality #3 is the most frequently used. You can use offset paper for printing on both sides, but that's not recommended for a sales proposal.

✔ **Bond.** Bond paper is used for one-page correspondence such as letters and it works in most photocopy machines. But bond paper doesn't have the opacity needed for two-sided printing. If you only print your proposals on one side of the paper, you can use bond paper. But be sure to use bond paper in weights greater than 24#. Don't use the same 20# bond paper that's sitting in your copy machine.

✔ **Weight.** The higher the paperweight number, the heavier the paper and the higher its cost. As you may guess, heavier weight paper also provides more opacity. You're probably using 20# bond paper in your copier, which is unsuitable for a proposal. Twenty-four pound (24#) bond paper should be the minimum quality paper for your proposals.

✔ **Opacity.** If you look closely at some of the white space on this page, you can see the words from the page behind it. In other words, the pages are slightly opaque. That's appropriate for a nearly 400-page book, but try to limit the opacity of the paper you use for your proposal. Heavier paper is more opaque than lighter paper and bond paper is not as opaque as coated paper.

✔ **Color.** You probably know that using colored paper increases opacity. But colored paper also reduces the contrast between the words and the background, making your proposal harder to read. Therefore, always print your proposals on paper that's white or a shade of white like ivory or cream. You may find that light tones of gray, blue, or brown will work for your proposals, especially if you are trying to get a look that is different. But don't use dark paper.

✔ **Surface.** One last thing to consider when selecting proposal paper is the paper's surface. Paper can have a smooth or a patterned surface and paper coatings range from dull to glossy. Go to an office supply or paper store to select a quality paper with a good look and feel for your proposals. For a few extra bucks, you can print your proposals on paper that really looks and feels great. Consider paper with a coating or pattern that can subtly differentiate your proposal from the competition.

Don't go overboard by using too many text colors, because an abundance of colors can slow readers down or make your message harder to understand and remember.

## Dividing it into bite-sized pieces

Use section dividers (or tabs) in your proposals. Dividers are a low-cost way to make your proposal stand out in the crowd. Dividers enhance your proposal's appearance and add readability to your proposal because they help readers separate, categorize, and find information. Use dividers to separate the proposal's table of contents, executive summary, and the five main sections. If you use appendixes in your proposals, use a divider to separate each appendix.

In fact, dividers can make a long proposal seem shorter. If your proposal is 25 pages long and you don't use dividers, readers may think it's a lot to read. After all, they're staring at big stack of paper. But if you use dividers, you cut the pile into bite-size pieces (probably three to five pages a bite).

### Using preprinted dividers

If all your proposals use the same main section names, then you can use preprinted dividers. However, if main section names change from one proposal to the next, use a copy center or other resource during the proposal's duplication process that has the ability to print and insert custom dividers.

### Guidelines for undivided success

So now that you're sold on using dividers, you need to know the details on what type of dividers to use.

Don't use dividers that:

✔ Extend beyond the proposal's cover. This looks cheap and creates the impression of poor quality.

✔ Are inexpensive and require you to type titles onto little pieces of paper.

Do use dividers that have a plastic or color coating to increase their durability and enhance your proposal's appearance.

Here's another tip: Make sure the font on your dividers matches a font used within your proposal. Doing so enhances your proposal's overall appearance.

## Binding and putting a cover on your proposals

You're now ready to package your proposals. You've picked the font, worked on format and layout, added tables and charts, picked colors and paper, and decided on dividers. You have the look that you want. You now need to put it in a nice package for the buyer. Packaging is important because your buyer will partially judge your proposal by its cover — by how it's packaged.

### Stapling doesn't get it

Never simply staple your proposals in the upper-left corner. Staples are not a binding option for sales proposals. Luckily, you have several easy and inexpensive binding options: wire, perfect, GBC, three-ring, and others. Some of these binding options you can use in-house. Other binding options may require you to go to copy center or printer. Visit your local office supply store, copy center, and printer to select the best binding option for your proposals. When you select a binding option, keep in mind that your proposal's binding should

✔ Be convenient for the proposal's reader.

✔ Be durable.

### Binding options may determine cover options

Obviously, the binding option you select may determine which cover options are available for your proposals. For example, if you use three-ring binders, your proposal's cover will be . . . a three-ring binder. Keep in mind that you can get three-ring binders with preprinted covers. Preprinted covers in your company's colors and with your company's logo can enhance the overall appearance of your proposal. Hey, if you use preprinted covers for your proposal, the buyer might assume that your company is stable and has been around for a long time. So, pick a binding option that allows you to use preprinted covers.

## Getting everyone an original

Always ask your contact or internal sponsor in the buyer's organization this question: "How many copies of the proposal will you need?" You can even consider putting this question on the application worksheet so that you don't forget (see Chapter 2 for more information on application worksheets).

You want to make sure that every decision maker gets an original proposal; in other words, don't give a "very best" copy to your prime contact and sub-par versions to everyone else.

The last thing you want to have happen is to have the buyer make copies of your proposal, staple the copies in the upper-left corner, and distribute the copies to the decision makers. What do you think will happen to your proposal's carefully crafted, high-quality look if your contact makes cheap copies for the decision makers?

For a few extra dollars you can send the very best to every one of the buyer's decision makers. You can't afford not to!

# Staples and proposals don't mix

In the mid-1980's, I was a co-owner of a firm that developed custom computer-based training (CBT) courseware, primarily for the financial services industry. CBT was pretty new, and many companies were starting to realize that CBT was a great way to train masses of people. Our staff was experienced and our company knew how to design and develop quality CBT courseware. Our firm was considered one of the leading CBT consulting firms in the financial services industry.

In our second year, we had an opportunity to bid on a medium-sized project for one of the largest banks on the West Coast. We followed our consultative sales approach and presented the bank with a good proposal. Except, we (I) did a bad job packaging the proposal. Actually, we didn't package the proposal at at all. You guessed it, we printed the proposal on normal printer paper and stapled it in the upper-left corner. My contact at the bank made four or five copies of our proposal so that each decision maker could read it.

One of our larger competitors was awarded the deal. My contact was kind enough to give us some feedback on our proposal. He said that most of the decision makers liked our approach. He told us that our price was a little less than the winner's. But the decision makers felt that we didn't consider their bank's business very important, because of the way we packaged our proposal. I probably don't need to tell you that we never repeated that mistake again!

# Chapter 13

# Using a Letter Proposal — When Shorter Is Smarter

. . . . . . . . . . . . . . . . . . . . . . . . . . . . . . . . . . . . . . . .

*In This Chapter*

▶ Understanding when to use a letter proposal

▶ Applying standard proposal structure to a letter proposal

▶ Comparing standard and letter proposals

. . . . . . . . . . . . . . . . . . . . . . . . . . . . . . . . . . . . . . . .

*W*hen you think about sales proposals, maybe the first thing that comes to mind is a three-ring binder filled with pages and pages of text, product specifications, complex tables, and marketing hype. Or maybe you think that a proposal has to be long to be good or you tie a proposal's length to its value — the longer a proposal, the better it must be. Maybe you think that you have to write long proposals because you sell a complex product. Or maybe the complexity of your product or service application adds length to your proposals.

You may be surprised to learn that not all effective proposals have to be long. Companies and professionals are occasionally in sales situations that call for smaller proposals. In certain situations, a five to ten page proposal is long enough and a letter format is very effective. In this chapter, I show you everything you need to know to write a *letter proposal*.

## Proposing in a Smaller Package

Question: Does a letter proposal contain all the logic and content requirements of regular, full-size proposal, just in a smaller package?

Answer: You bet.

A letter proposal is somewhere between an executive summary and one of your standard sales proposals. An executive summary is a proposal in miniature — it's a synopsis of the entire proposal. A standard sales proposal contains all the recommended components: a transmittal letter, an executive summary, the five recommended main sections, and supporting appendices. A letter proposal is a hybrid.

Table 13-1 shows the points of similarity and dissimilarity between a letter proposal and a full-length proposal.

| Table 13-1 | Comparing Standard and Letter Proposals | |
|---|---|---|
| *Proposal Section or Element* | *Standard Proposal* | *Letter Proposal* |
| Title page | x | |
| Subject line | | x |
| Transmittal letter | x | |
| Table of contents | x | |
| Executive summary | x | |
| Background information | x | x |
| Proposed solution | x | x |
| Implementation | x | x |
| Seller profile | x | x |
| Business issues | x | x |
| Approval (section) | | x |
| Appendixes (or attachments) | x | x |

A letter proposal contains the same information that you put in the five-section sales proposal. (See Chapters 4 through 10 for details on the five-section proposal.) However, a letter proposal only uses 6 to 10 pages to convey the information.

You may want to add appendixes to a letter proposal to control its length, just like you use appendixes with a full-sized proposal. However, use a different name for appendixes in a letter proposal. Call them *attachments* rather than *appendixes*. (See Chapter 11 for information about using appendixes in your proposals.)

# Deciding if Smaller Is Better

Designing and writing letter proposals is easy if you consider the letter proposal a shortened form of a standard proposal. You can use letter proposals the same way that you use regular proposals. You can and should integrate your letter proposal development process into your consultative sales process.

You may find that letter proposals work well in one of the following sales situations:

- You're selling an uncomplicated product with a low dollar value.

- A customer has received and accepted one of your standard proposals and you have the opportunity to sell an add-on.

- Sales for products or services that are not necessarily add-ons to a previous sale, but that you sell between large sales to an existing customer.

- The buyer's organization has only one or two decision makers who want a simple proposal to document an understanding that they've reached with you.

## How a letter proposal won $63,900 of add-ons

Bankman Technologies, Inc. (BTI), a bank data processing systems vendor, signed a major contract with Western State Bank to convert WSB's data processing functions from a service bureau to BTI's BankSystem 2000. The value of the proposal was $525,000. However, the project spelled out in the proposal didn't include converting the bank's tellers to BTI's system. Rather than writing another large proposal, the BTI sales professional used a letter proposal that addressed converting the WSB teller system to BTI's BankSystem 2000 Teller. The value of BTI's letter proposal was $63,900.

Using a letter proposal made sense for several reasons. First, Western State Bank was an existing BTI customer and had accepted an initial $525,000 proposal for the BankSystem 2000. Second, teller systems are an integrated component and a very logical add-on sale. Finally, the proposal was relatively small when compared to the initial sale: $63,900 versus $525,000.

Western State Bank's decision makers didn't need or want a full-size proposal from BTI. But they did want BTI to identify the specific non-financial and financial benefits of the teller system and they wanted a clear understanding of how BTI would implement the teller system hardware and software. The letter proposal was a quick and effective tool.

# Providing a Perfect Fit for Consultants

If you work for a small consulting firm or are an independent consultant, a letter proposal may work perfectly for you. Because your letter proposal is a condensed version of your standard proposal, you can easily educate the buyer's decision makers on all aspects of their improvement opportunity, your consulting capabilities, and the benefits of your proposed engagement.

Letter proposals work for small consulting firms and independent consultants because their deals are usually small in dollar terms and often not for a complex engagement with a staff of consultants.

Your buyers may find that a letter proposal doesn't seem to be as imposing as a standard proposal, even though your letter proposal's sales message can be just as compelling. Because a letter proposal is shorter, it's easier and faster to design and write. You can also add an acceptance section with signature lines to your letter proposal. This section makes approving your proposed engagement super-convenient. (I write about the acceptance section later in this chapter.)

For example, PresentPro Dynamics, Inc. (PPD) offers sales presentation design, development, and training services to its clients. A typical consulting engagement costs $10,000; some engagements can cost up to $20,000. PPD normally uses letter proposals because of the length and size of the average engagement: short-term and small.

However, PPD does use a standard proposal format for large contracts. For example, PPD recently proposed the design, development, and delivery of a presentation training program for a Fortune 1000 company. The contract was for $85,000 and involved the delivery of a customized half-day workshop at ten locations.

# Squeezing Proposal Content into a Letter Format

When you design and write a letter proposal always keep in mind that it's a standard proposal in letter format. You can use the same flow of information and ideas that you use in your standard proposal (the same five proposal sections). For example, the first several paragraphs of a letter proposal contain the buyer background information normally found in a section one of a standard proposal.

Because it's so short, a letter proposal doesn't need a table of contents or an executive summary. You can include a section for buyer approval instead of a separate contract or purchase order.

## The letter proposal components

Figure 13-1 gives you a quick look at what goes into a letter proposal. You can use the illustration to track the details in the following sections.

**Seller Company Name**
Address
City, State Zip
*(on the selling company's letterhead)*

Date

Buyer Contact Name
Contact Title
Company Name
Address
City, State Zip

Dear Mr./Mrs./Ms. Contact's Last Name:

**SUBJECT:** (Short title describing the proposal)

**Introduction:** One or two introductory paragraphs: "Thank you for inviting us to propose…"

**Main Body:** Same flow of information as in the five main sections of a standard proposal -- Background, Proposed Solution, Implementation, Seller Profile, Business Issues -- but condensed! Most parts no longer than one page.

**Closing:** One or two wrap-up paragraphs.

**Acceptance:** Optionally, a paragraph and signature line for the buyer to accept the proposal.

**Complimentary Close:** *Sincerely, Regards...*

**Name of Sender and Signature**

**Appendices (or Attachments):**

**Figure 13-1:**
Showing what goes into a letter proposal. Typically, such a letter is 6 to 8 pages long.

### Using the subject line for the title

A subject line in your letter proposal is like the title page of a standard proposal. Use it to link the buyer's improvement opportunity with your proposed product or service. See Chapter 11 for more information on a proposal's title.

### Using pieces of a transmittal letter

Put some key pieces of a transmittal letter at the beginning and end of your letter proposal. Start your letter proposal by explaining why you're submitting it to the buyer. And end your letter proposal by thanking your contact for his or her time and effort in helping you gather the information for the proposal. See Chapter 11 for more information on a proposal's transmittal letter.

### Including the five proposal sections

Use the five standard proposal sections in your letter proposal. Try to reduce each section to less than one page, but don't be too surprised if one or two sections in your letter proposal are longer than that. Chapters 4 through 10 provide detailed information about the five proposal sections.

### Getting the buyer to sign acceptance of the proposal

Make it easy for the buyer to approve your proposal by putting an acceptance section in your letter proposal. Figure 13-2 shows how this optional section can be designed. Note the signature and date line for an authorized buyer representative to approve your proposal. This section is optional; I recommend including it, but check with your attorney before doing so.

**Figure 13-2:**
A place
for your
customer to
accept your
proposal —
a conven-
ient option.

*Acceptance*

Please indicate your approval by signing the acceptance line below; keep one copy of this proposal for your files and return one to me for our records.

Accepted for: (Name of customer)

By: _____

Title: _____

Date: _____

Thank you again for the opportunity to submit this proposal for your consideration. I look forward to working with you and other members of the _____ staff.

Sincerely,

Before you add an acceptance section to your letter proposal, get some legal advice. Your attorney may want you to add some legal wording to your letter proposal or your attorney may want you to attach a contract to your letter proposal.

### Using appendixes like in a standard proposal

You can use appendixes (or attachments) to control the length of your letter proposals, just like you do with a standard proposal. Remember that length is critical with a letter proposal; the length should be no more than ten pages. Therefore, if you need to put details in your letter proposal, summarize the information and put the detail in an appendix. For a letter proposal, you should probably use the term *attachment* rather than *appendix,* but they're the same thing. See Chapter 11 for more information on appendixes.

Put the first page of your letter proposal on your company's standard business letterhead and use matching paper for all the other pages. Since it's in letter format, treat the letter proposal like you would a multiple-page letter. This means you need to put a page number on every page except the first.

The full text of a letter proposal appears on the CD. Check it out for ideas about structuring a letter proposal of your own.

# Part IV
# Getting It Right the First Time

The 5th Wave By Rich Tennant

@RICHTENNANT

BILL BLOWS THE SUMMATION

PRODUCT EXPANSION

"Well, I think this proposal meets all of your business needs. For the rest of your needs, I'd recommend a competent tailor, a low-fat diet and regular flossing."

## In this part . . .

Getting the buyer involved in the proposal development process ensures that your proposal contains exactly the information that the buyer needs to make a buying decision in your favor. This part presents some ideas for using the development of the sales proposal to create a sales partnership with the buyer.

This part also presents a process for developing sales proposal models and information — gathering tools for your company and its sales professionals.

Finally, this part presents the Sales Proposal RATER, a tool for evaluating your proposal from the buyer's viewpoint.

# Chapter 14

# Teaming with Your Buyer to Design and Produce the Proposal

### In This Chapter

▶ Understanding the roles and responsibilities of your proposal team

▶ Following the steps to design, write, and review your proposal

Yes, you read the chapter title correctly. The prospective buyer is willing to help you design and produce your sales proposal.

If partnering with your buyer on this crucial matter seems odd to you, you're probably thinking, "Why would the buyer *want* to help me with the proposal? What does the buyer gain?"

The answers are simple. You know that the buyer is very interested in finding ways to reduce or avoid costs, increase revenues, and improve operations. You know this because you have already helped the buyer identify some key improvement opportunities. The buyer's probably as interested in making those improvements as you are in selling your product!

So, a buyer can find working closely with you during the sales process and helping you design the content for its sales proposal very interesting, to say the least.

Remember that if you're following a consultative sales process, you are working closely with the buyer at every step of the process. No, you won't ask the buyer to actually help you write the proposal, but you can and should ask for help deciding on what goes into the sales proposal.

You need to make sure that the buyer's decision makers have the right information to make an informed buying decision. That's the main reason to team with the buyer as you develop your proposal.

In this chapter, I show you how to assemble an effective seller-buyer team aimed at producing the best possible sales proposal. And you know what I mean by *best:* a revenue producer.

# Forming Your Proposal Team

If you sell a complex product, you almost certainly seek input from people in your company. You also work closely with people in the buyer's company. The people whom you work with can be called your *proposal team*.

Don't think of your proposal team in terms of a project team or a sports team. More than likely, the team members will never meet as a group, although you may hold formal and informal meetings with team members from your company. It's also likely that some team members from the buyer's company may meet with team members from your company to analyze the buyer's current operations or to discuss the application of your product in the buyer's company.

Your proposal team is an informal group of people who help you write your proposal. They really represent your proposal development support team — they support your activities. You ask the team members for help and advice.

Part of your job is to coordinate team member communications. If you sell a complex computer system, for example, you may have to ask a systems analyst from your company for her advice on an installation issue that you want to include in your sales proposal. Before she can help you, she may need to talk with an analyst from the buyer's company; you make the calls and set up a meeting or telephone call between the analysts.

---

## Persuasive peddling

Put yourself on the buyer's side of the desk and think about how you may react if a peddler starts calling on you and has identified an improvement opportunity for your company. She claims that by using her company's product, your company can reduce costs. She spends a lot of time analyzing one aspect of your business to show how her proposed product can be installed, how it can work, and how it can save your company a pile of money.

During the process, she asks for some help in deciding what information about your company to use in her sales proposal and how to present this information so that it makes the most sense to your company's decision makers. During the

process, you begin to realize that this "peddler" is actually a good consultant and has really done a lot of work for you and your company. Her proposal presents some very interesting information. You realize that your input has helped her customize the sales proposal for your company. Her proposal presents some compelling reasons why your company should seriously consider moving forward with the purchase.

Besides, you get to present the proposal to your company's decision makers — the guys upstairs — which is always good for your career.

## *Selecting team members from the buyer's group*

Who you need to be in contact with in the buyer's organization depends on what you sell and how complex its application is in the buyer's business. For example, if you sell a big piece of machinery, you have to work with some engineers from the buyer's company. If you sell data processing services to financial institutions, you have to work with some back-office operations staff from the financial institution.

Some buyer team members are predictable no matter what you sell. You always want to have contact with the manager or managers in the buyer's company who would be impacted by your product. These team members help you decide what information to put in your sales proposal and how to present it.

Some buyer team members to consider and their areas of interest are listed on Table 14-1.

| Table 14-1 | Buyer Team Members |
|---|---|
| *If the team member's position is in . . .* | *They're interested in . . .* |
| Senior management | Financial, people, and operations improvement opportunities. |
| Financial management | Financial, people, operations, and investment performance improvement opportunities. |
| Functional management | How, when, and where you can improve their operations. |
| Purchasing | Price. You have to work with people from purchasing to develop the value proposition and then to make sure that they understand it. |

The most important team member from the buyer's team is your *internal sponsor* or *champion*. An internal sponsor can come from any of the areas listed in Table 14-1. However, your internal sponsor is probably a manager in the functional area that will be most affected by the purchase of your product. A typical internal sponsor or champion:

✔ Is usually a mid-level to senior-level manager

✔ Is your primary contact and mentor within the buying organization

✔ Usually acts like the manager or captain for the buyer's team members

## Your one indispensable team member

You need at least one person on your proposal team even if you're an independent management consultant — you need a proofreader for your proposal. Anyone can be a proofreader as long as he or she has reasonably good command of grammar and punctuation rules and has some ability as a writer.

# Selecting members from your group — the sales team

In most companies, sales professionals don't independently make company commitments. Most sales professionals don't define such things as custom service levels, production schedules, or multi-year pricing arrangements. They need to get help and input from others within their companies. This internal help and input comes from the seller's proposal team members. Your proposal team members may be representatives from production, systems development, operations, professional services, customer services, conversion services, accounting, and legal.

Some team members are going to be more important than others. Your legal department may have to get involved only if the buyer requests a change in the contract. On the other hand, a conversion services representative can have major input if you're proposing that the buyer convert to your company's service.

# Team roles and responsibilities

In a typical buyer-seller partnership, you and your internal sponsor can informally manage proposal development. You both manage and coordinate team members' activities.

Remember that the team members on the buyer side don't have formal roles and responsibilities in developing your proposal. Instead, your internal sponsor or coach usually helps coordinate introductions, meetings, and information-gathering activities between the buying and selling team members. Team members on the buyer's side usually help by identifying, researching, analyzing, and validating improvement opportunities.

However, your team members who work for your company can have more formal roles and responsibilities in your sales proposal development process. For example, if you sell a computer system, a representative from the systems development department might be responsible for establishing preliminary database specifications for the proposed systems implementation in the buyer's company. Or your company may require someone from your accounting department to develop the financial benefit calculations for all the company's sales proposals. Wouldn't that be nice?

## Building rapport and relationships

The interaction of the buyer and seller team members increases the buyer's exposure to your organization.

Here's how it works: You get the buyer's techies talking to your techies. Even though you can't understand what the techies are talking about, you know they're building rapport and relationships during the process. The rapport that you've developed with your internal sponsor expands to the proposal team members from both companies. It's human nature that folks who work together build rapport.

All this teamwork and the resulting relationships lead to the development of trust and confidence between the team members and two companies. This teamwork can become a consideration in the buyer's decision — the buyer is more inclined to pick a vendor that many of its people trust and feel comfortable working with over a company that the buyer doesn't know as much about.

# Organizing the Seller-Buyer Team Approach into Seven Steps

The following seven steps can help you with the timing and mechanics of using your informal buyer-seller proposal team to write a winning proposal.

1. **Establish the team.**

2. **Develop a skeleton proposal.**

3. **Get buyer approval of the skeleton proposal.**

4. **Write and edit the first draft of the proposal.**

5. **Get buyer approval of the draft proposal.**

6. **Finalize and present the proposal.**

7. **Get buyer approval — the sale.**

## Step 1: Establishing the team

This step is basically the formal kickoff. It only applies to those team members who work for your company.

Typical activities for this step include

- ✔ Establishing your internal team and defining its purpose and the buyer's improvement opportunity expectations
- ✔ Defining team members' roles and responsibilities
- ✔ Establishing the timeframes for completing the remaining steps of the proposal development process and defining the proposal's deadline
- ✔ Explaining the proposal writing processes and procedures that you plan to follow

If the sale that you're going after is a really big deal, then it's probably a good idea for you to hold an actual kickoff meeting to formally start the proposal development process in your company. This way, everyone on your team knows what's going on, how big the pending sale is, and how important it is for your company to get the deal. You can also let your company's team members know whether they will be working with people from the buyer's organization.

## Step 2: Developing a skeleton proposal

Imagine building a house without a blueprint. It would probably look pretty funny when you were done, right? Likewise, you need to have a blueprint to guide you as you write a proposal. A detailed skeleton proposal is your blueprint for developing a winning proposal. You can develop your skeleton proposal using this book's recommended proposal structure. You can start your proposal skeleton by using the proposal template that's on the CD that came with this book.

A skeleton is just bones, no meat. A skeleton proposal defines the structure and content of your proposal but doesn't include any detail (or includes very little detail). Your skeleton proposal can identify the main sections and subsections that you plan to include in your proposal. For each section or subsection, write a sentence describing its contents or use bulleted lists of the topics you plan to cover in each section or subsection. The skeleton proposal can also identify supporting appendices that you plan to include in your proposal.

If you use proposal models and still want to include the skeleton proposal steps, you can use your proposal models to reverse engineer standard skeleton proposals. In other words, you can use your proposal models, which are proposals that are 80 percent complete, to create consistent skeleton proposals for a buyer's review and approval. When you get the buyer to review and approve your skeleton proposal, it presents another good opportunity to work with the buyer and get its input.

I'm really in favor of proposal models and recommend that sales professionals use them as often as possible. However, if you use proposal models, I don't think that you should miss the benefits of the buyer-seller team in a consultative sales process. Even if you use a proposal model, you can still use a buyer-seller team.

## Step 3: Getting buyer approval of the skeleton proposal

Some sales professionals call the skeleton proposal a *straw man* proposal because it gives them a chance to present their proposal's logic, content, and direction to their internal sponsor. The nice thing about the skeleton proposal is that designing and writing one doesn't take much time or effort. Getting buyer approval of a skeleton proposal:

✔ Presents an opportunity to easily incorporate any buyer recommendations and suggestions into your final proposal's design

✔ Begins the all-important buyer ownership process for your proposal

✔ Increases the chances that your development activities will be productive because the buyer has okayed the blueprint for your sales proposal

## Step 4: Writing and editing the first proposal draft

You may find that the most difficult part of your entire proposal development process is actually writing the proposal. Certainly, your skeleton proposal helps; however, you still have to sit down and write the proposal. Writing proposals becomes easier over time, but designing and writing winning proposals is never effortless — even if you make things easy on yourself by following this book's recommended proposal structure.

Consider developing proposal models for each of your products or services. Starting with a model can really make you a more effective writer of sales proposals. In Chapter 15, I show you in more detail how to use proposal models and supporting sales tools.

Consider using these steps to write and edit the first draft of your custom sales proposal:

1. **Write the main sections in the order that they appear in your proposal.**

   Doing so helps you develop a logical flow of information and ideas. Writing your proposal sections in order also increases the continuity and consistency of your proposal.

2. **As you write the proposal, decide where you want to reference each appendix.**

   By identifying appendix references as you write the proposal draft, you can make sure that your proposal contains accurate cross-references.

3. **Print a draft of the proposal, proofread it, have someone else proofread it, and make corrections.**

4. **Give copies of your proofread and corrected proposal draft to the proposal team members who work for your company. Ask your team members to read it and give you their comments and corrections.**

   You can hold a team meeting to review any major concerns your proposal team members may have and get their approval of the proposal draft, if necessary.

## Step 5: Getting buyer approval of the first proposal draft

You're ready to present the first draft of your proposal to your internal sponsor for review. Make sure that you mark the proposal as "Draft" or "Draft Copy Only — Not For Distribution." If you don't, you run the risk of the draft proposal being copied and sent to others in the buyer's organization. Hey, you run that risk even if you do mark your proposal as a draft copy.

Tell your internal sponsor that you want to use his review as a "sanity check" for your proposal. In other words, let your internal sponsor know that you're giving him a chance to review your proposal because you want to make sure it meets his company's needs and expectations. Of course, the internal sponsor's review can also help you avoid unnecessary surprises or embarrassments — inaccuracies or inconsistencies about the buyer's improvement opportunities, current operation, or whatever else.

If possible, try to meet with your internal sponsor to discuss his proposal comments and suggestions. During the meeting with your internal sponsor:

✔ Spend some time reviewing the critical buyer-specific information in the proposal, particularly the buyer's numbers (the key financial measures used to measure the buyer's improvement opportunity).

✔ Make sure you get agreement with your internal sponsor on the buyer's needs and objectives contained in the proposal.

✔ Carefully review the product application and its features and the resulting non-financial and financial benefits with your internal sponsor. Make sure he understands how your product or service is going to work in his company.

✔ Review your implementation plans and make sure your internal sponsor agrees with your estimated timeframes and understands the buyer's implementation team commitment levels.

## Step 6: Finalizing and presenting the proposal

More than likely, your internal sponsor's review will cause you to make some changes to your proposal. After you make these changes, you're ready to submit the final proposal to the buyer for review and approval by its decision makers. *Note:* If you have to make many changes to your proposal after reviewing the proposal draft with your internal sponsor, you may want to repeat the fifth step.

## Step 7: Getting buyer approval — the sale

Most sales professionals expect to close every deal. That doesn't happen, even though you give your buyers world-class sales proposals. Your *proposal close ratio* can't be 100 percent. However, you can have a good close ratio if you follow an integrated consultative sales and proposal development strategy.

Chapter 21 gives you some good ideas on how to develop and deliver a winning presentation for your proposal. But start thinking about your presentation as you write the final proposal. The five main proposal sections and their sequence provide an excellent basis for developing an accompanying proposal presentation. If your presentation highlights the critical elements of each proposal section, then your presentation will parallel your proposal's flow of information and ideas. If your presentation follows the flow of your proposal, you make it very easy for the decision makers to follow along, ask questions, or take notes in their copies of the proposal.

# Chapter 15

# Bringing Your Company Up to Proposal Speed

. . . . . . . . . . . . . . . . . . . . . . . . . . . . . . . . . . . . . . . . .

### In This Chapter

▶ Deciding if you're ready to integrate two crucial processes

▶ Developing proposal models and worksheets

▶ Following some implementation project steps

▶ Deciding if proposal automation is the next step

. . . . . . . . . . . . . . . . . . . . . . . . . . . . . . . . . . . . . . . . .

*P*erhaps it's time for your company to give its potential customers a better sales proposal. It doesn't matter if you're an independent consultant — a company of one — or if you work for a large company. You've been selected (or you volunteered) to put a more effective sales proposal development process in place. You accept the assignment and you need a plan. This is the chapter you need.

In this chapter, I provide a plan — guidelines and steps for developing sales proposal models and application worksheets.

## Deciding if Your Company Is Ready to Integrate the Processes

A key to writing winning sales proposals is integrating consultative selling with proposal development. In other words, you or your company's sales professionals have to get to know the buyer, and your proposal has to reflect that knowledge. Although integrating your selling process with your writing process may make sense to you, other people in your company, like other sales professionals or senior management, may not embrace the concept. If this is the case, you need to determine whether your company is ready to make the changes that are necessary in order to integrate the processes.

Answering the following questions can help you decide if your company is ready.

### Do your company's sales professionals follow a consultative sales process?

If they do, go to the next question. If they don't, you and your company face a major challenge. Before your sales professionals can be expected to gather the type of buyer-specific information that's needed to write a good sales proposal, they need to know how to sell consultatively. Read Appendix A to find some resources that can help. Your company may want to consider an onsite workshop conducted by a sales training organization in order to teach the sales professionals how to sell consultatively.

### Do your company's sales professionals incorporate gathering the buyer information that's needed to write a sales proposal into the selling process?

The most likely situation is that your company's sales professionals already gather and process lots of buyer-specific information. Much of this information is probably the same information that's needed to write buyer-focused proposals. But the sales professionals probably need a place to systematically record this stuff so that all the buyer information isn't just in their heads or buried in their notes. Here's where an application worksheet comes in handy.

If your company's sales professionals don't gather the buyer information needed to write a sales proposal, go to the previous question — your company's salespeople lack consultative selling skills.

### Is your company's senior management committed to helping sales professionals make a change in the way they sell and how they develop sales proposals?

If senior management is ready to help your company's sales professional make the change, go to the next question. However, if senior management isn't behind the change, you have a major sales job in front of you. You need to convince senior management that the company needs to adopt a consultative sales process and integrate it with a proposal development process. Keep reading — you're going to get some help in this chapter. Part V of this book also has lots of relevant tips.

### Does your company's senior management understand what it will take to integrate a consultative sales process with a proposal development process?

If your company's senior management wants the sales professionals to sell consultatively and write winning proposals, then senior management is waiting for someone (you) to tell them what needs to be done, how long it's going to take, and how much it's going to cost. Sounds like a project. Thanks in advance for volunteering. Keep reading because you will get some help.

If your company's senior management doesn't understand what it will take to integrate the processes, you need to sell them on the concepts, guidelines, and ideas in this book. Maybe you need to write an internal sales proposal. See Chapters 17 and 18 for some help.

# Understanding the 80/20 Rule, Proposal Models, and Application Worksheets

You need to understand these concepts before starting your new process integration project:

- ✔ The 80/20 rule for designing proposals
- ✔ Proposals models
- ✔ Application worksheets

*Note:* Chapter 2 goes into each of these concepts in more detail. If you haven't already read Chapter 2, you may want to check it out.

## 80/20 rule

Your proposals should follow an 80/20 rule: 80 percent of the wording in your company's sales proposal is the same for most customers; the remaining 20 percent is buyer specific.

Only 20 percent of your wording needs to change from one customer to the next.

## Proposal models

Proposal models are based on the 80/20 rule. A proposal model is a proposal that is 80 percent complete. Twenty percent of its wording is missing — it has some critical information gaps. These gaps provide places to insert the buyer-specific information (the 20 percent) that's needed to convert the proposal model into a custom proposal.

If you sell different types of products, you need a proposal model for each product that you sell.

## Application worksheet

An application worksheet is a proposal development tool. The application worksheet contains the questions that sales professionals need to ask and the topics they need to cover with a buyer. Getting answers to the questions and covering the topics on the worksheet ensures that the sales professional gets the 20 percent (the buyer-specific information) needed to write a custom proposal. The application worksheet is an integral part of a consultative sales process and helps convert the proposal model into a custom proposal.

Proposal model + application worksheet = custom proposal

(80% + 20% = 100%)

# Developing the Proposal Model and Application Worksheet

Before your company can get up to speed, it needs to create two tools for each product it sells: a proposal model and an application worksheet.

You can reverse engineer an application worksheet and create a proposal model by using a completed sales proposal as the starting point. You want the completed proposal to follow the five-part structure that I detail in Chapters 4 to 10.

Go through each section of your completed proposal and identify the standard wording (the 80 percent) and the buyer variables (the 20 percent). The buyer variables are parts of your proposal that change from one buyer to the next. (Remember that these percentages are approximate.)

Develop your application worksheet by writing a question or phrase that will prompt a sales professional to get the information needed for each of the buyer variables that you've identified. You can arrange the questions or phrases into a bulleted list or arrange them in a table that the sales professional must complete.

Now turn the completed proposal into a proposal model by deleting the buyer variable information. Doing so leaves some spaces and blank lines. The buyer information that sales professionals gather with the application worksheet will find a home in one of these spaces or blank lines in the proposal model.

Use the sample application worksheet on the CD to help you design worksheets for your proposal models.

When you've completed your worksheet, it should include questions that prompt for some or all of these buyer-specific information requirements:

- ✔ Basic information: company name and address; contact names, titles, and phone numbers; and so on

- ✔ Business description: industry type, number of locations, annual revenues, and so on

- ✔ The business's needs and objectives that relate to the proposed product

- ✔ Decision-making and buying processes

- ✔ Key decision makers and their expectations and influences on the buying decision

- ✔ The buyer's selection criteria

- ✔ Product application definition variables (variables that define the application of your product in the buyer's business)

- ✔ Product features, generic benefits, and buyer-specific benefits

- ✔ Financial benefit analyses variables, formulas, and worksheets

- ✔ Implementation variables (variables that define the implementation of your product in the buyer's business — team, schedule, commitment levels, and so on)

# Following a Development Project

If you're managing a full-blown project to create proposal models and application worksheets, this section is for you.

Designing, developing, writing, testing, and implementing a proposal model and its accompanying application worksheet is a significant project for your company. You need to start with a commitment from senior management to change the way the company's sales force deals with its customers throughout the sales process. But sometime during the project, the sales force itself has to buy into the project.

Expect that some sales professionals may view the changes as a lot of unnecessary effort — they'll have difficulty understanding why the company wants to elevate the importance of an administrative document (which is how they view the sales proposal). Other sales professionals may readily embrace the integrated processes. These sales professionals will like the proposal models and find the application worksheets help them during their sales process. These sales professionals will quickly realize that all this new stuff makes them more consultative, helps them close more business, and really provides them with a great opportunity to raise their level of professionalism.

The following steps provide you with a blueprint for creating a detailed plan to implement consultative sales and proposal development processes in your company. Because your company is unique, you need to carefully evaluate your situation, market, customer base, resources, needs, and objectives before undertaking the project.

You may confuse this chapter with what you read in Chapter 14 — how to team with the buyer to write a proposal. Chapter 14 assumes you have a proposal model that you will follow when teaming with the buyer to write a winning proposal. This chapter helps you design the proposal models your sales professionals can use when they team with a buyer to sell consultatively and write a winning proposal.

## Step 1: Establishing the project team

Recruit representatives from other departments in the company to participate on the project. Start with those departments that have some direct involvement with sales, working with prospective customers, and pricing or defining the application of your company's products for prospective customers. Sales, marketing, product management, and customer service representatives are the most logical candidates for your project team. However, don't overlook the production, accounting, and legal departments. I'm not going to give you any numbers for how many people should be on the team, as every situation is different. Use your common sense and base your decisions on the size of your company and the complexity of the project.

Make sure that you get a commitment to support the project from each team member's manager. Also be sure to define team member roles and responsibilities on the project and communicate them to all the team members.

## Step 2: Defining project goals and objectives

Hold a project kickoff meeting to: 1) explain the project and define its goals and objectives and 2) introduce the team members and identify their roles and responsibilities. Make sure that all the team members understand the expected project outcomes or deliverables — the proposal models and supporting application worksheets. Identify which of the company's products will be the basis for developing the proposal models and worksheets. Also, establish a schedule for Steps 3 through 11.

At this Step 2, make sure that you:

✔ Define the proposal's format and layout: type, graphics, and color.

✔ Establish packaging specifications: paper, binding, and dividers.

# Step 3: Developing a proposal model outline

Build an outline of the proposal model by defining and titling the main sections and subsections of the proposal model. Write one or two sentences that describe the contents of each section and subsection or write a bulleted list of the primary topics that are covered. Review Part II of this book to help you with the proposal's sections and subsections.

Where possible, identify the buyer-specific information that's needed to complete each section and subsection. For example, section one (the buyer's background information) should contain some information about the buyer's current operations. Identify what buyer-specific information is needed to complete that subsection in your outline. Defining buyer information requirements early in the process helps you develop the application worksheet.

As you develop the proposal model outline, try to identify which subsections require supporting appendices and identify the appendices by name in the outline. This helps you write the proposal and identify where each appendix will be referenced in the proposal.

Distribute the completed proposal model outline to your team members and ask for their comments and suggestions. You can schedule a meeting to review comments and suggestions as a team. Make changes to the outline as needed.

# Step 4: Drafting and approving the proposal model

Using the outline as a blueprint, write a proposal model draft. Follow the agreed-upon proposal layout and format. Distribute a copy of the draft to all the project team members and ask for their comments and suggestions. You may want to schedule another meeting to review the team member's comments and suggestions. After reviewing the team member's comments and suggestions, make changes as needed to the proposal model. Get approval from the team of the proposal model.

# Step 5: Developing the application worksheet

Using the proposal model as the basis, reverse-engineer an application worksheet. Create an application worksheet that will help you gather all the information that's needed to fill in the blanks in the proposal model.

# Step 6: Defining the sales and proposal process integration

Define how the company and its sales professionals can integrate the consultative sales and proposal development processes. You need to get the sales professionals on your team heavily involved at this point. They must decide how the company's sales professionals can use the application worksheet and proposal model during the sales process. Make sure the team members, especially the sales professionals, consider the following two issues when they integrate the processes.

## Integration requires a consultative sales process

If your company's sales professionals have been using a consultative sales process, they don't have to change the way they sell very much, although they may find that the worksheets help them more clearly define what buyer-specific information to gather and process.

However, if your company's sales professionals haven't been selling consultatively, plan to get them some major league help as a key part of your project. The company can't expect major changes in the sales professionals' behavior simply because they were handed some new proposal models and worksheets. The team needs to include a consultative-sales training program in the project. Make sure that the person who delivers the training program makes the proposal models and worksheets an integral part of the training program.

## Worksheets are for internal use only

The worksheets are sales tools designed for internal use by the company's sales professionals only. The sales professionals need to understand that they are responsible for gathering the buyer-specific information identified on the worksheets. A sales professional should never hand the worksheet to a prospective customer and ask the contact person to fill out the worksheet — behavior like that is not consultative or professional.

# Step 7: Defining proposal systems requirements and production procedures

Don't expect stunning results if you simply distribute the application worksheets and proposal models as Word files and tell the sales professionals to start using them.

Define what systems, processes, and procedures the company and the sales professionals need to use to generate a custom proposal using the models and application worksheets.

Consider what word-processing, printing, and binding systems will be needed to produce a sales proposal that reflects your company's quality standards. Develop production procedures that make it easy for sales professionals to generate a proposal using the worksheets and proposal models that have been developed.

See Chapter 12 to get some ideas on producing a quality proposal. Later in this chapter, see the section on automating the process for more information about proposal production systems.

# Step 8: Developing performance measurements

Make sure your company gets a good return on its investment by creating a system to measure the success of your sales proposals. Your company can use a *proposal close ratio* (PCR) to measure the effectiveness of your combined selling and writing processes. In order to measure PCR, your company must track the outcome of every proposal that gets written. Your sales proposals can have one of four outcomes:

- **Won.** The buyer accepted your sales proposal.

- **Lost.** The buyer rejected your sales proposal but selected one of the competitor's sales proposals instead.

- **Pending.** The buyer received your sales proposal but its decision is pending. In other words, your sales proposal is in the buyer's hands but it hasn't made a decision.

- **Abandoned.** The buyer didn't reject your sales proposal and accept a sales proposal from a competitor. Instead, the buyer simply decided not to do anything. For whatever reason, it abandoned any plans to take advantage of the improvement opportunity that's defined in your proposal.

### Calculating the proposal close ratio (PCR)

You calculate an individual's, a region's, or your entire company's proposal close ratio (PCR) as follows:

> Number of proposals closed ÷ total number of proposals written = proposal close ratio

### Evaluating your PCR

A high PCR (50 percent or higher) can mean your company's sales proposals and integrated processes are very effective. Your work creating a proposal model and application worksheet paid off.

A high PCR could also mean that your company's sales professionals are only generating sales proposals for those prospects whom they feel are very likely to buy your company's products. Another possibility is that they're not counting all of their sales proposals in the measurement.

A low PCR (20 percent or lower) can indicate a problem with your sales proposals or the integrated consultative sales and proposal development processes. You may need to reevaluate everything — the sales process, proposal models and worksheets, proposal development systems, processes and procedures, and how all this stuff is integrated. A low PCR can also indicate that the sales professionals are writing too many proposals. Some sales professional may use the new sales proposals as a crutch. These sales professionals write proposals before the buyer is ready to receive one. Or, sales professionals are generating proposals with minimal or sketchy buyer information rather than following a consultative sales process. In other words, they shortcut the consultative sales process and minimize the need to understand the buyer's unique situation. These are tell-and-sell guys writing boilerplate sales proposals.

Your company may want to calculate a PCR for each sales professional. This can make it easy to spot the winners and underachievers. Perhaps the underachievers just need some more help.

## Step 9: Pilot testing

Run several pilot tests using real prospective buyers and buying situations before introducing the integrated processes, new proposal models and worksheets, and new systems and procedures to the entire sales force. Make sure the entire project team gets to review the results of the pilot test. Thoroughly debrief the sales professionals involved in the test. Get their reactions to everything. Find out what works and what's confusing. If possible, interview or survey the buyers' decision makers — the sales proposal recipients — to get their reactions and impressions. Make revisions as needed to the proposal models, application worksheets, systems, processes, and procedures.

# Step 10: Implementing the integrated processes and project deliverables

Finally, the project team can roll out the new proposal models and worksheets. Remember that you need to properly position the integrated processes, proposal models, worksheets, procedures, and systems with the sales professionals. Don't just present these changes and materials to the sales force and expect their immediate acceptance. If you just put all this new stuff out into the field, expect to have a disaster. The sales guys will ignore it.

Include as part of your project the development and delivery of a workshop in which the sale professionals get some hands-on experience with all the new stuff. The sales professionals need to understand some key things if you want to have successful implementation. They need to understand:

- ✔ Why the proposal models contain what they do
- ✔ How to use the worksheets and how the buyer-specific information from the worksheets fits into precise places in the proposal models
- ✔ How to use the systems, processes, and procedures to produce a custom proposal. (The word processing system, perhaps a system for sending a completed worksheet to a centralized proposal production department, maybe a procedure where the sales manager first reviews the worksheet with the sales pro before going to production, and so on.)

Consider using examples from the proposals generated during the pilot test to help you develop your workshop materials. Case studies always seem to help people relate new concepts and systems to real-world situations.

Plan for an introductory period as part of the implementation phase. During an introductory period, expect to give some sales professionals additional help. Make sure that if a sales professional is having a problem, he or she can make a call to get help. Treat your sales professionals like you would customers, because they are your project's customers.

Implementation can last a couple of weeks or months, depending on the complexity of the sale and the length of a typical sales cycle.

# Step 11: Monitoring results

Monitoring results is an ongoing activity that can originate from your project. Your company, especially its sales managers, needs to monitor the results of the integrated sales and strategic proposal development processes. They may find that using the proposal close ratio is an easy and effective way to evaluate individual and group performance and process effectiveness.

# Automating the Process — Now or Later?

After everyone in the company realizes that the new proposal models and worksheets really do work, the next thing they may want to do is to automate the proposal *production* process. Automating proposal production can be the next step in your current project or it can be a future project. It means your company acquires or develops a computer system that generates custom sales proposals based upon the input of buyer-specific information.

Before automation, you need to have working proposal models and worksheets. Your proposal automation system takes all the information on an application worksheet and inserts it into the proper places in a proposal model to generate a custom proposal. The system then outputs the proposal into your word processing system so that you can make minor edits, as needed. (Aren't you glad you volunteered for this project?)

## Deciding if your company is an automation candidate

Before you go ahead with automation, evaluate whether your company is a good candidate. Use the criteria in Table 15-1 to help you decide.

| Table 15-1 | Proposal Automation Criteria |
|---|---|
| *Criteria* | *Considerations* |
| Number of sales professionals | If your company employs many sales professionals, automating the production process makes sense; cost-justifying automation is easier when many people benefit. |
| Geographic dispersal the sales professionals | If your company's sales professionals are spread out all over the country, automating sales proposal production helps insure content consistency. |
| Proposal production time and cost | Calculate how long it takes and how much it costs to write a proposal without an automated production system. If a sales professional has to spend 4 to 5 hours writing a sales proposal, that's costly. Further, the sales professional's time would be better spent selling. |

| Criteria | Considerations |
|---|---|
| Number of products sold | If your company needs proposal models for many products, automating proposal production makes main taining and controlling the proposal models easier. Sales professionals will have only one source for the models: the automated proposal production system. |
| Frequent changes to product offerings | If your company frequently makes changes to its product offerings, then automating production helps ensure that sales professionals use the most current version of a proposal model. |

# Identifying the benefits of automated proposal production

Automating proposal production in your company provides non-financial and financial benefits.

### Identifying non-financial benefits

Table 15-2 presents some of the features that you can expect to have in an automated proposal system and the resulting non-financial benefits. Remember that non-financial benefits are those benefits that are difficult to measure in monetary terms.

| Table 15-2 | Non-Financial Benefits |
|---|---|
| *System Feature* | *Benefits* |
| Proposal model database | Sales professionals simply select an appropriate pro-posal model from a sales proposal database. |
| | Proposal model database easily deployed and updated so everyone has access to the most current proposal versions. |
| Online input of buyer-specific information | Sales professionals enter buyer-specific information on formatted input screens either to a standalone PC, server, Intranet, or Internet-based system. |
| | Optionally, the company's contact management or customer relationship management system contains the buyer-specific information fields needed to gener-ate a custom sales proposal. |

*(continued)*

**Table 15-2 *(continued)***

| System Feature | Benefits |
|---|---|
| Proposals generated in word-processing system format | Sales professionals can easily edit generated proposals and add their final changes.<br>Everyone already uses the word-processing system. |
| Activity and management reporting | Sales professionals and management should have easy access to proposal activity and status reporting. For example, the system should report the dollar value and number of proposals won, lost, pending, and abandoned year-to-date for the company, division or region, and individual.<br><br>Sales professionals and management should be able to access the Proposal Close Ratio for the company, division or region, and individual. |

### Calculating financial benefits

You can calculate the financial benefits of automating proposal production by comparing current (and manual) production costs and times to those of the automated system. Use these key performance indicators:

- Number of proposals written annually
- Average time needed to write a custom proposal
- Average hourly rate (including benefits) of a sales professional and anyone else involved in writing proposals

Use the key performance indicators to calculate the cost to write and generate one proposal using the current manual process.

## Spotting potential problems with automation

You should be aware of two potential problems if you decide to automate proposal production:

- **Design deficiencies:** If your proposal models or worksheets have any design deficiencies, these deficiencies can limit a sales professional's ability to gather and process the right client information. In other words, the system may not request or provide a place for the sales professionals to input some appropriate (and needed) buyer-specific information. This can force the sales professionals to make many manual changes to the generated proposals. There goes the financial benefit.

✔ **Not following a consultative sales process:** Problems can arise if the sales professionals don't follow a consultative sales process. They may simply input client information that lacks substance or depth. In other words, even the best automated proposal system can't cover for sales professionals who don't (or don't want to) understand the buyer's unique situation.

The proposals generated from both of the above problem situations can lack compelling reasons for the buyer to make a change. The automated system will have helped the company's sales professionals turn out these deficient proposals in record time.

# Chapter 16

# Rating Your Proposal

· · · · · · · · · · · · · · · · · · · · · · · · · · · · · · · · · · · · · · · · · · · · · · ·

### In This Chapter

▶ Introducing the five elements of quality customer service

▶ Evaluating your proposal with the Sales Proposal RATER

▶ Using the electronic version of the Sales Proposal RATER

· · · · · · · · · · · · · · · · · · · · · · · · · · · · · · · · · · · · · · · · · · · · · · ·

*W*hat if you could evaluate the quality and effectiveness of your proposal from a buyer's viewpoint? Do you think that you could more easily design and write winning proposals? You can do the next best thing if you ask a colleague to read and rate your proposal (or read and rate it yourself). If you use the Sales Proposal RATER that I present in this chapter, you have an opportunity to correct deficiencies in your proposal before the decision makers use it to make their final buying decision.

## Using Five Quality Customer Service Dimensions

Experts on customer service offer lots of solid, practical advice. Among my favorite short collection of tips is the group of five presented in the book *Delivering Quality Service,* authored by Valerie A. Zeithaml, A. Parasuraman, and Leonard L. Berry (Free Press). The authors list five elements of delivering quality customer service: reliability, assurance, tangibles, empathy, and responsiveness. High quality customer service must embody all five of these attributes, the authors say, and I agree.

### Selling is customer service during the sale

You probably agree with me that you provide a form of customer service during the sales process, especially if you sell consultatively. If selling represents customer service before the sale, your sales activities can and should embody the five aspects of quality customer service that are identified in *Delivering Quality Service.*

One point I make throughout this book is that the consultative sales and proposal development processes should be integrated. If you agree that your sales proposal represents the end product or deliverable of these two integrated processes, then your sales proposal also should contain the five elements of good customer service: reliability, assurance, tangibles, empathy, and responsiveness.

Selling and customer service are intangible, which makes it somewhat difficult to evaluate and measure their quality. However, your sales proposal is a tangible product. As such, it's fairly easy to evaluate the quality of your sales proposal.

### Sales proposal quality dimensions

I created my Sales Proposal RATER by using the five aspects of quality service that are contained in *Delivering Quality Service.* The RATER gets its name from the first letters of each of these aspects.

- ✔ **Reliability** reflects the seller's ability to identify creative and practical business solutions that help the buyer achieve its goals and objectives.

- ✔ **Assurance** increases the buyer's trust and confidence in the seller's ability to deliver successful results.

- ✔ **Tangibles** enhance and differentiate the communication of the seller's message and invite readership by the proposal's content, structure, and overall appearance.

- ✔ **Empathy** reflects the seller's thorough understanding of the buyer's unique business environment, operations, organization, improvement opportunities, needs, and objectives.

- ✔ **Responsiveness** demonstrates the seller's willingness to work closely with the buyer to understand its unique situation, present viable business solutions, and ensure the achievement of the promised results.

## Using the Sales Proposal RATER

The five aspects of quality provide the foundation for the RATER. Each quality aspect has five specific evaluation points or questions in the RATER. Each evaluation point or question receives a score of 1 to 5.

## Two ways to use the RATER

You can use the RATER in one of two ways. You can:

✔ Self-rate one of your sales proposals

✔ Ask a business associate to rate one of your sales proposals.

I think you get a more objective evaluation if a business associate reads and evaluates one of your sales proposals. A business associate probably doesn't know as much about your buyer and the proposed product as you do. Therefore, when she reads and evaluates your sales proposal, she can more readily identify content deficiencies and information gaps. In other words, if you really want to evaluate your proposal from a buyer's viewpoint, get someone else to do it for you.

If a business associate is going to rate your sales proposal, don't just give her a draft copy of the proposal. Package your proposal like you would package it for a buyer. This way your nicely packaged proposal can really make your evaluator feel like she's on the buyer's side of the desk. Actually, one of the evaluation points or questions under the tangibles category addresses the proposal's appearance, so putting your sales proposal in a nice package may get you an extra point or two.

To rate a proposal's quality from the buyer's viewpoint, follow these steps:

1. **Carefully read the entire sales proposal**

   Don't just skim through the proposal. Read and evaluate the proposal from the viewpoint of a decision maker who has to make a buying decision for the company. Read the entire proposal first and then answer or score the questions on the RATER.

2. **Use the scale below to score each evaluation point or question under the five categories.**

   Use the space below each question for notes or to explain why and how you scored the question the way you did.

3. **Total the scores for each of the five categories.**

### Sales Proposal RATER Scale

| Score | Rating | Comments |
| --- | --- | --- |
| 5 | Excellent/Yes | Exceptional quality |
| 4 | Above average | High quality; only minor revisions needed to reach level 5 rating |
| 3 | Average | Acceptable; needs more than minor revisions to reach level 5 rating |

| Score | Rating | Comments |
|-------|--------|----------|
| 2 | Below average | Substandard; needs major revisions to reach level 5 rating. |
| 1 | Unacceptable/No | Does not reach minimum quality levels — requires a complete revision or restart. |

# Reliability

Does the sales proposal:

Present a solid business solution that meets the buyer's expectations and helps the buyer capitalize on its improvement opportunity? ___

Effectively describe the seller's proposed product or service and clearly define how its application will work in the buyer's unique environment? ___

Describe all of the fees, prices, and expenses the buyer will incur? ___

Present product features or service capabilities and convert them into buyer-specific non-financial benefits? ___

Present product features or service capabilities and convert them into buyer-specific financial benefits? ___

RELIABILITY TOTAL ___

# Assurance

Does the sales proposal:

Assure the buyer that 1) the seller is experienced and has qualified management and staff to fulfill the contract or engagement and 2) provide appropriate background and historical information about the selling organization? ___

Present the seller's project management or implementation methods and/or business practices for delivering on the contract or engagement? ___

Define the buyer's and seller's implementation or engagement roles and responsibilities and their commitment levels? ___

Provide a schedule of major engagement, project, or implementation activities? ___

Provide customer references that are easy to verify and that demonstrate a solid track record? ___

ASSURANCE TOTAL ___

# Tangibles

Does the sales proposal:

Focus on the customer and provide a logical flow of information and ideas for the reader? ___

Convert the intangible elements of the proposal into tangibles, such as schedules, flow diagrams, process tables, graphics, or charts? ___

Effectively use supporting appendixes to 1) control the length of the main proposal sections and 2) provide the reader with more detailed information? ___

Demonstrate high standards for writing, grammar, punctuation, format, layout, appearance, and overall readability? ___

Contain an executive summary that is a proposal in miniature? Does the executive summary condense the essence of the entire proposal into no more than two to four pages? ___

TANGIBLES TOTAL ___

# Empathy

Does the sales proposal:

Reflect a thorough understanding of the buyer's business operations? ___

Clearly define the buyer's improvement opportunity — how it could reduce costs or increase revenues? ___

Clearly define the buyer's short-term needs and long-term objectives for achieving the improvement opportunity? ___

Propose a product or service whose application will: 1) work in the buyer's unique business and 2) help the buyer meet its needs and objectives? ___

Propose a solution that fits within the buyer's timeframe? ___

EMPATHY TOTAL ___

# Responsiveness

Based solely on the sales proposal's contents, does the sales proposal:

Reflect the sales professional's willingness to ask questions, gather information, and gain a thorough understanding of the buyer's business and unique improvement opportunity? ___

Reflect the seller's willingness to identify the buyer's unique business improvement opportunity and present a custom application of its products or services? ___

Present (or offer to present) and review the final proposal with the buyer (or a buying committee) to answer questions and clarify issues? (YES = 5 or NO = 1) ___

Convey that the seller is willing to support the buyer in achieving the promised results after the sale? ___

Seem integrated with the seller's consultative sales process? (YES = 5 or NO = 1) ___

RESPONSIVENESS TOTAL ___

# Analyzing the RATER's Scores

After evaluating each of the five qualities of a sales proposal using the Sales Proposal RATER, you can use Figure 16-1 to draw a profile of the proposal as a whole. To form a quick picture, simply mark an X at the point on the scale corresponding to the numerical score for each of the five qualities. Table 16-1 helps you interpret your scores.

**Figure 16-1:** You can plot the overall power of a proposal by marking an X at the score for each of the five qualities.

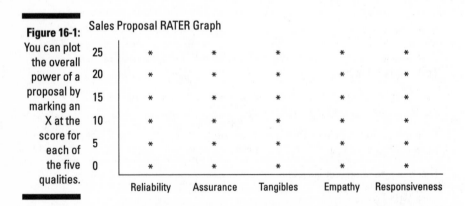

Sales Proposal RATER Graph

| Table 16-1 | Sales Proposal RATER Score Values |
|---|---|
| **Total Score** | **Rating/Comments** |
| 21 to 25 | Excellent; exceptional quality |
| 16 to 20 | Above-average quality; only minor revisions needed |

| Total Score | Rating/Comments |
|---|---|
| 11 to 15 | Average quality; needs more than minor revisions to reach top ratings |
| 6 to 10 | Below-average quality; needs major revisions |
| 0 to 9 | Unacceptable; requires complete revision or rewrite |

# Getting more diagnostic help from the automated Sales Proposal RATER

The CD in the back of this book contains an automated version of the Sales Proposal RATER. The automated version of the RATER is identical to the one in this book, except that, for each evaluation point or question, the automated Sales Proposal RATER contains a comment or recommended corrective action. There are approximately 120 comments or corrective actions, total, in the automated RATER. You see about 25 of these, based on the score you give to each item in the RATER.

The 120 comments and recommended corrective actions in the automated Sales Proposal RATER help you identify and correct deficiencies or information gaps in your sales proposals. For example, the first reliability evaluation point or question is

> Does the proposal present a solid business solution that meets the buyer's expectations and helps the buyer capitalize on its improvement opportunity?

If the person evaluating your proposal gives this evaluation point a score of 5, the automated Sales Proposal RATER responds with the following comment:

> Your proposal does an **excellent** job identifying the buyer's business improvement opportunity and its expectations before presenting a business solution. As a result, the buyer realizes that the seller: 1) understands its unique situation and 2) is proposing a business solution with a product or service that clearly matches its needs and objectives and can help it make or save money.

However, if the person evaluating the proposal gives this evaluation point a score of 1, the automated Sales Proposal RATER responds with the following comment:

Your proposal is **unacceptable** in this area. It doesn't identify the buyer's business improvement opportunity and its expectations. It also does a poor job presenting a business solution. A total rework is needed for this part of your proposal. Begin by making sure that your proposal clearly describes the buyer's unique situation. Next, clearly identify the buyer's expectations. Then propose a product or service that clearly matches the buyer's needs and objectives. And, finally, explain how the buyer can make or save money. Scores of average and below in this area may indicate that you're not following a consultative sales process — you're not thoroughly analyzing the buyer's business situation and presenting (or explaining) a viable business solution.

## Combining the paper-based and automated Sales Proposal RATERs

You may find that using both the paper-based and automated Sales Proposal RATERs helps you design and write winning proposals. Consider following these steps in order to use both RATERs:

1. **Make a paper copy of the Sales Proposal RATER by copying the appropriate pages from this chapter of the book.**

2. **Give a business associate the sales proposal you want evaluated and the paper copy of the Sales Proposal RATER.**

3. **After your business associate completes her evaluation and returns the completed (scored) RATER, access the automated Sales Proposal RATER system on your computer and enter the scores your business associate assigned to the 25 evaluation points or questions.**

4. **Print a copy of the Sales Proposal RATER, which includes the scores, comments, and recommended corrective actions.**

5. **Use the printed output from the automated Sales Proposal RATER to identify areas in the sales proposal that need improvement.**

# Part V

# Selling on the Inside: The Internal Sales Proposal

The 5th Wave    By Rich Tennant

"GET READY, I THINK THEY'RE STARTING TO DRIFT."

## In this part . . .

Not every sale you make is to an outside buyer. On occasion, you may have a brilliant idea that you want to sell to your boss or the company's senior management. This part presents the process to use and introduces the structure and contents of a *recommendation report* — an internal sales proposal.

# Chapter 17

# Inside Job: Selling an Improvement Opportunity to Your Own Company

*T*he success of your company is very important to you, and you pay close attention to the way things work internally. So one day you identify a new technique or procedure that can really help your company — an improvement opportunity staring you in the face, right at home. You believe this opportunity has a high probability of reducing or avoiding costs or increasing revenues. Does this sound familiar? Of course, these are the same exciting opportunities you identify for other companies as you apply the *consultative selling process* (see Chapters 5 and 6).

In most other chapters in this book, I write about how you can craft a sales proposal to win business — proposals that are intended for an outside organization.

This chapter is different. Here, I apply the techniques covered elsewhere in the book to one of the trickiest sales proposal challenges you can encounter: selling your boss and colleagues on an improvement opportunity for your *own* company.

If you can implement your solution or idea without committing company resources, you probably just have to ask your boss for an okay to proceed. But what if you need to get others in the company to help you? What if your solution or idea requires new equipment or software? In these situations, you probably need to sell your solution or idea to your boss or to the company's senior management.

You first need to convince your boss or senior management (the company's decision makers) that you've identified an improvement opportunity and one or more viable solutions. You also need to define the *value proposition* for the company — how the company will benefit financially or non-financially if the decision makers decide to implement your solution. (I write about value propositions in Chapter 7.)

This chapter covers the whole process, from thinking through your strategy for advancing an improvement opportunity inside your company, to sidestepping political booby traps, to preparing the internal sales proposal, which I call a *recommendation report.*

# Deciding How to Proceed: Big Deal or Little?

Before you run off and start writing a recommendation report — your internal sales proposal — you may want to consider two issues. Both relate to size:

- ✔ Consider the size of the improvement opportunity and your proposed solution.
- ✔ Take into account the size of your company.

Suppose you work for a very large company and the improvement opportunity you've identified only affects the employees working in your department. You first should talk to your immediate boss to get her insight and reactions. Perhaps someone else in your department has identified this improvement opportunity before and it was implemented but didn't work. Or maybe your boss wants you to put your thoughts in writing. If that's the case — and you don't need to go through an elaborate process to get the information that's needed in your written report — you may want to skip to the next chapter to learn about the structure and contents of a recommendation report.

But what if your improvement opportunity is really a big deal? What if the improvement opportunity you identified affects people in other departments, requires expensive purchases, or affects the way your company does business? Before you do anything, you should always discuss your improvement opportunity with your immediate boss to get her thoughts and approval to proceed. If your improvement opportunity involves other departments or affects the company's business operations, you may need help from other employees to fully evaluate your idea. You (or your boss) may need to get approval from the company's senior management to proceed.

Don't make a major production out of recommending a small change that only affects a small part of your company — or amounts to small change, literally. How small is small? It's all a matter of scale. A $50,000 reduction in costs for a company whose annual revenues are $1 million represents a 5 percent increase in pretax profits, and that's a *big* deal!

No matter how big or small your company or what kind of improvement opportunity you've come up with, talk to your boss first. If you work for a small company and your improvement opportunity doesn't cost a lot to implement or doesn't affect others within the company, perhaps she will let you go ahead with the change without any recommendation report.

## Following established policy and procedures

If you work for a big company, you may be required to follow established policy and procedures for recommending a change. If that's the case, you probably can't use the exact steps and types of documents that I recommend in this chapter, but you can still get valuable information and ideas by reading on. If your company doesn't have a process for evaluating improvement opportunities and recommending internal changes, the four-step process presented in this chapter offers a very workable approach for selling and implementing new ideas within your company.

## Watching out for internal politics

How big or small your company is doesn't matter when it comes to one thing — you should be prepared to deal with some internal politics when writing a recommendation report. Another employee in your department may feel threatened or resent you for identifying the improvement opportunity and a solution or idea before he did. If your improvement opportunity affects other departments or the entire company, expect to experience some resentment for identifying it.

If the improvement opportunity you identify makes it appear as though another department or manager isn't doing a good job, you can *really* expect to experience some resentment and political heat. Some employees and managers may feel so threatened by your improvement opportunity and solution that they may try to keep you from evaluating the opportunity and submitting a recommendation report. They may play hardball internal politics with senior management to derail your recommendation report.

The best way to avoid the internal politics that can surround your recommendation report is to keep its contents as non-personal as possible — in other words, don't name names. For example, if the improvement opportunity identified in your recommendation report exposes the inefficient operations or bad decisions of a department, don't name the department manager who is allowing his department to operate inefficiently or has made some bad decisions. Just state the facts surrounding the improvement opportunity without laying blame on anyone.

# Following a Four-Phase Internal Selling Process

The four-phase process that I recommend for managing an internal improvement opportunity isn't my original creation. A large financial service company (a $4-plus billion commercial bank) that I worked for in the early 1980s used it to initiate and manage all major improvement opportunity projects. For two years, I was a project manager at the bank and learned a lot about how to sell to senior management. I know that the process worked extremely well for the bank and was an effective way for senior management to evaluate the merits of the improvement opportunities and proposed solutions presented for their consideration and make informed decisions.

The four-phase process gives your company's senior management the opportunity to terminate an improvement opportunity project if it fails to deliver the promised financial and non-financial benefits — the *value proposition* for your company.

Here are the four phases of the process:

1. **Concept**
2. **Recommendation**
3. **Implementation**
4. **Operation**

## 1. Concept phase

The concept phase gives anyone in your company a means to identify and document an improvement opportunity. As the phase name implies, you only need to identify the *concept,* — the improvement opportunity — in this phase. You don't need to write your internal sales proposal — the recommendation report — at this point. During the concept phase you:

✔ Identify the improvement opportunity.

✔ Define, in general terms, how the improvement opportunity can benefit your company.

✔ Request the commitment of specific resources that you need for evaluating the improvement opportunity during the recommendation phase.

✔ Communicate your improvement opportunity and possible ways to achieve the opportunity in writing to senior management.

### Position paper: Concept phase deliverable

A position paper is the end product or deliverable from the concept phase. A position paper is the initial vehicle you use to communicate the improvement opportunity to your company's senior management. Your position paper defines the improvement opportunity and provides estimates of the resources (money and employee's time) needed to:

✔ Evaluate the improvement opportunity (study the situation and write a recommendation report).

✔ Implement the improvement opportunity, if senior management approves the project identified in the recommendation report.

See the section in this chapter on writing a position paper for detailed information on the suggested format and content of a position paper. (Don't confuse a position paper and recommendation report. You write the recommendation report *after* you write the position paper. I cover recommendation reports in Chapter 18.)

Use the position paper model on the CD to help you write a winning position paper.

### Getting the position paper approved

Submit your position paper to whatever level of management must approve the resources requested for the next process phase, the recommendation phase. If your boss can authorize the resources needed for the next project phase, then submit your position paper to your boss. If resources from other divisions or departments within your company are needed for the next phase, then you or your boss must get the resource commitments from the relevant department managers before seeking approval of the position paper from a senior manager.

After the other department managers commit the resources for the next phase, you can submit your position paper to your boss, or perhaps your boss's boss, for approval. If your position paper is approved, you're ready to move on to the second process phase, the recommendation phase. One word of caution: You may want or need to get the resource commitments in writing from all the impacted department managers.

Suppose your position paper identifies the need to integrate the purchasing, accounts payable, and inventory control functions in your company. This integration can help your company's bottom line and is the improvement opportunity. Other employees from within your company are needed to do an in-depth evaluation of these three functions and write a recommendation report. Your position paper should identify the need for representatives from each of the following departments: purchasing, accounting, information technology, auditing, and warehouse. You or your boss needs to discuss the improvement opportunity with the appropriate department managers and get their commitment to assign a representative from their respective departments to the recommendation phase of the improvement opportunity project.

# 2. Recommendation phase

As the name of this phase implies, the recommendation phase provides for an in-depth evaluation of the improvement opportunity that you identify in your position paper. If your position paper identifies the need for representatives from other divisions or departments within your company to participate during this phase, then a team of people will be involved in the recommendation phase. You may want to call this team the *recommendation team* or *study team*.

### Recommendation report: Recommendation phase deliverable

The recommendation report is jointly written by the recommendation team members and is the end product or deliverable from the recommendation phase. The recommendation report is the internal sales proposal. This report is a formal document, which provides a detailed feasibility analysis of the identified improvement opportunity and the proposed product. The recommendation team leader submits the recommendation report to the company's senior management for approval.

Later in this chapter, I give you the details on a recommendation report.

### Roles and responsibilities of the recommendation phase

Writing a recommendation report can be a big deal and a lot of work. You may want to clearly define the roles and responsibilities of the people on the recommendation team. Table 17-1 identifies the people who you may want to bring on board as you write the recommendation report.

| Table 17-1 | Roles and Responsibilities for the Recommendation Phase |
|---|---|
| *Position and Description* | *Role and Responsibility* |
| **Steering committee:** Division or department managers or senior management, usually from the affected divisions or departments. | Guides the preparation of the recommendation report. |
| **Steering committee chairperson:** A division or department manager, usually from the division or department that identified the improvement opportunity. | Directs the steering committee and presents the recommendation report to company's senior management. |
| **Recommendation team leader:** Usually a representative from the division or department that will use the proposed product. | Provides in-depth knowledge of the improvement opportunity defined in the position paper.<br><br>Completes the recommendation report on time and within budget, as defined in the position paper.<br><br>Ensures that the recommendation team's recommendations are feasible for implementation.<br><br>Presents the recommendation report to the steering committee. |
| **Recommendation team members:** Representatives from the divisions or departments that will be affected by the improvement opportunity or implementation project if the recommendation report is approved. | Provide the knowledge and expertise needed to evaluate the improvement opportunity.<br>Prepare an assigned section of the recommendation report.<br><br>Represent their divisions or departments on the recommendation team.<br><br>Communicate the recommendation team's findings and decisions to their respective divisions and departments. |
| **Advisors:** Managers or supervisors from the divisions or departments that will be affected by the improvement opportunity or implementation project if the recommendation report is approved. | Assist recommendation team members with the detailed and functional knowledge necessary to complete the recommendation report. |

### Getting the recommendation report approved

You may want to consider the following steps to obtain approval of a recommendation report within your company:

1. **The recommendation team reviews and approves the final draft of the recommendation report.**

2. **The recommendation team leader presents the recommendation report to the steering committee for review and approval.**

3. **Upon approval by the steering committee, the steering committee chairperson presents the recommendation report to the company's senior management for review and approval.**

4. **If the company's senior management approves the recommendation report, they commit resources for the next phase of the improvement opportunity project — the implementation phase.**

## 3. Implementation phase

The implementation phase is the time period during which people design, develop, test, and implement the proposed product using purchased equipment, outside consulting services, and so on, if necessary (or during which the product is acquired). Implementation is limited in scope to the improvement opportunity and the product identified in the approved recommendation report, although the project's steering committee can expand or contract the project's scope.

The steering committee can terminate the project during the implementation phase if:

✔ The improvement opportunity that's identified in the recommendation report is found to be unfeasible during implementation or will be unfeasible during operation.

✔ The value proposition of the improvement opportunity doesn't meet the expectations created by the recommendation report.

Your company may follow a project management methodology for managing and controlling internal projects. If that's the case, the implementation of the improvement opportunity proceeds like any other internal project for your company. If your company doesn't follow a formal project management methodology, you may have just identified another improvement opportunity for your company (oh no, another recommendation report to write).

### Roles and responsibilities for the implementation phase

Whether your company follows a project management methodology or not, you may want to define the roles and responsibilities of the individuals who are committed to the implementation phase of the project. Table 17-2 identifies the implementation team and other resources that your company may commit to the implementation phase.

| Table 17-2 | Roles and Responsibilities for the Implementation Phase |
|---|---|
| *Position and Description* | *Role and Responsibility* |
| **Steering committee:** Division or department managers or senior management, usually from the affected divisions or departments. | Provides general guidance for the implementation of the approved product. |
| **Steering committee chairperson:** A division or department manager, usually from the division or department that identified the improvement opportunity. | Assumes final accountability for the implementation of the approved product. |
| **Project manager.** | Ensures that the implementation efforts follow standard procedures.<br><br>Ensures that the implementation project is completed on time, within budget, and as specified in the recommendation report.<br><br>Ensures that the new (or acquired) product interfaces and integrates with the company's existing operations.<br><br>Reports project progress and any significant variances to the steering committee |
| **Implementation team members:** Representatives from the divisions or departments that are needed to support the implementation project. | Provide the resource commitments identified in the recommendation report.<br><br>Participate on the implementation project under the direction of the project manager.<br><br>Represent their divisions or departments on the implementation team.<br><br>Communicate the implementation team's decisions and the project status to their respective divisions and departments. |

*(continued)*

**Table 17-2** *(continued)*

| Position and Description | Role and Responsibility |
|---|---|
| **Advisors:** Managers or supervisors from the divisions or departments affected by the improvement opportunity or implementation project. | Assist implementation team members with the detailed and functional knowledge necessary to complete the project. |

## My most important recommendation report

Several years ago, I was the manager of new product development for a company that provided data services to financial institutions. Training our customers' employees to use the data processing systems was one of the biggest problems this company had. Every time the company converted a customer to its systems, all the customer's employees had to learn how to use the new systems. Some of the customers had high turnover rates, especially in their clerical positions, which meant there were always new employees who needed training. The training department of the data services company struggled with conversion and ongoing customer training demands.

In late 1983, I read some articles about how organizations were using computer-based training (CBT) to teach everything from philosophy at large universities to online functions on mainframe computer systems. Using CBT to train customers' employees seemed to make a lot of sense. I discussed my CBT improvement opportunity idea with my boss, who was a division manager. He agreed that CBT may work for the company and asked that I write a report for him to present to senior management. I wrote a CBT recommendation report, although I didn't have the luxury of a recommendation team.

The report recommended that our company create a CBT department and develop CBT courseware for a new deposit system we recently purchased from a software vendor. The recommendation report pointed out the benefits of our company using the CBT courseware to train our customers' employees. Even more importantly, the report recommended that we sell the deposit system CBT courseware, after we developed it, to other financial institutions that licensed the deposit system for internal use.

My boss presented the recommendation report to senior management. The report was approved, setting in motion a chain of events that led to the formation of a CBT department, development of courseware for computer-based training, licensing the system to banks, and new six-figure sales revenues to my employer.

Two and a half years later, sensing a personal opportunity, I resigned as vice president and manager of the CBT department to start my own company, Electronic Learning Systems, that specialized in consulting on computer-based training and the development of custom courseware. In less than two years, my company was generating revenues of more than $1.2 million. A year after that, we sold the company to a software company that wanted a professional services division.

In short, a recommendation report led to some big things in my career and my life. Computer-based training was very, very good to me.

# 4. Operation phase

The operation phase provides for the transfer of responsibility for the new product from the implementation team to the user division or department.

Before the initiation of the new product into operation, the user division or department must accept all aspects of the new product. After the new product is accepted, responsibility for the new product is transferred from the implementation team to the user division or department. The implementation team can then celebrate with irrational exuberance for one night before returning to their respective cubicles.

*Note:* Your recommendation report can recommend that your company implement a new product or service. However, the user division or department that will be responsible for managing the new product or service may not be prepared to take over management after the implementation phase. If that's the case, make sure the user division or department defines an organizational structure that will accept responsibility for operating the new product or service when it goes into production.

### Conducting a post-implementation review

Following the acceptance of the new product by the user division or department (and at least one week after the post-implementation party), the implementation project team may want to conduct a post-implementation review. This review should evaluate the operational performance of the new product as soon as an evaluation is feasible.

The post-implementation review can compare the actual financial and non-financial benefits of the new product with those benefits that were identified in the recommendation report. The project manager should distribute the post-implementation report to the steering committee, the division and department managers affected by the new product, and the implementation team members.

# Writing a Position Paper

A position paper is the end product or deliverable from the concept phase of the four-phase internal improvement opportunity process presented in this chapter. A position paper:

✔ Represents the start of an internal process for selling senior management on the need for obtaining a new product to help the company

✔ Identifies the improvement opportunity available to the company.

✔ Identifies the estimated resource commitment required to implement the new product that will allow the company to take advantage of the available improvement opportunity

Use the position paper model on the CD to help you write a winning position paper.

## Format and content

An interoffice memorandum format works well for writing a position paper because it allows you to clearly define the nature and purpose of the position paper by using the following divisions:

✔ **TO:** The division or department manager who needs to approve the commitment of resources to proceed to the next process phase, the recommendation phase.

✔ **FROM:** The person or persons who identified the improvement opportunity.

✔ **SUBJECT:** The improvement opportunity and the new product that's needed to take advantage of the opportunity. The subject line is really the position paper's title; see Chapter 11 to learn how to create a compelling title.

Of course, you still have a lot of writing to do after you fill in the to, from, and subject lines. Table 17-3 defines the recommended position paper sections and the content of each. There aren't any hard and fast rules about length, but 3 to 6 pages for each section is reasonable.

| Table 17-3 | Position Paper Sections |
|---|---|
| *Section Name* | *Description/Comments* |
| **Concept** | A description of the improvement opportunity and the proposed product that's needed to capitalize on the improvement opportunity. |
| **Background Data** | Historical information detailing the events that led to the current situation. |

| Section Name | Description/Comments |
|---|---|
| **Magnitude of the Proposed Product** | This section has three subsections:<br><br>**Benefits Anticipated:** An *estimate* of the financial benefits (the reduced or avoided costs or increased revenues) associated with the improvement opportunity and the proposed new product. A list of the non-financial benefits the company can expect from implementing the new product.<br><br>**Implementation Effort:** An *estimate* of the resources required for the recommendation and implementation phases of the project. These estimates should include:<br><br>    Project team staffing levels and costs<br><br>    Capital expenditures<br><br>    Project expenses<br><br>**Implementation Schedule:** The *anticipated* duration of the recommendation and implementation phases and the operational date of the new product. |
| **Commitment Required for the Recommendation Phase** | The resources needed for the recommendation phase — what it will take to evaluate the improvement opportunity and write the recommendation report. This section has three subsections:<br><br>**Steering Committee:** The division or department managers recommended for the steering committee and the recommendation for the steering committee chairperson.<br><br>**Project Study Team:** The persons recommended for the recommendation team and the recommendation for the recommendation team leader.<br><br>**Other Expenses:** Estimate and give a brief description of any expenses that will be incurred during the recommendation phase. For example, travel expenses for fact-finding trips. |

## Supporting documentation

You may want or need to include some supporting documentation with your position paper, which may include the following:

- ✔ Commitments for the proposed recommendation team members.
- ✔ Reports, memoranda, statistical analyses, and so on used to write the position paper.

Attach any supporting documentation to your position paper that you think the person who will approve your position paper wants to see.

*Note:* I recommend obtaining written commitments from the managers of each proposed recommendation team member. If you have written commitments, the team members' managers are less likely to renege on their commitments of the member's time, time that is needed to analyze the improvement opportunity and write the recommendation report.

# Chapter 18

# Writing an Internal Sales Proposal

• • • • • • • • • • • • • • • • • • • • • • • • • • • • • • • • • • • • • • • • •

## In This Chapter

▶ Writing a recommendation report

▶ Writing the five main report sections

▶ Adding finishing touches to your report

• • • • • • • • • • • • • • • • • • • • • • • • • • • • • • • • • • • • • • • • •

*Y*our recommendation report is an internal sales proposal from you, and perhaps others, to the senior management of your company. It contains the findings of a feasibility analysis for an improvement opportunity and identifies the available solution to take advantage of the improvement opportunity. Most recommendation reports try to convince senior management to implement a new product.

You can write a recommendation report by yourself. But your feasibility analysis can be more thorough and the content of your report more comprehensive if you use a team of people. And if you use a team and your idea doesn't work, you can spread the blame!

See Chapter 17 for more information about the four-phase process for selling and managing internal improvement opportunity projects. The four-phase process involves senior management, division or department managers, and others within your company.

## Writing a Recommendation Report

The intent of your recommendation report is to provide senior management, your company's decision makers, with ample information on which to make an informed decision about an available improvement opportunity. Your recommendation report must identify:

✔ An improvement opportunity that's available for your company

✔ One or more viable business solutions or ideas for taking advantage of the opportunity

✔ The commitments of time and money that the company must make to implement one of the available solutions or ideas

✔ How your company can reduce or avoid costs or increase revenues — the *value proposition*.

Use the recommendation report model on the CD to help you write a winning recommendation report.

## *How this inside document differs from an outside sales proposal*

Your recommendation report differs from a sales proposal in two major ways:

✔ Your recommendation report usually contains more than one alternative for taking advantage of the improvement opportunity. In other words, your recommendation report may compare the advantages and disadvantages of competing products.

✔ Your report contains the conclusions and recommendations of the recommendation team (or you, if there was no team) who conducted the feasibility analysis and wrote the report. As your recommendation report's name implies, your team is recommending (and requesting) to senior management that they approve the implementation of the product selected from the alternatives.

## *Deciding on format*

Your recommendation report is a formal, internal document. Remember that senior managers in your company are the recipients of your report, so it should reflect your best thinking and writing. (These people may give you a big promotion or fat bonus if they think you're doing a great job.)

You don't need to spend a lot of money packaging a recommendation report, but you do want to use some binding process to make it look professional. Don't just staple your recommendation report in the upper left-hand corner. See Chapter 12 for ideas on packaging your recommendation report.

## *Writing the Five Main Sections*

Figure 18-1 shows you the five main sections of a recommendation report, along with chapter references where you can find details about writing those sections. If the figure seems familiar, it is: You may have noticed a very similar one elsewhere in this book with different words in the boxes. But, language aside, the five parts of a recommendation report correspond closely to the five parts of a sales proposal.

Here's a rundown of everything that should go into a complete recommendation report:

✔ Title Page

✔ Table of Contents

✔ Executive Summary

✔ Five main report sections:

- Statement of the improvement opportunity: be sure to cover your company's present operations and needs and objectives

- Background and Purpose of the recommendation report

- Available Alternatives (two or more)

- Conclusions and Recommendations

- Implementation: Schedule and Resource Commitments

✔ Attachments

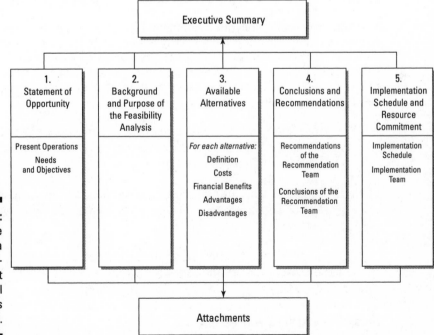

**Figure 18-1:** Your guide to building a recommend-ation report (an internal sales proposal).

Write the five main recommendation report sections like you would the main sections of a sales proposal. Follow these guidelines:

✔ Write the five sections in such a way that a flow of information and ideas is established for the reader.

✔ Emphasize the business issues associated with the improvement opportunity more than the technical issues. Remember that your company's senior management is probably more interested in reducing or avoiding costs or increasing revenues than they are in learning about the technical details of a new product.

✔ Look at the recommendation report from a recipient's viewpoint. Don't assume, just because you're writing an internal report, that every decision maker is fully knowledgeable about the improvement opportunity. Make sure your recommendation report educates decision makers who may have limited knowledge about some aspects of the improvement opportunity.

You may want to skim Chapter 3 to review why documents like sales proposals and recommendation reports play a key role in the decision-making process for a company's senior management.

## Stating the improvement opportunity

The first main section of your recommendation report, the statement of the improvement opportunity, must clearly define the business problem facing your company or the business opportunity available to your company. You should start this section with a strong sentence that leaves no doubt in the reader's mind that you have identified an improvement opportunity for your company. Here are some examples:

- *Over the last two years, the operating services division has experienced a 48 percent turnover rate within its customer service representative positions.*

- *Offering facilities management services to the largest 20 percent of the existing customers can generate new revenues for PrintPro.*

- *The current mainframe-based property management system costs $700,000 in annual operating and maintenance expenses.*

### Present operations subsection

After you identify the available improvement opportunity in your recommendation report, you need to tell the decision makers how the company operates today. Explain the aspects of the company's current operation that relate to the improvement opportunity. Include enough information about the current operations so the decision makers understand the what, why, and how of the improvement opportunity.

The present operations subsection also needs to include the relevant *key performance indicators*. Remember that later on in your recommendation report, you need to calculate the financial benefits of the recommended solution. To calculate the financial benefits of the recommended solution, you first need to measure the current costs and revenues associated with the improvement opportunity. In other words, you need to know how much the improvement opportunity costs your company today in higher costs or reduced revenues. After you have a number for the current costs or reduced revenues, you have the basis for calculating the financial benefits your company can get from the recommended solution. Read more about key performance indicators in Chapters 2 and 3.

### Needs and objectives subsection

To write a recommendation report, you and your recommendation team members need to do a feasibility analysis of the improvement opportunity and available solutions. If you and your team do a thorough job on the feasibility analysis, you should be able to easily list your company's *short-term needs* and *long-term objectives* associated with the improvement opportunity. My point is, if you thoroughly study the improvement opportunity you should be able to describe what your company needs to do in the short-term and what your company should expect from the recommended solution in the long-term.

For example, if the improvement opportunity for your company sounds like this:

> The current mainframe-based property information management system costs $700,000 in annual operating and maintenance expenses.

Then your recommendation report may include the following short-term needs and long-term objectives:

> The Accounting and Information Technologies divisions identified the following property information management system needs:
>
> • Convert the property information system from a mainframe application to a more cost-effective server-based application.
>
> • Reduce internal and external support costs.

- Incorporate barcode readers and scanners to facilitate biannual property and equipment inventories.

- Improve *ad hoc* reporting capabilities to improve property relocation and reassignment processes.

The two divisions also identified the following property information system objectives:

- Provide Web-enabled access to the property information management system to allow authorized company employees to work remotely (telecommute).

- Add digital images to all property records.

## Covering the background and purpose of the feasibility analysis

The second main section of your recommendation report lets the decision makers know the how and why of the improvement opportunity, feasibility analysis, and resulting report. Your recommendation report needs to provide the decision makers with the following information:

- ✔ Background and historical information about the events that created the improvement opportunity.

- ✔ A brief discussion of the people within the company who identified the improvement opportunity and how it was identified.

- ✔ Why one or more division or department managers felt strongly enough about the improvement opportunity to commit resources to complete the feasibility analysis and write the recommendation report.

This second main section of your recommendation report puts the improvement opportunity in perspective for the decision makers. This section explains what was going on inside or outside the company that caused someone to take a closer look at the situation.

Try to make the background and purpose of the feasibility analysis section fit on one page. Keep it on a business level. If the improvement opportunity is the result of someone's bad decision or was caused by someone who allowed a small problem to become a much larger problem, don't try to assign blame in this section. Just explain the facts. (If senior managers want to reprimand someone for creating a problem or not doing his job, they can easily find out who messed up.)

Here's an example that you can use as a model:

The idea of offering complete facility management services for our largest customers' copy centers was conceived by several account executives and field service representatives. Part of the idea to offer facility management services stems from several large PrintPro customers experiencing similar operational problems:

- Difficulty in recruiting, hiring, and retraining competent staff to staff their copy center operations.

- An increasing number of emergency service calls to correct equipment problems that could have been easily corrected by a competent and trained operator.

- Frequent requests for on-site training sessions to train new copy center employees.

Some of our account executives have noted that several large PrintPro customers are reluctant to replace or update their out-moded equipment with more advanced copiers. Although most of these large customers want their businesses to use the advanced network interface functions and features of the latest copiers, they feel that their copy center staff makes this impossible. They feel many of the copy center employees are reluctant to learn or incapable of understanding digital interface operations.

After several months of formal and informal discussions, Larry Kramer (senior account executive) and Bill Fisher (field service manager) wrote a facilities management services position paper and submitted it to their department managers, Sheila Wilson and Andy Pettit, for approval. Because trends in both departments supported the key points of the position paper, Ms. Wilson and Mr. Pettit committed resources from their departments to partici-pate in the study. They also obtained recommendation team member commitments from the marketing, customer service, and accounting departments.

The purpose of the recommendation team is to evaluate the feasi-bility of offering complete facilities management services to the largest 20 percent of PrintPro's customers.

## Presenting the alternatives

The third main section of your recommendation report serves two purposes:

- ✔ Identifying and defining the primary methods of taking advantage of the improvement opportunity
- ✔ Comparing and contrasting these alternatives (usually competing products).

You can easily accomplish the two purposes of the available alternatives section by breaking your discussion of each alternative into five components.

- ✔ **Definition:** A brief description of the product.
- ✔ **Costs:** A summary of all the capital expenditures, employee salaries, and other expenses associated with the implementation of this alternative. (Use an attachment for the detailed cost analysis of each alternative.)
- ✔ **Financial benefits:** A summary of the financial benefits associated with this alternative — the reduced or avoided costs or increased revenues.
- ✔ **Advantages:** A list of reasons why this is an attractive alternative that's better than other alternatives or the existing situation.
- ✔ **Disadvantages:** A list of reasons why this is, perhaps, not the best alternative or as good as the existing situation.

*Note:* The advantages of one alternative often are the disadvantages of another alternative. And the disadvantages of one alternative often are the advantages of another alternative. Here's how it works with the PrintPro example. One alternative is to offer the facilities management service, which has one advantage of adding new revenue for the company. Another alternative is to do nothing (not offer the new service) which has a disadvantage of not adding new revenue for the company.

The following example shows how the PrintPro recommendation team can present two alternatives in their recommendation report. Boldfacing the important words makes them easier for the decision makers to find.

### Alternative #1: Offer full-service facilities management services.

This alternative requires PrintPro to market, sell, and provide copy center facilities management services to existing and new customers. PrintPro would establish a facilities management department to staff, manage, and control copy centers operations at customer locations. PrintPro would assign fulltime staff to assume responsibility for the total operation of a customer's copy center. One fulltime account executive would specialize in selling PrintPro facilities management services. Facilities management services would be provided under three- to five-year contracts.

The annual costs for Alternative #1 are as follows:

Department management and administration:        $150,000

Sales including commissions:                     $100,000

Other department expenses and overhead:          $50,000

Total annual costs:                              $300,000

The financial benefits for Alternative #1 are as follows

Each PrintPro facilities management location would generate from $50,000 to $75,000 in annual pretax profits, depending on the copy and reproduction equipment in use and production volumes.

Four (4) existing PrintPro customers have signed letters of intent to become facilities management sites if the service becomes lavailable. Estimated annual pretax profits from these four sites are $235,000. Two additional existing customers have requested facilities management sales proposals from PrintPro; profits from these two additional sites would allow the facilities management department to reach a breakeven point during the first year of operation.

See Attachment B: Facilities Management Cost Analyses for details.

There are several advantages of Alternative #1

- PrintPro can gain a new source of revenue tied to multi-year management contracts.

- PrintPro can control staff quality, expertise, and training at its facilities management sites.

- PrintPro's on-site facilities management staff can ensure customers receive quality service while fully utilizing all the functions and features of the copy and reproduction equipment.

- PrintPro can change its marketing and sales focus for the facilities management customers from selling equipment to selling service supported by PrintPro equipment. PrintPro facilities management staff can decide when to upgrade equipment at each copy center based on the customer's desire to receive more advanced and sophisticated services.

The disadvantages of Alternative #1 are:

- PrintPro's facilities management department's annual operating costs are $300,000.

- PrintPro has to recruit, hire, and train management and production staff for its facilities management sites.

- By offering facilities management services to its largest customers, PrintPro would trade high-margin equipment sales or lease and maintenance contracts for lower margin facilities management services.

**Alternative #2: No change to current operations.**

Under Alternative #2, PrintPro would not make any changes to its current operation. PrintPro would continue to market, sell, maintain, and support copiers and reproduction equipment for existing and new customers.

There are no new or incremental costs associated with Alternative #2.

The financial benefits for Alternative #2 are the same as PrintPro currently realizes from selling or leasing, maintaining, and supporting copiers and other reproduction equipment.

Alternative #2 does have several advantages:

- PrintPro can avoid the risks associated with offering a new, unproven, and lower margin service to its largest customers.

- PrintPro can avoid annual operating costs of $300,000 for a facilities management department.

- PrintPro does not need to recruit, hire, and train management and production staff for facilities management sites.

There are some disadvantages to Alternative #2:

- Frequent requests for on-site training sessions to train new copy center employees.

- PrintPro can continue only to sell or lease, maintain, and support copiers and other reproduction equipment in an ever more competitive market.

- PrintPro can miss an opportunity to offer a new service to existing and new customers.

- PrintPro can miss an opportunity to gain a new revenue source with multi-year contracts.

- Some PrintPro customers can experience poor quality service because their copy center staffs may lack the knowledge and ability to utilize the equipment's functions and features.

# Coming to conclusions and making recommendations

The fourth main section of your recommendation report records the conclusions and recommendations that a majority of the recommendation team agreed upon.

### Conclusions of the recommendation team subsection

This subsection in your report should be one or two paragraphs that:

- ✔ Identify which alternative the team thinks is most feasible — in other words, the alternative which the team recommends
- ✔ Briefly discuss why each of the other alternatives was not selected

### Recommendations of the recommendation team subsection

This subsection in your recommendation report:

- ✔ Names the division or department that will be responsible for the new product when it becomes operational.
- ✔ Names who will serve on the project's steering committee during the implementation phase.

## Implementation: Covering the schedule and use of resources

The fifth and last section of your recommendation report defines the implementation project schedule and identifies the team of people needed to implement the recommended alternative.

Chapter 8 can give you many ideas for creating an implementation section. Chapter 8 covers implementation for sales proposals, but the sections are similar in sales proposals and recommendation reports. The difference is that recommendation reports need to contain less information about your company's way of doing things.

Identify when the implementation project will start and end. If your company uses a project management methodology, list the phases and their planned start and stop dates.

For each implementation team member, list the following:

- ✔ Name
- ✔ Functional job title
- ✔ Their time commitment, as a percentage of their total workweek, by project phase

Use a table to make this subsection easy to read. Check out Chapter 8 for the details on using tables in an implementation section.

# Creating a Title Page

The title page should clearly identify the nature of your document, so put "Recommendation Report" on the top line. Your title page should also include the following information:

- ✔ **Title of the study**: Include the improvement opportunity in the report's title. For example, if the improvement opportunity you've identified for your company reduces inventory levels and costs, "Reducing Inventory Levels and Costs" would be a good title!
- ✔ **Date started:** The date that you or, even better, the recommendation team started the study or feasibility analysis.
- ✔ **Date completed:** The date the study or feasibility analysis was completed.

- ✔ **Recommendation team:** Recommendation team members listed in alphabetical order with an asterisk (*) next to the recommendation team leader's name.

- ✔ **Advisors:** Recommendation team advisors listed in alphabetical order.

- ✔ **Steering committee:** Members of the steering committee, with two asterisks (**) next to the chairperson's name.

- ✔ **Company name:** Your company's name

- ✔ **Sponsoring division or department:** The name of the division or department within your company that identified the improvement opportunity and initiated the feasibility analysis.

Putting all this information on the title page of your recommendation report may seem like a bit much. But if your company has an internal process for evaluating improvement opportunities or your company decides to follow the four-phase process that I present in Chapter 17, having this information on your title page makes sense because one page identifies the what, who, and when of the report.

Read the section in Chapter 11 on how to create a compelling title for a sales proposal for more help titling your recommendation report.

# Deciding What to Attach to Your Recommendation Report

The purpose of attachments (or *appendixes*) is to support the information in your recommendation report. Table 18-1 lists some of the attachments you may want your recommendation report to include.

| Table 18-1 | Recommendation Report Attachments |
|---|---|
| *Attachment* | *Comments* |
| Cost analysis | A cost analysis for each of the alternatives. |
| Dissenting opinions | If any of the recommendation team members disagree with the conclusions and recommendations reached by the majority of the recommendation team, a memo from the dissenting team member can be an attachment to the report. |

*(continued)*

**Table 18-1** *(continued)*

| *Attachment* | *Comments* |
| --- | --- |
| Purchasing requisitions | If the recommended alternative calls for the purchase of hardware, software, or other equipment, attach a purchase requisition to the recommendation report. If senior management approves your report, make it easy for them to authorize the purchase of the materials needed for implementation. |
| Staff increase requests | If the recommended alternative calls for new hires, attach the appropriate staff increase request documents to the recommendation report. Again, you're making it easy for senior management to authorize the increases. |
| Detailed implementation tasks | The detailed tasks used to support the implementation schedule subsection. |
| Other supporting documentation | Any statistics, reports, memoranda, articles, and so on used during the feasibility analysis and to write the recommendation report. |
| Internal resource commitment authorizations | Any internal authorizations needed in your company for an implementation project, for example, implementation team member commitments from their division or department managers. |
| Technical reviews | Technical review by the information technology division or other divisions, if needed. |

# Part VI
# The Part of Tens

"FIRST HARRY SOLD BOWLING BALLS, SO HE TOOK ME BOWLING. THEN HE SOLD GOLF CLUBS, SO WE TOOK UP GOLF. NOW HE'S SELLING SURGICAL INSTRUMENTS, AND FRANKLY I HAVEN'T HAD A FULL NIGHT'S SLEEP SINCE."

## In this part . . .

Every *For Dummies* book has a bunch of tips that coincidentally come in groups of ten. You'll find three topics in this part: ways to make your proposal close more business, things a buyer wants to see in your proposal, and tips for presenting your proposal to the buyer.

# Chapter 19

# Ten Surefire Ways to Make Your Proposals Close More Deals

### In This Chapter

▶ Following the consultative sales process

▶ Using proposal models

▶ Making the quality obvious

*W*riting a winning sales proposal may never be an easy task, but you can make sure your proposals have a better chance of winning if you follow the advice in this chapter.

## Focus on the Buyer

A winning proposal is always buyer focused. Don't start your sales proposal with a section about your company; that's egocentric. Instead, start your proposal with a section that's all about the buyer. Make sure this first proposal section defines the buyer's improvement opportunity, current situation, key financial measures, and needs and objectives. Make sure that the buyer knows that you understand its company and unique situation before you write the rest of your proposal.

## Follow a Consultative Sales Process

If you want to write a compelling proposal, you need to know lots about the buyer. You need to gather and correctly analyze the appropriate buyer information. And you need to follow a consultative sales process to do so.

During your consultative sales process, you can spend time working with the buyer to understand its unique business and operations and discuss how your proposed product or service can work for the buyer. Your proposal should reflect what you've learned during the sales process. If you don't follow a consultative sales process, you can't know enough about a buyer to write a very good sales proposal. But you *can* write a boilerplate proposal — a proposal that reads like a poorly written brochure.

# Describe the Application

Your sales proposal should explain how your proposed product or service can work in the buyer's business — the application. By including your product or service application description in your proposal, you can answer many questions that the buyer may have. A clearly defined application also can give you the base you need to identify buyer-specific benefits. Your product or service application can be the key piece of information that the buyer's decision-makers need to have in order to make an informed buying decision. Besides, describing the application of your product or service in the buyer's business is a basic part of consultative selling.

# Present Financial Benefits

Your proposal needs to present the buyer's value proposition. Part of your *value proposition* is how your proposed product or service can help the buyer reduce or avoid costs or increase revenues — the financial benefits of your product or service. Your proposal needs to include buyer-specific financial benefits based on the buyer's numbers, its *key financial indicators*. The financial benefits you include in your sales proposal can provide compelling reasons for the buyer to make a change — a basic function of consultative selling. Financial benefits are part of your value proposition for the buyer.

# Present Non-Financial Benefits

Some benefits of your proposed product aren't easily measured in monetary terms but they still are part of the value proposition. Make sure that your proposal converts product features (or service capabilities) into non-financial benefits for the buyer. This conversion is a key part of consultative selling, especially if the non-financial benefits you identify are buyer specific.

# Define the Implementation

Let the buyer know that your company has been there, done that. Use one section of your proposal to tell the buyer how you plan to install the proposed product or implement the proposed service. Be specific. Answer the questions that the buyer may have about how you will implement the project, how long it will take, and who will be. If you do a good job designing and writing your proposal's implementation section, the buyer's decision makers will feel less risk if they decide to buy the product from you. The point is to make it clear to the buyer that you've implemented the product before — that you've been there, done that.

# Include Information about Your Company

Your sales proposal should assure the buyer that your company can deliver on the contract. Including information about your company can help differentiate you from the competition. If you don't know what to put in the proposal to describe your company, pretend that you're the buyer. Answer the questions you might ask a sales professional if you were on the buyer's side of the desk.

# Define the Business Issues

The buyer's decisions makers are probably more interested in the business aspects of your proposed product or service than the technical aspects. Don't overwhelm your proposal's readers with a lot of technical details.

Make sure that your proposal helps the buyer's decision makers understand why and how your technology can improve their business, but use an appendix to explain all the technical stuff, like how your new electric widget can make a network run faster.

# Use Proposal Models

Develop a proposal model (or models) for your company and make sure that everyone in your company's sales force uses it (or them). Remember that your sales proposals represent your company when your sales professionals aren't present. A proposal that wins business doesn't read like a hodgepodge of ideas and writing styles, so a good model for your sales professionals to use is a great first step to having winning proposals.

Your proposal model can reinforce the need for your company's sales professionals to follow a consultative sales process.

Your company hired its sales professionals because they're good at selling; some of them may not be the best writers — another reason to have a good model in place.

## *Show a Commitment to Quality*

Your sales proposals are critical customer communications documents and represent your company when your sales professionals aren't in front of buyers. Spend the time and effort needed on your proposal's content, design, and packaging to produce sales proposals that convey the best possible impression of your business to potential buyers.

# Chapter 20

# Ten Things a Buyer Expects to See in Your Sales Proposal

*In This Chapter*

▶ Giving your buyer all the information that's needed

A buyer's decision makers want to make an informed buying decision. Your sales proposal needs to contain the critical information that helps them make that decision. A well-written and professionally packaged sales proposal should fulfill and exceed the buyer's information needs.

## A Description of the Buyer's Improvement Opportunity

Decision makers want to know that you understand their business and have identified a viable improvement opportunity for their company. If your proposal doesn't give them that impression, they question the reliability of your proposed solution. If you do your homework on the buyer, it shows in your proposal. Describing the improvement opportunity is standard operating procedure if you follow a consultative sales process.

## A Description of the Buyer's Needs and Objectives

To set the stage for your proposed product, your sales proposal first must identify the buyer's *confirmed* needs and objectives. The buyer's decision makers are very likely to make a positive buying decision when your proposed product satisfies confirmed needs and objectives. Plan to spend some time working with your buyer to understand its needs and objectives. You can use this knowledge to develop a custom application of your product for the buyer. This is another standard operating procedure for consultative sales professionals.

# A Description of the Proposed Product and Its Application

One section of your proposal should give the buyer a general idea of what your product is all about — what it does and how it works. Make sure you include a description of optional product components. Your proposal must also explain how you plan to apply your proposed product in the buyer's business. Your proposal must describe exactly how your product can be installed (or how your service can be provided). If your proposal doesn't do a good job explaining your product's application, the buyer will be left with some unanswered questions.

Don't expect the buyer to try to figure out the details of your product and its application — that's your job and the buyer won't do it for you.

# The Buyer's Clearly-Defined Value Proposition

The non-financial and financial benefits of your product are very important to the buyer. Both benefit types combine to form the *value proposition* for a buyer — how your product will improve the buyer's business and lead to reduced or avoided costs or increased revenues. If your proposal doesn't define the benefits the buyer will realize, how do you expect the buyer's decision makers to make an informed buying decision?

# How You Plan to Deliver on the Contract

Part of your sales proposal must describe your company's standard implementation (or project management) methods or business practices. You describe the steps, phases, and activities that your company normally follows to implement your proposed product. Your sales proposal also can identify what resources (specifically the people) you will use for the project and how long you plan to take to get the job done. By including this information in your proposal, you let the buyer know that your company has been there, done that. The section can give the buyer confidence in doing business with your company.

# Customer References

Customer references let the buyer's decision makers know that their company isn't the first to buy your product. Easily verifiable customer references make it easy for a prospective buyer to talk to someone who has experience with your company. Including customer references in your proposal says a lot about your company's track record. It says that your customers (or at least the ones you use as references) have had positive experiences with your company and its products.

# Some Information about Your Company

The seller profile section of your proposal gives the buyer a bunch of reasons why it wants to buy your products and do business with you instead of one of your competitors. But don't use this section of your proposal to impress the buyer with how big your company is or how many employees and locations you have. The buyer may equate the size of your company with the price of your product and start talking with one of your smaller competitors. Instead, use this section to impress the buyer with your company's unique qualifications. Impress it with your company's business philosophy, quality programs, or customer service approach.

# A Complete Description of Fees, Prices, and All Other Costs

Your proposal must disclose and detail the buyer's total cost. As you might expect, the buyer needs this information to make a decision. The more detail about cost that you include in your proposal, the fewer surprises your buyer and you will have.

Make sure that your proposal lets the buyer know about everything that you expect it to pay for as part of the deal.

# Quality

The quality of your proposal's appearance is as important as the quality of its substance. Your sales proposal is a business document that must project a professional image to the buyer's decision makers. Always remember that your sales proposal represents your company when the sales professional isn't in front of the buyer. The quality of your proposal's appearance and organization should be as good as the quality of your brochures or Web site. The buyer expects nothing less.

# A Professional Package

Put your proposal in a professional package. The buyer's decision makers don't expect to get a leather-bound sales proposal, but they do expect more than pages of copier or printer paper stapled in the upper-left corner. Plan to spend a few dollars to professionally package each sales proposal. And make sure that all your sales professionals package their proposals in a similar way. Remember that your sales proposal is the first deliverable the buyer receives from your company.

# Chapter 21

# Ten Tips on Presenting Your Sales Proposal

*In This Chapter*

▶ Building your presentation around your proposal

▶ Avoiding some common mistakes

*N*ever pass on the chance to present your sales proposal to the buyer, whether your presentation is only to your internal sponsor or to the buyer's decision makers. If you present the sales proposal to your internal sponsor, then your presentation is like a conversation rather than a presentation to a group of people. However, if you really get lucky, you (and probably your competitors) are asked to pitch your deal to the buyer's decision makers. Besides presenting the key elements of your sales proposal during this formal presentation, expect to clarify some information and to answer some tough questions that the decision makers may have about the deal.

Presenting your sales proposal in person gets you in front of the buyer one more maybe in front of the buyer's decision makers for the first time — and that's always good. But your performance must be top notch.

# Make Sure that the Buyer Can Read Your Sales Proposal in Advance

Don't hand your sales proposal to the buyer's decision makers just before your presentation. If you do, the decision makers will split their attention between you and the proposal. You stand a better chance of holding the decision makers' attention if you send your proposal to them well ahead of your presentation date. Doing so gives them a chance to read and study your proposal. Some decision makers may even take notes and jot questions in the margins. However, expect that some decision makers may not have looked at your sales proposal until the presentation; they'll be the ones flipping through the proposal as you present. If they really like what you're saying, the intensity of their flipping may increase.

# Give Every Decision Maker an Original Copy

Don't send one sales proposal to the buyer and expect your internal sponsor to make copies. You know what will happen: Some overworked member of the sponsor's staff will make photocopies and staple them not very carefully in the upper-left corner, wiping out all the care and attention you have invested in a professional-looking presentation. The solution is easy. Simply find out how many decision makers from the buyer's organization need a proposal and produce an "original" for everyone. For a few dollars, you can make sure that every decision maker experiences the full effect of your sales proposal's packaging. After you get the deal, your winning proposal can be sitting on the credenza or in the bookcase of all the decision makers' offices. Make sure it looks good!

# Use Your Sales Proposal to Organize the Presentation

*Successful Presentations For Dummies,* by Malcolm Kusher, says this about organizing material for a presentation:

> "Patterns play a critical role in how we assign meaning and how we interpret messages . . . While patterns are infinite in variety, certain ones appear over and over again. Here are a few of the most common patterns for presentations:
>
> **Problem/solution:** State a problem and offer a solution. . . ."

If you follow the structure I recommend in *Sales Proposals Kit For Dummies*, your proposal has a problem/solution pattern. Use that pattern for your presentations as well.

Your proposal's first section identifies the buyer's improvement opportunity (a business problem that can be solved). Your second proposal section contains the solution, including the solution's benefits. To complete your presentation, you can follow the flow of information and ideas from the next three sections of your sales proposal: implementation, seller profile, and business issues.

If you organize your presentation using your proposal's structure as the basis, your audience can easily follow along in their copies of the proposal.

# Give Your Presentation and Sales Proposal the Same Look

If you use overheads, slides, or presentation software to develop visual aids, your presentation should be an extension of your sales proposal. Use some of the visual elements from your sales proposal, such as its layout and format, font, colors, and graphics, to make your presentation match your proposal. For example, the font used for main headings in your sales proposal can also be used for headings in your presentation's visual aids. Taking the time to match the look of your presentation with the look of your proposal may not seem worthwhile, but your attention to detail will impress the buyer, even if it does so subliminally.

# Keep It Simple

If you use visual aids for your presentation, don't put too much information on the overheads, slides, or screens. Keep your presentation simple. Don't get carried away with too many fonts, fancy graphics, or elaborate color schemes in your presentation. The rule in Chapter 12 about sales proposals is also relevant to presentations: The easier it is for you to make, the easier it is for your readers (or audience) to read.

# Avoid Too Much Text

Your slides or overheads should be just an outline. Don't put everything you're going to say on a slide, show the slide to the audience, and then read the slide! That's boring and unprofessional.

On each slide or overhead you use, try and use about five lines of text, with six or fewer words per line.

# Use Builds

A *build* is a series of slides or overheads in which each successive slide adds another bullet point to a list of bullet points. As you design and write various sections of your sales proposal, think about how you can use builds to communicate that information in your presentation. For example, if your product description includes components, then use builds to present the components in your presentation. You can use builds for presenting much of the material in your proposal: the buyer's needs and objectives, features and benefits, and project phases and deliverables. Just don't use builds on every overhead or slide. Doing so eventually may distract and annoy the audience.

# Use Infographics

You probably use *infographics* such as tables, charts, maps, and graphs in your sales proposals. Consider using infographics in your presentation. Infographics can enhance communications, improve readability, and make your complex concepts easier to understand. You can use tables in your presentation, but don't try to copy complicated tables from your sales proposal and expect to use them in your presentation (see the advice earlier about avoiding too much text).

Think about using a bar chart in your presentation to present your planned implementation or project schedule. The bar chart can be easier to understand than an overhead with a list of phases and start and stop dates. Use maps to communicate where your company does business or office locations. Communicate trends and make comparisons in your presentation with graphs.

# Refer to the Sales Proposal during Your Presentation

Don't forget to use your sales proposal during the presentation (remember, your proposal is why you're doing this presentation). As you discuss key points during the presentation, refer the decision makers to specific pages in the proposal, especially to the stuff that you want to make sure they read. For example, when you talk about how your company plans to implement the proposed product, you can say something like "Please turn to page twelve of the proposal to see the team of people we will use to implement the new system. As you can see, we've identified the team members and their roles and responsibilities for the project."

# Practice Your Presentation

If you do a great job designing and writing your sales proposal, preparing for the presentation should be easy. Since your sales proposal contains exactly the information that you need to convey to the buyer, you already have an in-depth understanding of the material. However, even if you think that you know the material in your presentation backwards and forwards, don't overlook the need to rehearse. *Successful Presentations For Dummies* by Malcolm Kusher says this about rehearsing a presentation:

> "Rehearsal is probably the most neglected area of speech-making. People run out of time. They think that rehearsing is unnecessary. They ignore it, and they pay the consequences."

# Part VII

# Appendixes

The 5th Wave    By Rich Tennant

SALES MANAGEMENT PICNIC

"Remember — chit-chat first."

# In this part . . .

As you read my book, you may want to check this part for leads to more information on aspects of proposal writing of special concern to you. I list a large number of references — books, Web connections — in Appendix A.

Appendix B tells you all about what's on the CD that accompanies *Sales Proposals Kit For Dummies*. Among other useful items, the CD includes a sample sales proposal, a sales proposal model template, worksheets, and my very own Sales Proposal RATER — a nifty tool that you can use to measure the power of your sales proposals (or proposals from the competition that just happen to fall into your hands). The CD is a real workhorse, and Appendix B is your harness.

# Appendix A

# Resources in Books and on the Internet

## Books on Selling

Alessandra, Tony and Barrera, Rick. *Collaborative Selling*. New York: John Wiley & Sons, 1993.

Bosworth, Michael. *Solution Selling*. Chicago, Illinois: Irwin Professional Publishing, 1995.

Hanan, Mack. *Consultative Selling*. New York: AMACOM, 1990, 1985, 1973, and 1970.

Hanan, Mack. *Key Account Selling*. New York: AMACOM, 1993.

Hopkins, Tom. *Selling For Dummies*. Foster City, California: Hungry Minds, 1995.

Miller, Robert and Heiman, Stephen. *Strategic Selling*. New York: Warner Books, 1985.

Parinello, Anthony. *Selling to VITO, the Very Important Top Officer*. Holbrook, Massachusetts: Adams Media Corporation, 1994, 1999.

Rackham, Neil. *Major Account Sales Strategy*. New York: McGraw-Hill, 1989.

Willingham, Ron. *Integrity Selling*. New York: Doubleday, 1987.

## Books on Sales Proposals and Business Writing

Kantin, Robert. *Strategic Proposals, Closing the Big Deal*. New York: Vantage Press, 1999

Kantin, Robert and Hardwick, Mark. *Quality Selling Through Quality Proposals.* Cincinnati, Ohio: International Thomson Publishing, 1994.

Lindsell-Roberts, Sheryl. *Business Writing For Dummies.* Foster City, California: Hungry Minds, 1999.

Pfeiffer, William S. *Proposal Writing, The Art of Friendly Persuasion.* Columbus, Ohio: Merrill Publishing Company, 1989.

Sant, Tom. *Persuasive Business Proposals.* New York: AMACOM, 1992.

Tepper, Ron. *How to Write Winning Proposals for Your Company and Client.* New York: John Wiley and Sons, 1989.

# Books on Related Stuff

Gookin, Dan. *Word 2000 For Windows For Dummies.* Foster City, California: Hungry Minds, 1999.

Kushner, Malcolm. *Successful Presentations For Dummies.* Foster City, California: Hungry Minds, 1995.

Tiffany, Paul and Peterson, Steven. *Business Plans For Dummies.* Foster City, California: Hungry Minds, 1997.

Wang, Wally and Parker, Roger C. *Microsoft Office 2000 For Windows For Dummies.* Foster City, California: Hungry Minds, 1999.

# Books on Accounting

I include this section in case you need help developing compelling financial benefits.

Finkler, Steven A. *The Complete Guide to Finance & Accounting for Non-Financial Managers.* Englewood Cliffs, New Jersey: Prentice-Hall, 1983.

Hilton, Ronald W. *Managerial Accounting.* New York: McGraw-Hill, 1991.

Thomsett, Michael C. *Winning Numbers.* New York: AMACOM, 1990.

Tracy, John A. *Accounting For Dummies, 2$^{nd}$ Edition.* Foster City, California: Hungry Minds, 2001.

# Sales-Related Web Sites

**SalesForce.com** (www.salesforce.com): A top-notch Web site with everything you need to know about sales.

**Sales and Marketing Management** (www.salesandmarketing.com): A magazine for sales and marketing professionals.

**Sales Doctors** (www.salesdoctors.com): Seeking cures for the common close.

**Selling Power** (www.sellingpower.com): Your daily guide to sales success, this Web site also has a magazine for sales professionals.

# Sales Proposals Web Sites

**SalesProposals.com** (www.salesproposals.com): Sales proposal software, design tips, books, and consulting services. Get proposal and worksheet/questionnaire templates and software demonstrations from SalesProposals.com on the CD in the back of this book.

**Sant Corporation** (www.santcorp.com): Software and services to help with sales letters, RFP responses, presentations, and generating proposals.

**Pragmatech Software** (www.pragmatech.com): Pragmatech sells a complete suite of integrated proposal automation software.

**Eposal.com** (www.eposal.com): An online sales proposal system.

# Presentations Web Sites

I include this section in case you want help developing a top-notch winning presentation for your proposal.

**PresentationPro** (www.presentationpro.com): This Web sites aims to help you create a presentation that packs a wallop without having to hire an expensive designing firm.

**PresentationStreet.com** (www.presentationstreet.com): A site that sells images, backgrounds, photos, and video clips that can energize your presentation.

# Appendix B

# About the CD

## System Requirements

Make sure that your computer meets the minimum system requirements shown in the following list. If your computer doesn't match up to most of these requirements, you may have problems using the software and files on the CD.

- ✔ A PC with a Pentium or faster processor; or a Mac OS computer with a 68040 or faster processor

- ✔ Microsoft Windows 95 or later; or Mac OS system software 7.6.1 or later

- ✔ Some files require Microsoft Excel 97 or higher

- ✔ At least 32MB of total RAM installed on your computer; for best performance, we recommend at least 64MB

- ✔ A CD-ROM drive

- ✔ A sound card for PCs; Mac OS computers have built-in sound support

- ✔ A monitor capable of displaying at least 256 colors or grayscale

- ✔ A modem with a speed of at least 14,400 bps

If you need more information on the basics, check out these books published by Hungry Minds, Inc.: *PCs For Dummies,* by Dan Gookin; *Macs For Dummies,* by David Pogue; *iMacs For Dummies* by David Pogue; *Windows 95 For Dummies, Windows 98 For Dummies, Windows 2000 Professional For Dummies, Microsoft Windows ME Millennium Edition For Dummies,* all by Andy Rathbone.

# Using the CD with Microsoft Windows

To install items from the CD to your hard drive, follow these steps:

1. **Insert the CD into your computer's CD-ROM drive.**

2. **Click the Start button and choose Run from the menu.**

3. **In the dialog box that appears, type** d:\start.htm.

   Replace *d* with the proper drive letter for your CD-ROM if it uses a different letter. (If you don't know the letter, double-click My Computer on your desktop and see what letter is listed for your CD-ROM drive.)

   Your browser opens, and the license agreement is displayed. If you don't have a browser, Microsoft Internet Explorer and Netscape Communicator are included on the CD.

4. **Read through the license agreement, nod your head, and click the Agree button if you want to use the CD.**

   After you click Agree, you're taken to the Main menu, where you can browse through the contents of the CD.

5. **To navigate within the interface, click a topic of interest to take you to an explanation of the files on the CD and how to use or install them.**

6. **To install software from the CD, simply click the software name.**

   You'll see two options: to run or open the file from the current location or to save the file to your hard drive. Choose to run or open the file from its current location, and the installation procedure continues. When you finish using the interface, close your browser as usual.

*Note:* We have included an "easy install" in these HTML pages. If your browser supports installations from within it, go ahead and click the links of the program names you see. You'll see two options: Run the File from the Current Location and Save the File to Your Hard Drive. Choose to Run the File from the Current Location and the installation procedure will continue. A Security Warning dialog box appears. Click Yes to continue the installation.

To run some of the programs on the CD, you may need to keep the disc inside your CD-ROM drive. This is a good thing. Otherwise, a very large chunk of the program would be installed to your hard drive, consuming valuable hard drive space and possibly keeping you from installing other software.

# Using the CD with Mac OS

To install items from the CD to your hard drive, follow these steps:

1. **Insert the CD into your computer's CD-ROM drive.**

   In a moment, an icon representing the CD you just inserted appears on your Mac desktop. Chances are, the icon looks like a CD-ROM.

2. **Double-click the CD icon to show the CD's contents.**

3. **Double-click** `start.htm` **to open your browser and display the license agreement.**

   If your browser doesn't open automatically, open it as you normally would by choosing File⇨Open File (in Internet Explorer) or File⇨Open⇨Location in Netscape (in Netscape Communicator) and select *SalesPropKit FD*. The license agreement appears.

4. **Read through the license agreement, nod your head, and click the Accept button if you want to use the CD.**

   After you click Accept, you're taken to the Main menu. This is where you can browse through the contents of the CD.

5. **To navigate within the interface, click any topic of interest and you're taken you to an explanation of the files on the CD and how to use or install them.**

6. **To install software from the CD, simply click the software name.**

# What You'll Find on the CD

The following sections are arranged by category and provide a summary of the software and other goodies you'll find on the CD. If you need help with installing the items provided on the CD, refer back to the installation instructions in the preceding section.

*Shareware programs* are fully functional, trial versions of copyrighted programs. If you like particular programs register with their authors for a nominal fee and receive licenses, enhanced versions, and technical support. *Freeware programs* are free, copyrighted games, applications, and utilities. Unlike shareware, these programs do not require a fee or provide technical support. *GNU software* is governed by its own license, which is included inside the folder of the GNU product. See the GNU license for more details.

Trial, demo, or evaluation versions are usually limited either by time or functionality (such as being unable to save projects). Some trial versions are very sensitive to system date changes. If you alter your computer's date, the programs will "time out" and will no longer be functional.

# Sample Forms and Reports

This section lists the various forms from the book as well as some extras thrown in especially for the CD. Each form is available to you as a PDF file and almost every form is available as a Rich Text File (.rtf). You'll need Adobe Acrobat Reader (available on this CD) to view and print the PDF files. You can use your favorite word processor to view, print, and edit the .rtf files.

# Sales Proposal Kit

The CD-ROM contains the following sales proposal tools, examples, and demonstration software:

| Name | Comments/Description |
| --- | --- |
| Sales Proposal Model Template - Product | Proposal model skeleton for a product with section and subsection titles; fully formatted Microsoft Word document including title page, page numbers, and automated table of contents. |
| Sales Proposal Model Template - Services | Same as the sales proposal template for a product but designed for the sale of services. |
| Sample Proposal | Sample proposal for a software product in Adobe Acrobat (pdf) format. |
| Sample Worksheet | Sample sales tool for gathering the client information needed to write the sample proposal; Adobe Acrobat (pdf) format. |
| Sales Proposal RATER-Demo | For Windows. A program that you can use to evaluate a proposal from the buyer's viewpoint. Provides diagnostics and prescriptive advice 25 quality evaluation points. |

| Name | Comments/Description |
|------|---------------------|
| Sales Proposal Architect - Demo | For Windows. A demonstration version of a software program designed by Bob Kantin, the author of *Sales Proposals Kit For Dummies*. Sales Proposal Architect is a unique program that automates the design and development of a sales proposal. The program follows the structure and content guidelines for sales proposals presented in this book. (www.salesproposals.com) |
| Sales Proposal Architect User Guide | The user guide for Sales Proposal Architect; Adobe Acrobat (pdf) format. |
| Sales Proposal Architect - Quick Start | A two-page guide for installing and running Sales Proposal Architect; Adobe Acrobat (pdf) format. |

# Writing a Recommendation Report — Your Internal Sales Proposal Kit

The CD-ROM also contains the following tools for selling an idea within your own company.

| Name | Comments/Description |
|------|---------------------|
| Position Paper Template | Position paper template — a skeleton of a document that you can use to get approval to undertake a feasibility analysis; fully formatted Microsoft Word document. |
| Recommendation Report Template | Recommendation report template — a skeleton of a document with section and subsection titles that you can use to document the findings, conclusions, and recommendations of your feasibility analysis; fully formatted Microsoft Word document including title page, page numbers, and automated table of contents. |

# Presentation Pro

For Windows. If you need some professional help to develop a Microsoft PowerPoint presentation to present your sales proposal to the buyer's decision-makers, the CD-ROM in *Sales Proposals Kit For Dummies* also includes software and sample presentation templates from PresentationPro, Inc. (www.presentationpro.com).

# Software

## Acrobat Reader

Evaluation version.

For Macintosh and Windows. Acrobat Reader, from Adobe Systems, is a program that lets you view and print Portable Document Format, or PDF files. The PDF format is used by many programs you find on the Internet for storing documentation, because it supports the use of such stylish elements as assorted fonts and colorful graphics (as opposed to plain text, or ASCII, which doesn't allow for any special effects in a document). You can also get more information by visiting the Adobe Systems Web site, at www.adobe.com.

## Internet Explorer

Commercial version.

For Macintosh and Windows. Internet Explorer, from Microsoft, is one of the best-known Web browsers available. In addition to the browser, this package includes other Internet tools from Microsoft: Outlook Express 5, a mail and news reading program; Windows Media Player, a program that can display or play many types of audio and video files; and NetMeeting 3, a video conferencing program.

If you have a version of Windows 98, 2000, or NT that already includes Internet Explorer 5.5, don't install the CD-ROM version. Instead, go to Microsoft's Web site at www.microsoft.com/windows/ie/download/windows.htm and see what updates are available to fix errors and security problems in the version you have.

## *Netscape Communicator*

Commercial version.

For Macintosh and Windows. Netscape Communicator, from Netscape Communications, is one of the best-known Web browsers available. The CD-ROM installs Netscape Communicator Version 4.7. You also have the option of installing Real Player G2 (to play streaming audio and video files) and Winamp (to play MPEG3 files).

You can find information about Netscape Navigator from its Help menu or at its Web site, home.netscape.com.

# *Troubleshooting*

I tried my best to compile programs that work on most computers with the minimum system requirements. Alas, your computer may differ, and some programs may not work properly for some reason.

The two likeliest problems are that you don't have enough memory (RAM) for the programs you want to use, or you have other programs running that are affecting installation or running of a program. If you get an error message such as Not enough memory or Setup cannot continue, try one or more of the following suggestions and then try using the software again:

- ✔ **Turn off any antivirus software running on your computer.** Installation programs sometimes mimic virus activity and may make your computer incorrectly believe that it's being infected by a virus.

- ✔ **Close all running programs.** The more programs you have running, the less memory is available to other programs. Installation programs typically update files and programs; so if you keep other programs running, installation may not work properly.

- ✔ **Have your local computer store add more RAM to your computer.** This is, admittedly, a drastic and somewhat expensive step. However, if you have a Windows 95 PC or a Mac OS computer with a PowerPC chip, adding more memory can really help the speed of your computer and allow more programs to run at the same time. This may include closing the CD interface and running a product's installation program from Windows Explorer.

If you still have trouble installing the items from the CD, please call the Hungry Minds, Inc. Customer Service phone number at 800-762-2974 (outside the U.S.: 317-572-3993) or send email to techsupdum@hungryminds.com.

# Index

# Notes

# Notes

# Notes

# Notes

# Notes

# Notes

# Hungry Minds, Inc.
# End-User License Agreement

**READ THIS.** You should carefully read these terms and conditions before opening the software packet(s) included with this book ("Book"). This is a license agreement ("Agreement") between you and Hungry Minds, Inc. ("HMI"). By opening the accompanying software packet(s), you acknowledge that you have read and accept the following terms and conditions. If you do not agree and do not want to be bound by such terms and conditions, promptly return the Book and the unopened software packet(s) to the place you obtained them for a full refund.

1. **License Grant.** HMI grants to you (either an individual or entity) a nonexclusive license to use one copy of the enclosed software program(s) (collectively, the "Software") solely for your own personal or business purposes on a single computer (whether a standard computer or a workstation component of a multi-user network). The Software is in use on a computer when it is loaded into temporary memory (RAM) or installed into permanent memory (hard disk, CD-ROM, or other storage device). HMI reserves all rights not expressly granted herein.

2. **Ownership.** HMI is the owner of all right, title, and interest, including copyright, in and to the compilation of the Software recorded on the disk(s) or CD-ROM ("Software Media"). Copyright to the individual programs recorded on the Software Media is owned by the author or other authorized copyright owner of each program. Ownership of the Software and all proprietary rights relating thereto remain with HMI and its licensers.

3. **Restrictions on Use and Transfer.**

    **(a)** You may only (i) make one copy of the Software for backup or archival purposes, or (ii) transfer the Software to a single hard disk, provided that you keep the original for backup or archival purposes. You may not (i) rent or lease the Software, (ii) copy or reproduce the Software through a LAN or other network system or through any computer subscriber system or bulletin-board system, or (iii) modify, adapt, or create derivative works based on the Software.

    **(b)** You may not reverse engineer, decompile, or disassemble the Software. You may transfer the Software and user documentation on a permanent basis, provided that the transferee agrees to accept the terms and conditions of this Agreement and you retain no copies. If the Software is an update or has been updated, any transfer must include the most recent update and all prior versions.

4. **Restrictions on Use of Individual Programs.** You must follow the individual requirements and restrictions detailed for each individual program in Appendix B of this Book. These limitations are also contained in the individual license agreements recorded on the Software Media. These limitations may include a requirement that after using the program for a specified period of time, the user must pay a registration fee or discontinue use. By opening the Software packet(s), you will be agreeing to abide by the licenses and restrictions for these individual programs that are detailed in Appendix B and on the Software Media. None of the material on this Software Media or listed in this Book may ever be redistributed, in original or modified form, for commercial purposes.

5. **Limited Warranty.**

   **(a)** HMI warrants that the Software and Software Media are free from defects in materials and workmanship under normal use for a period of sixty (60) days from the date of purchase of this Book. If HMI receives notification within the warranty period of defects in materials or workmanship, HMI will replace the defective Software Media.

   **(b)** HMI AND THE AUTHOR OF THE BOOK DISCLAIM ALL OTHER WARRANTIES, EXPRESS OR IMPLIED, INCLUDING WITHOUT LIMITATION IMPLIED WARRANTIES OF MERCHANTABILITY AND FITNESS FOR A PARTICULAR PURPOSE, WITH RESPECT TO THE SOFTWARE, THE PROGRAMS, THE SOURCE CODE CONTAINED THEREIN, AND/OR THE TECHNIQUES DESCRIBED IN THIS BOOK. HMI DOES NOT WARRANT THAT THE FUNCTIONS CONTAINED IN THE SOFTWARE WILL MEET YOUR REQUIRE-MENTS OR THAT THE OPERATION OF THE SOFTWARE WILL BE ERROR FREE.

   **(c)** This limited warranty gives you specific legal rights, and you may have other rights that vary from jurisdiction to jurisdiction.

6. **Remedies.**

   **(a)** HMI's entire liability and your exclusive remedy for defects in materials and workman-ship shall be limited to replacement of the Software Media, which may be returned to HMI with a copy of your receipt at the following address: Software Media Fulfill-ment Department, Attn.: *Sales Proposals Kit For Dummies*, Hungry Minds, Inc., 10475 Crosspoint Blvd., Indianapolis, IN 46256, or call 1-800-762-2974. Please allow four to six weeks for delivery. This Limited Warranty is void if failure of the Software Media has resulted from accident, abuse, or misapplication. Any replacement Software Media will be warranted for the remainder of the original warranty period or thirty (30) days, whichever is longer.

   **(b)** In no event shall HMI or the author be liable for any damages whatsoever (including without limitation damages for loss of business profits, business interruption, loss of business information, or any other pecuniary loss) arising from the use of or inability to use the Book or the Software, even if HMI has been advised of the possibility of such damages.

   **(c)** Because some jurisdictions do not allow the exclusion or limitation of liability for conse-quential or incidental damages, the above limitation or exclusion may not apply to you.

7. **U.S. Government Restricted Rights.** Use, duplication, or disclosure of the Software for or on behalf of the United States of America, its agencies and/or instrumentalities (the "U.S. Government) is subject to restrictions as stated in paragraph (c)(1)(ii) of the Rights in Technical Data and Computer Software clause of DFARS 252.227-7013, or subparagraphs (c) (1) and (2) of the Commercial Computer Software - Restricted Rights clause at FAR 52.227-19, and in similar clauses in the NASA FAR supplement, as applicable.

8. **General.** This Agreement constitutes the entire understanding of the parties and revokes and supersedes all prior agreements, oral or written, between them and may not be modified or amended except in a writing signed by both parties hereto that specifically refers to this Agreement. This Agreement shall take precedence over any other documents that may be in conflict herewith. If any one or more provisions contained in this Agreement are held by any court or tribunal to be invalid, illegal, or otherwise unenforceable, each and every other pro-vision shall remain in full force and effect.

# Installation Instructions

The *Sales Proposals Kit For Dummies* CD offers valuable information that you won't want to miss. To install the items from the CD to your hard drive, follow these steps.

## For Microsoft Windows Users

1. **Insert the CD into your computer's CD-ROM drive.**

2. **Open your browser.**

3. **Click Start⇨Run.**

4. **In the dialog box that appears, type D:\START.HTM**

5. **Read through the license agreement, nod your head, and then click the Accept button if you want to use the CD — after you click Accept, you'll jump to the Main Menu.**

6. **To navigate within the interface, simply click on any topic of interest to take you to an explanation of the files on the CD and how to use or install them.**

7. **To install the software from the CD, simply click on the software name.**

## For Mac OS Users

1. **Insert the CD into your computer's CD-ROM drive.**

2. **Double-click the CD icon to show the CD's contents.**

3. **Double-click** `start.htm` **to open your browser and display the license agreement.**

   If your browser doesn't open automatically, open it as you normally would by choosing File⇨Open File (in Internet Explorer) or File⇨Open⇨Location in Netscape (in Netscape Communicator) and select *SalePropKit FD*. The license agreement appears.

4. **Read through the license agreement, nod your head, and click the Accept button if you want to use the CD.**

5. **To navigate within the interface, click any topic of interest and you're taken you to an explanation of the files on the CD and how to use or install them.**

6. **To install software from the CD, simply click the software name**

For more complete information, please see the "About the CD" appendix.

# FOR DUMMIES
# BOOK REGISTRATION

**Register This Book and Win!**

## We want to hear from you!

Visit **dummies.com** to register this book and tell us how you liked it!

- ✔ Get entered in our monthly prize giveaway.

- ✔ Give us feedback about this book — tell us what you like best, what you like least, or maybe what you'd like to ask the author and us to change!

- ✔ Let us know any other *For Dummies* topics that interest you.

Your feedback helps us determine what books to publish, tells us what coverage to add as we revise our books, and lets us know whether we're meeting your needs as a *For Dummies* reader. You're our most valuable resource, and what you have to say is important to us!

Not on the Web yet? It's easy to get started with *Dummies 101: The Internet For Windows 98* or *The Internet For Dummies* at local retailers everywhere.

Or let us know what you think by sending us a letter at the following address:

*For Dummies* Book Registration
Dummies Press
10475 Crosspoint Blvd.
Indianapolis, IN 46256

...FOR DUMMIES™

**BESTSELLING BOOK SERIES**